LOVE AND LOSS

In Life and in Treatment

Have you ever wondered what a therapist really thinks? Have you ever wondered if a therapist truly cares about her patients? Have you tried to imagine the unimaginable, the loss of the person most dear to you? Is it true that "'tis better to have loved and lost, than never to have loved at all?"

Love and loss are a ubiquitous part of life, bringing the greatest joys and the greatest heartaches. In one way or another all relationships end. People leave, move on, die. Loss is an ever-present part of life. In *Love and Loss*, Linda B. Sherby illustrates that in order to grow and thrive, we must learn to mourn, to move beyond the person we have lost while taking that person with us in our minds. Love, unlike loss, is not inevitable but, she argues, no satisfying life can be lived without deeply meaningful relationships.

The focus of *Love and Loss* is how patients' and therapists' independent experiences of love and loss, as well as the love and loss that they experience in the treatment room, intermingle and interact. There are always two people in the consulting room, both of whom are involved in their own respective lives, as well as the mutually responsive relationship that exists between them. Love and loss in the life of one of the parties affects the other, whether that affect takes place on a conscious or unconscious level.

Love and Loss is unique in two respects. The first is its focus on the analyst's current life situation and how that necessarily affects both the analyst and the treatment. The second is Sherby's willingness to share the personal memoir of her own loss which she has interwoven with extensive clinical material to clearly illustrate the effect the analyst's current life circumstance has on the treatment.

Writing as both a psychoanalyst and a widow, Linda B. Sherby makes it possible for the reader to gain an inside view of the emotional experience of being an analyst, making this book of interest to a wide audience. Professionals, from psychoanalysts, psychotherapists, and bereavement specialists, through students in all the mental health fields, to the public in general will resonate and learn from this heartfelt and straightforward book.

Linda B. Sherby is a psychotherapist, psychoanalyst, and supervisor in private practice in Boca Raton, Florida.

PSYCHOANALYSIS IN A NEW KEY BOOK SERIES
Donnel Stern
Series Editor

When music is played in a new key, the melody does not change, but the notes that make up the composition do: change in the context of continuity, continuity that perseveres through change. Psychoanalysis in a New Key publishes books that share the aims psychoanalysts have always had, but that approach them differently. The books in the series are not expected to advance any particular theoretical agenda, although to this date most have been written by analysts from the Interpersonal and Relational orientations.

The most important contribution of a psychoanalytic book is the communication of something that nudges the reader's grasp of clinical theory and practice in an unexpected direction. Psychoanalysis in a New Key creates a deliberate focus on innovative and unsettling clinical thinking. Because that kind of thinking is encouraged by exploration of the sometimes surprising contributions to psychoanalysis of ideas and findings from other fields, Psychoanalysis in a New Key particularly encourages interdisciplinary studies. Books in the series have married psychoanalysis with dissociation, trauma theory, sociology, and criminology. The series is open to the consideration of studies examining the relationship between psychoanalysis and any other field—for instance, biology, literary and art criticism, philosophy, systems theory, anthropology, and political theory.

But innovation also takes place within the boundaries of psychoanalysis, and Psychoanalysis in a New Key therefore also presents work that reformulates thought and practice without leaving the precincts of the field. Books in the series focus, for example, on the significance of personal values in psychoanalytic practice, on the complex interrelationship between the analyst's clinical work and personal life, on the consequences for the clinical situation when patient and analyst are from different cultures, and on the need for psychoanalysts to accept the degree to which they knowingly satisfy their own wishes during treatment hours, often to the patient's detriment.

LOVE AND LOSS

In Life and in Treatment

Linda B. Sherby

Routledge
Taylor & Francis Group

NEW YORK AND LONDON

First published 2013
by Routledge
711 Third Avenue, New York, NY 10017

Simultaneously published in the UK
by Routledge
27 Church Road, Hove, East Sussex BN3 2FA

Routledge is an imprint of the Taylor & Francis Group, an informa business

Library of Congress Cataloging in Publication Data
Sherby, Linda B.
   Love and loss in life and in treatment / authored by Linda B. Sherby
   – 1st ed.
      p. cm.
   1. Loss (Psychology)   2. Love – Psychological aspects.   3. Grief.
   4. Psycholanalysis. I. Title.
   BF575.D35S54 2013
   155.9´3-dc23   2012036216

ISBN: 978-0-415-88893-6 (hbk)
ISBN: 978-0-415-88894-3 (pbk)
ISBN: 978-0-203-83136-6 (ebk)

Typeset in Garamond
by HWA Text and Data Management, London

Printed and bound in the United States of America by
Walsworth Publishing Company, Marceline, MO.

IN MEMORY OF MY HUSBAND,
GEORGE EDWARD BRANDEBERRY,

AND
IN APPRECIATION OF ALL MY PATIENTS
WHO HAVE SO GENEROUSLY SHARED
THEIR LIVES WITH ME

CONTENTS

FOREWORD

Donnel B. Stern

I have often thought about writing a book that portrays life as a psychoanalyst. I mean really portrays it – an affectively alive book that lets readers know what it's like to live a life at the same time that you're doing treatment every day. How the life influences the work and the work influences the life. I have thought of writing a novel (who knows, maybe I still will) and I have thought of writing a memoir. Well, I don't have to worry about the memoir anymore, because Linda Sherby has written it, and she has done it in a way that I hope and believe will draw readers from inside psychoanalysis and outside it. It is easy to imagine this book crossing the ordinary barriers that separate professional books from books of general interest. In fact, if there is any justice in this world, it will cross those barriers. It is the one psychoanalytic book I have read that most deserves to become widely popular. More than that, it is the one psychoanalytic book I have read that really would be fascinating to people who are not themselves psychotherapists. Once you've read it, see if you don't agree: anyone who is a reader will find this book hard to put down. And yes, I do know how unexpected it is to say that about a book in a series written for psychoanalysts.

The problem anyone trying to write a memoir about being a psychoanalyst faces is the integration of the life and the work. In fact, I think that's probably the problem for anyone trying to write a book about what life as any particular kind of worker is like. Has it ever occurred to you how rare it is to read a book about the nature of work? We have many books about love. But there are so few about work. Work can seem to pale when set against the passion of life, so that as soon as you start to describe the life, the work takes a back seat.

Oh, there are certain seeming exceptions: actors and actresses, rock stars and other prominent musicians, famous painters, dancers, and so on. A few creative geniuses in business, government, and academics. But think about it. When you read those books, it's the rare exception for the focus to be on the work. It's the work that brings to attention the subject of the biography or autobiography; but it's the life, lovers, and friends of that person that is the stuff of the book.

And that's what so unusual here. Linda Sherby is hardly a celebrity. That's not why her life interests us. She is an everyday person. Well, sort of. An everyday person who can write like the wind. One of my favorite novels happens to be Laurens Van Der Post's *A Story like the Wind*, which concerns the lives of the Bushmen of Africa.

Love and Loss, despite having nothing to do with the Bushmen, is a story like the wind. It grabs you in a way that you're not used to being grabbed by anything in the psychoanalytic literature. Unless some other duty calls, if you are a psychotherapist you are not likely to put this book down until it ends. And if you're not a psychotherapist – well, you're not likely to put it down, either. It is that gripping.

How did Linda Sherby do this? Why has she been able to write something so thoroughly compelling? I think I know why she could do it, and why I didn't. The reason I couldn't figure out how to do it myself was that I didn't have a particular theme relating the life and the work. Linda does. With enormous generosity of spirit, she has allowed us to know everything she can think to tell us about her life with her husband, George, whose illness and eventual death is the thread along which the pearls of her narrative are strung. As Linda works with her patients, we understand how it is for her; we feel what it is like for her to live her life, to love and lose George. It's indelible. Linda gives it to us straight and to the heart. All of us have been there, even if we have never lost a spouse. We have lived with heartache while we continued to want to help other people with everything we had. But never has anyone come back from a place like that with a narrative that braids the life and the work together as Linda has done here. That's what's unique about *Love and Loss*. That's why Linda could do it when I, and no doubt many others, could not manage it. She has been willing to supply the thread of life along which the pearls of work could make a necklace.

I have every confidence that George was as committed to this book as Linda herself has been. The book was, and is, an act of courage for both of them, and it came at no little sacrifice. It would have been easier not to write it. It is a memorial to George, and to Linda's devotion to George, and it is a gift to its readers.

INTRODUCTION

I write this book as a psychoanalyst and as a widow. I write it as someone who knows with every fiber of my being that love and loss are a ubiquitous part of life, bringing the greatest joys and the greatest heartaches. In one way or another all relationships end. People leave, move on, die. Loss is an ever-present part of life, from the first separation from our mother's body, through growing up and leaving home, through navigating the break-up of relationships, through the dying of those we love, to the final loss of our own death. In order to grow and thrive, we must learn to mourn, we must both move beyond the person we have lost while taking that person with us in our minds. If we fail to achieve this delicate balance, we live our lives either bogged down in endless pain or incapable of being connected with others in a deep, meaningful way. *Love and Loss* examines both my own and my patients' struggles with loss and mourning, illustrating that seemingly unbearable pain can be both born and transformed.

The book itself is one of the ways I have dealt with my personal mourning, the death of my husband. It is one of the ways I have been able to both hold on to him and to the relationship I so cherished, while engaging in the process of letting go. Goethe wrote, "We die twice: first, when we die, and then when those who knew us and loved us die" (cited in Kernberg, 2010). This quote captures one of my prime motivations for writing this book, the desire to keep a part of both my husband and our relationship alive by putting it on paper, recording it, seeing it in black and white. Since I can no longer have him as my living, breathing husband, I at least have this book that partially captures our life and our love.

Unlike loss, love is not inevitable, but no satisfying life can be lived without it. Intense and connected relationships are integral to our growth and fulfillment as human beings. Love and loss intertwine throughout our lives, forever present in one form or another. And just as love and loss exist in life, so too do they exist in treatment. Every therapeutic relationship begins with the assumption of an ending. From the first time a patient walks into a therapist's office, the expectation is that they will one day say good-bye. During the course of treatment, many feelings transpire between patient and analyst, including feelings of caring and love. Both patient and therapist are also likely to confront loss, not only from the termination of the treatment itself, but losses that arise in their respective lives, be it divorce, physical impairment, aging, or death.[1]

1

The primary focus of this book is how patients' and therapists' independent experiences of love and loss, as well as the love and loss they experience in the treatment room, intermingle and interact. There are always two people in the consulting room, both of whom are involved in their own respective lives, as well as in the intense, mutually responsive relationship between them. Thus, at any one moment, both patient and analyst are being affected, both consciously and unconsciously, by their immediate interaction, by their own history and dynamics, and by their own and the other's present life circumstances, all of which exist simultaneously and stimulate thoughts, feelings, conflicts, and fantasies in each party. Love and loss in the life of one of the parties affects the other, whether that effect takes place on a conscious or unconscious level.

Psychoanalysts have long understood that what the therapist brings to the consulting room must be examined and understood. Earlier analysts were most concerned about how the therapist's history and conflicts affected the treatment situation, while more contemporary analysts have drawn attention to the continual conscious and unconscious interaction between both members of the dyad. Both points of view are crucial and must be attended to in any treatment. I believe, however, that what the therapist brings to her sessions because of her current life situation – although certainly affected by her past history and the uniqueness of the patient/therapist dyad – has been insufficiently examined. A therapist will have different concerns, feelings, and stresses if she is getting married or divorced, if a child is about to be born or to leave for college, if a spouse is ailing or a parent dying. Regardless of how therapists might strive to keep their personal lives, concerns, or feelings out of the treatment room, they are inescapable. A therapist who has miscarried will react differently to a pregnant patient than a therapist who has three healthy children at home. A therapist whose mother has just died may well respond in a different manner to an excessively demanding patient than she did prior to her mother's death. There are always two people in the consulting room, each living lives in the present. Their mutual interactions become entwined leading at times to great confusion and at other times to profound connection or insight. It is these current life circumstances and their affect on the treatment that I will explore in this book.

My personal desire to memorialize my relationship with my husband and my professional interest in examining how an analyst's present life affects the treatment come together in *Love and Loss*. To achieve these two goals, both personal and professional, I present extensive, in-depth clinical material, as well as a good deal of autobiographical information. Such self-disclosure is unusual for a psychoanalyst and I have undertaken it with the knowledge that it may carry profound effects for me both with present and future patients, as well as with professional colleagues. Psychoanalysis began as a profession in which the analyst attempted to reveal nothing, thereby encouraging the patient to transfer onto the analyst his own imaginings and past history. Much has changed over the years and greater self-disclosure is seen not only as acceptable, but inevitable. Still, the autobiographical facts that I reveal are more extensive than what is widely practiced and I do realize there are implications in what I have chosen to do. Although I certainly have not revealed everything about myself, if my patients read this book they will have far greater information about me than is generally the norm. I could say that privacy in the age of the Internet has become impossible anyway and, to some extent, this is true. Patients do have more information about us than they have had in the past. But I cannot comfortably fall back on this rationalization.

What I will say is that when I saw patients during my husband's illness and eventual death, I found that they were able to take in and often grow from a significant amount of disclosure on my part. Additionally, and not surprisingly, I found that different patients took in different amounts of information, that they reacted differently and that their responses were very much in line with who they were as people. The therapist's adage, "Everything is grist for the mill," is indeed operative here. Anything can be examined and understood. Do I think I may have made my future life as an analyst more difficult for myself? Quite possibly. But obviously it is a consequence I have been willing to accept for both personal and professional reasons.

I have also written this book with the hope that it will be read, not only by psychoanalysts and psychotherapists, not even only by those studying to become analysts or therapists, but by the general public. I am a staunch believer in the value and efficacy of psychoanalysis and recognize that its message has been lost in both the myths of its past and the desire for instantaneous cures within our overall culture. Psychoanalysis as a profession needs to be both humanized and seen for what it actually is. Analysts are caring but fallible human beings whose in-depth treatment method has relevance in today's world. As a rule, analysts are neither totally detached from their patients nor engaged in unethical sexual behavior with them. They are neither superior, overly intellectualized practitioners nor cavalier charlatans only in it for the money. Generally, therapists are thoughtful, considerate human beings who give people the time and space to explore their own minds, to be listened to and to be heard, perhaps for the first time.

Because I hope this book will appeal to a wide audience, I have used little professional jargon. When such words seemed unavoidable I define them as simply as possible. In addition to presenting copious clinical material, I have also attempted to provide a window into my thinking process. I want you, the reader, to see my uncertainties, my unanswerable questions, and my willingness to put not only my patient, but myself under a microscope that examines and investigates, but does not judge. This is yet another form of self-disclosure, as I provide you an entry into my mind as a therapist.

This brings me to the patients presented in the book. Most of them are composites of patients I have worked with over the course of my forty plus year career. This means that although I have attempted to remain true to the patient or idea I am trying to present, I have incorporated aspects of many patients, such as family histories, physical appearance, or presenting problem, to create one viable, true-to-life patient. Sometimes the composites draw not only from patients, but from friends, acquaintances, or even my own imaginings. A few of the patients presented, with their consent, are almost entirely true depictions with just minor changes such as names, places, or slight deviations from actual fact. To those patients I would like to express my great appreciation for both their courage and their willingness to open themselves to the scrutiny of others. Although actual case histories would have been preferable in every instance, my patients' best interests and confidentiality must always come first. In some instances I felt it would be deleterious to ask patients for permission to write about them, in other cases I had no idea how to contact the patients nor did I think it would be helpful to reappear in their lives after many years.

To bring the complex relationship between patient and therapist to life, I have also used considerable dialogue. This dialogue is not based on verbatim transcripts and in only rare instances does the dialogue represent direct quotes from my notes written either during or after specific therapy sessions. Mostly the dialogue flows from my own mind as I attempt to capture the intensity of a particular interaction, the significance of a certain dream, or the repeated struggle between the desire for and terror of change and growth. I have made every effort to stay true to both my own voice and those of my patients. You, the reader, will decide how well I have succeeded.

JOURNEYS[1]

I am following the gurney that carries my husband, George Edward Brandeberry, to the hospice facility where he will die.

With me is Melodee, George's daughter. Lacing her arm through mine she says, "The last journey."

She is referring to the tribute I read at my husband's eighty-third birthday party just one week before. In that tribute I spoke of the wondrous journey of our relationship, the amazing trips we took all over the world, and the tortuous journey of the last sixteen months as we dealt with the fear, pain, and uncertainty of his increasing health problems. The party was bittersweet. We knew that George would enter the hospital the Monday following his party. He was jaundiced. We thought he needed gallbladder surgery. We didn't know if he could survive general anesthesia. But I held out hope. After all, I never believed he would see this birthday. The previous year, on his eighty-second birthday, his PSA, the number that indicates the insidious rise of prostate cancer, had jumped precipitously despite chemotherapy. Yet here he was, one year later, still fighting for his life. I hoped that my husband's strength and tenacity would carry him through yet another crisis.

Now, as we follow the gurney, I say nothing. The decision to put George into hospice was difficult, but not agonizing. Even this final time, George took care of me. Once in the hospital we discovered that George's jaundice was due not to his gallbladder, but to growths in his bile ducts that were blocking their drainage. It was not good news. His oncologist did not think it was a metastasis of his prostate cancer, but possibly an entirely different cancer. The bile ducts had to be drained, and a biopsy of the growths was necessary to determine the type of cancer. Neither procedure could be done immediately because my husband had to be off his blood thinners for several days to prevent excessive bleeding. So we waited. And George grew weaker. Finally they made an attempt to drain the bile. George became nauseated, his heart, which was already severely compromised, became too unstable. They stopped.

They were to try again the next day. Before that second attempt, our internist came into the room and asked George if he stopped breathing during the procedure whether he wanted to be resuscitated.

Much to my surprise, this man who had fought and fought and fought to live said, "No. It's enough already."

5

"I'm not arguing with you," I began.

"Yes you are," he interrupted.

"No, I'm not, I just want to ask you one question. Are you doing this for you or for me?"

"For me," he replied. I believed him. He had had enough. He was ready to stop fighting.

George made it through the second procedure, but his body was breaking down. The charge nurse and George's cardiologist asked if I had considered hospice.

I made the decision, choosing a hospice facility I visited years before when a patient of mine was dying of ovarian cancer.

I called Melodee who had been with me and George for over a week. I also called George's grandson, Luke, and Luke's girlfriend, Emily. We had hired Emily to be George's companion and my helpmate for the past year. She stayed with George so that I could see patients, attend to my ninety-seven-year-old mother, and generally deal with life outside of George and his illness. She was perfect for George: kind, loving, and concerned, without being anxious, intrusive, or hovering.

While I waited for them to arrive, I called patients. Despite all the medical crises of the past sixteen months, more than half of my patients did not know of my husband's illness. Those patients I told that a family member was dying, that I needed to take some time off from work, and that I would contact them when I was ready to return. For those patients who did already know, I said that my husband was dying and that I would contact them when I was ready to return. I immediately heard my patients' anxiety, their fear that I would never come back to work. I reassured them. I knew I would resume working. I just wasn't sure exactly when.

Melodee, Luke, and Emily arrived at George's hospital room. We cried and hugged and told George and each other how much we loved one another. George's voice was very weak. It was hard for him to make himself heard unless we stood close by. I stepped towards the foot of the bed so that Luke and Emily could say their tearful good-byes. George opened his arms and clearly, distinctly, loudly proclaimed, "I love you, Linda." I rushed into his arms sobbing.

And here Melodee and I are, following the gurney through the side door of the hospice. I don't like the man who is wheeling my husband. It's odd how clearly I remember him: a big, fat man with a missing front tooth, a caricature of the "dumb oaf" frequently portrayed in the slapstick comedies that I have always disliked. I see him as someone incapable of compassion, and I want my husband to be lovingly carried on his final journey. Or perhaps he is just someone to allow me to feel disgruntled, someone to take me away from my pain.

They are expecting us. My husband is taken immediately to his room, S105. It is as I remembered it, airy, light, welcoming. Each room is private. And quiet. There are no nurses bustling around with medication, no PA system summoning doctors, no call buttons, and no IVs. Melodee and I go immediately to talk with the head nurse on duty. She is a short, squat woman who tells us about the facility – we can come and go whenever we wish, on weekends and nights the front door is locked but we can come in the side door by just pressing the buzzer, there is a refrigerator for any food we want to bring but we should put our name on it so that it isn't eaten by someone else. She has read my husband's chart. She tells us that he will be kept comfortable. He will be fed and given whatever pain medication or sleeping pills he needs.

I ask one question, a quintessential me question. "I know you can't say for sure, but how long do you think it will be?" When dealing with that which is totally unknowable, I always want to know, I want to gain some semblance of control over that which is entirely uncontrollable. Our doctors learned not to answer these questions. This nurse says, "Two weeks." I feel ambivalent about her response: both relieved and concerned. He'll still be with us, with me. I don't have to let him go just yet. But since we know the outcome, isn't it best to get it over with? I don't want him to suffer. I don't want my suffering prolonged. I've been in a state of almost-mourning for so long. I'm ready, I think, to begin the actual process. But another hug, another kiss, certainly that's reason enough to keep him around as long as possible.

Melodee and I go into my husband's room. He is, for him, somewhat agitated. "There you are. Where have you been?"

"We had to speak with the nurse," I reply defensively. But I realize immediately that I have been insensitive. How could I leave George alone and abandoned in a new place, his last place?

"I'm sorry," I say. I caress his face and kiss him, his skin no longer jaundiced, his cheek smooth except for a hint of stubble, his lips warm and welcoming as always. He is not at all skeletal, not ravaged by cancer. Quite the contrary. With all his medications for pain and his tremendously limited capacity to walk he has gained an enormous amount of weight. Although not a vain man, George hated the weight gain. He had been thin his whole life and now said that he felt like "a beached whale." He has lost his silky, wavy silver hair to the chemotherapy treatments. His goatee and mustache are mere fragments of their former states. His bright blue eyes are still blue, but have lost some of their luster.

But in so many ways, he is still the person he has always been.

"Who's going to pay for all this?" George asks.

"Don't worry," I reply, "It's covered by Medicare." Reassured that he's not excessively burdening me, he moves to his second concern.

"What about Emily?"

I know what he is asking. Once he is dead, what will she do for a job? What will she do for money?

"Don't worry, George," I tell him, "I won't abandon Emily."

George is again reassured. He tells Melodee and me to go home. It's late. We're tired. We haven't eaten. I tell him I'll bring Hadley, our six-month old piebald miniature dachshund in the morning. We say our good-nights.

From the time I first became involved with George almost thirty years before, I worried about his dying. It wasn't an unrealistic worry since he was twenty-one years my senior. And loss and separation were especially difficult for me. I could cry at airports watching total strangers hug good-bye. George, referring to my constant worry would say, "I'll only die once, but you'll die a hundred times." It wasn't, however, my death that I worried about, but his. And I probably thought about his dying thousands and thousands of times, not hundreds. Sometimes the thoughts were spurred by actual medical emergencies. Sometimes they just flew unbidden into my head and I would rehearse one imagined death or another. Now, however, it is for real. All that went before was a dress rehearsal. This is the real thing.

By morning George has lapsed into unconsciousness. Not yet realizing that he has begun his process towards death, I put our frisky puppy into his bed. He seems to startle awake. But it is only momentary. He is breathing, but no longer with us. He was given only a sleeping pill the night before. No other medication was necessary. My husband has made his decision. Just as he fought against all odds month after month to live, he has now decided to let go, to allow himself to die, to go quickly without a tortuous, drawn out ending.

All day I sit watching my husband with Hadley in my lap. It is unusual for her to be so calm and sedate. But today she lies contentedly in my lap while I stroke her and stroke her. Her fur is soft and silky. George and I both loved texture – tactile stroking, softness, fabrics or fur or skin that felt warm, inviting. Hadley has all that. She is a mixture of short and long-haired, mostly white, with brown markings down her back. She has long cocker spaniel like ears and a feathery white tail she wags almost all the time, looking as though she is waving a frayed flag in the wind.

Over the past sixteen months, my husband had begun to express a desire for a dog, although he would always add, "But it's not fair. I couldn't take care of it." Early in our marriage we had Brenna, a loving, smart combination black Labrador and German Shepherd whom George loved dearly. After we had to put her down, George said, "No more dogs." On several occasions I tried to change his mind, but he was adamant. We had cats, but no dogs. As George became sicker, more housebound, more vulnerable, he would watch countless animal shows on television, and his desire for a dog increased. I considered surprising him with one for his eighty-second birthday, but then decided I simply couldn't take care of one more being. But after a period when George's health had improved, I decided to take the risk. We got Hadley. I called her my happy dog. As it happened, George's health crashed two weeks later. Hadley was my last present to George and his most fortuitous, final present to me. So now I sit and stroke Hadley and stare at my husband.

Throughout the day various staff enter the room. They check to make sure that George isn't uncomfortable. They turn him, empty the bag with the draining bile, empty the bag with his urine that is becoming increasingly dark. The nurse we first talked to told us the urine gets darker as the patient nears death. The staff is kind, respectful, unintrusive.

As the day turns to early evening, the staff asks if Melodee and I plan to spend the night. It isn't until Melodee says that she wants to, that I realize they are telling us they think George will die that night. Does it make sense to say that I am shocked? Too soon, I think, too soon. But I had to know. I did know. I knew as soon as I saw

George that morning. And yet. And yet. Am I still not ready to let go? Can I not accept the reality of his being gone from me forever? Can I not accept the reality of losing this man who had embraced life with such strength and courage and who always, always cherished me? Reality breaks through my denial. Of course we'll spend the night.

We try to make ourselves comfortable on the two reclining chairs. Sleep seems impossible. At some point a doctor comes into the room. I remember that he is tall and thin and young. I remember that I tell him I don't know how he does this work. I know his response is kind, but I don't remember what he says.

At some point when the aides are tending to George, Melodee sees that his toes have begun to curl. "It won't be long now," she says.

I look at her incredulously. She nods at me.

"It's true," she says. "The toes curl when you're going to die." She had been through a similar death watch with her mother-in-law.

I must have dozed. It's 2:30 a.m.

"I think he stopped breathing," Melodee says.

I'm instantly at his side. He looks the same. The same in death as in life. Melodee and I stand at either side of his bed, looking at him, touching him. I try to take off his wedding ring. It won't come off. I panic.

"Don't worry," Melodee says. Like her father, figuring things out in the physical world comes naturally to her. She goes into the bathroom and gets the bar of soap. She lubricates George's finger. She slides off the ring. She hands it to me. We stand there looking at him, this man we both so dearly loved. We're not crying then. We're not talking. Just looking.

I leave to tell the staff that George has died. The nurse and an aide come into the room. They listen to his heart. They confirm what we already know. We pack up: Hadley, blankets, books. We take one last look.

We leave.

1

FALLING IN LOVE IN TREATMENT AND IN LIFE[1]

In the summer of 1982 Alyce Carhart chose me as her therapist. This was no ordinary choosing. She had read a book, *Getting Free: Women and Psychotherapy* (Hinton, Sherby and Tenbusch, 1982), I had co-authored with two other women therapists. Since our names were listed alphabetically, I was the second author. Nowhere in the book could you tell which of us had written any particular section. Our pictures did not appear. It was years before the advent of the Internet and the possibility of patients Googling prospective analysts. Knowing nothing factual about me, Alyce still chose me. She wrote, told me she was a twenty-year-old college student, that she had read the book and wanted to see me in therapy. I sent a return letter, telling her that I would soon be leaving on vacation and that I was not taking any new patients until my return. Since she was attending a university sixty miles from my office, I also suggested it might be preferable for her to see a therapist closer to her school. She wrote back and told me she would wait until I returned. Although I felt leery about the apparently inexplicable attachment she already felt towards me, I agreed.

Opening the door to my waiting room I invite her in. I am struck immediately by her large, brown, doe-like eyes that seem simultaneously beseeching and defiant. She sits across from me, perched on the edge of the brown chair. I have to remind myself that she's a college student. She feels much younger to me, a still chubby, awkward adolescent.

"I've been imagining what you'd look like," she says, smiling tentatively. "I did pretty well. I knew you'd have brown hair. Just like me. And I knew you'd have a warm smile. And you do." Alyce's own smile broadens, dramatically altering her appearance. The fear drains from her eyes and, for a moment, she looks not like a terrified deer, but an energized young woman ready to take on the world. The window into the radiant Alyce shuts quickly. She looks furtively around the office. "Can I sit over there?" she asks, gesturing to a Victorian love seat that sits against the wall between our two chairs. "I don't like having my back to the windows."

"Of course," I reply. "Sit wherever you're comfortable." I am already aware that I am looking at a very troubled young woman. Part of me wants to shy away, but I can feel the pull towards Alyce, the desire to provide her with a sense of safety, a desire to allay her fears. Getting up from the chair, I see her hesitation. Where will she sit on the love seat, closest to me or furthest away? She chooses the latter. At that time I have no idea how significant the issue of seating will become in her treatment.

"While you were away I wondered if I even needed to be in therapy. I should be able to handle things on my own. But I don't seem to be able to. I didn't even go back to school this semester. I felt too scared. I'm living at home. I'm not sure that's any better. They're more scary than school. That's one of the things I don't understand. I seem to be doing lots of things I don't understand these days. Or maybe it's not that I'm doing them, it's more like things keep happening to me. Weird things. Like sometimes I wonder if I've been selected for something special. But I don't know who selected me or for what. Besides, who cares about me? No one. So how could I be selected?" She looks at me expectantly.

Feeling as though I'm swimming through a morass, I fall back into my traditional therapist mode. "Can you tell me a little about your background? Your family? Do you know what it is you're scared of? Can you tell me why you were so determined to have me as your therapist?"

"Are you saying you won't be my therapist?" she asks frantically.

"No, no," I hasten to reassure her. "I'm just trying to understand more, including why you chose me."

"I'm adopted," she declares, as if this should explain everything. When I don't respond she continues. "I hate my parents. My mother's a witch. All my father does is scream. And I'm not scared. Did I tell you that I'm scared? I'm not. I just don't like school. I can't concentrate. I keep thinking of things. Who wants to learn dumb math anyway. I just want everyone to leave me alone! I just want to do what I want to do."

"And what do you want to do?" I ask.

"I don't know. [Pause.] No, that's not true," she says tentatively. "I want to write. And I want to find my real mother! And, no, don't ask me," she says suddenly defiant, "I don't do either! I don't write and I don't look for my mother. I don't do anything! Just ask my parents, my fake parents, they'll tell you! Oh, and by the way, they want to talk to you. I know you have to see them because they'll be the ones paying you, but you can't tell them anything. That's right, isn't it? You can't tell them anything? But you will see me, you will won't you?" she asks, the defiance replaced by supplication.

And so began one of the most tumultuous treatments of my career. In that first session I saw Alyce as a frightened, confused, child-like young woman who was terrified by her own vulnerability and who was fighting off psychotic thoughts. I was immediately drawn to her, hooked by her underlying fragility covered by a defensive and defiant toughness. That night I went home and told my husband that I had made my first lifetime commitment to a patient. I knew about being scared. I also knew about appearing strong while shaking on the inside.

I'm sitting on my bed, watching Mommy as she pulls up her stockings. Mommy, Daddy and I all share a bedroom. We live in a three-room apartment in Brooklyn. I want her to hurry. It's Saturday morning. I want to get to Gram and Gramps' in time to go to Jones Beach. It takes over an hour to get to their apartment in the Bronx. I spend most weekends with Gram and Gramps. I love it there. Usually Gramps comes to get me after school on

Friday and we take the long, crowded subway ride back to their apartment, standing all the way. But Grandpa had to work this Friday. The cafeteria where he works at night as a baker must have needed him to come in during the day.

Daddy is just getting out of bed. He worked very late last night. At Frosted Food Field. *He usually works late.* Frosted Food Field *is a frozen food trade paper. I'm not exactly sure what that is, but I know that Daddy owns it and that they write articles about frozen foods and that in order to make money they have to sell advertising for the magazine. Mommy works there too. They both work hard. And Daddy worries a lot about money. I don't know how he ended up doing what he does. It's not what he wanted to do. He wanted to be a scientist. He's real smart. Both he and Mommy graduated from college. Daddy seems to know everything. And he talks in these big words. He's always telling me to use the dictionary when I read. But I usually don't.*

Daddy has to get up now. That's a problem. Mommy tried to wake him earlier, like he asked her to, but she couldn't. Not even putting cold water on him. He's always hard to get up in the morning.

He sits up, passes his hand through his thick, curly brown hair. "What time is it?" he asks in his clipped, British-sounding voice. I know he's not British. But he still sounds British.

"Ten-thirty," Mommy answers.

"You Goddamn bitch," Daddy screams. "I thought I told you to wake me at nine."

"I tried to wake you, Eddie, but you wouldn't respond," she says in her quiet, even voice.

"Can't you ever do anything right?" he yells, turning the clock around to face him. "All I ask is that you wake me on time and you can't even do that!!! You're a stupid, stupid bitch."

Mommy ignores him, walking to the closet to get a blouse. I look down at my bed and begin pleating and unpleating the white sheet. I'm shaking inside. Maybe outside too. I'd like to go hide, but I don't know where to go. His voice is so loud.

Daddy gets up, hikes his striped pajama bottoms over his big stomach and walks rapidly towards the bathroom, brushing Mommy aside as he goes. Before the door slams shut he screams, "Get me something to eat."

I look up at Mommy. She knows I want to leave. And I know she'll get his breakfast. We won't make it to the beach. She still has to finish getting dressed, make-up. We'll be too late.

Unlike my mother, as I get older, I fight back, despite the fear that never leaves me. It's a Saturday morning. We're now living in a two-bedroom apartment. We moved so that I could go to Midwood High School, supposedly the best public high school in Brooklyn. I'm sitting at the kitchen table finishing a bowl of Rice Krispies. My mother's there too, reading the paper. Our green parakeet, Sunshine, chirps in his cage in the corner. My father walks back and forth from the bathroom, shaving. He likes having an audience, even when he shaves. He's pontificating about the state of the world: the difficulty Kennedy's having getting his legislation through Congress, the knee-jerk reaction against everything Russian, the evils of the Catholic Church. He doesn't require a response. Suddenly he turns toward Sunshine's cage, immediately beet-red and screaming.

"What is it with that Goddamn bird?! If he doesn't shut the hell up I'm going to kill him!"

My response is instantaneous. "If you touch that bird I'll never speak to you again!" I'm shocked. I can't believe I said that. I've never yelled at Daddy before. I go to my room, shutting the door behind me. I'm shaking and crying and pleased with myself all at once. Perhaps I'm stronger than I think. Perhaps I can protect Sunshine, even if I am scared inside. I didn't really, really think Daddy would hurt Sunshine. But he's such a bully! I wanted to stop his bullying. And just in case, I wanted to protect the helpless little bird.

In the end, my mother intervenes, defends my father, explains the stresses in his life, tells me how upset he is and gives me the task of mending the breach. And so, for many, many years I do what my mother asks. I apologize to my father.

Within two weeks of beginning treatment, Alyce decompensated into a florid psychosis. I saw her two and then three and sometimes four times a week. In addition, she often called me between sessions, sometimes pleading that I make her better, sometimes railing against my incompetence.

She walks carefully into my office, as though she is aware of every step she takes. "You don't hear it, do you?" she asks.

"Hear what, Alyce?"

"That voice. That voice that keeps saying I'm bad."

Regardless of how many times I have sat with psychotic patients, the experience, and especially the initial experience, is an eerie one fraught with anxiety and tension. It is as if I have entered an alien world where I have to put aside my own logic and reason and leap into this foreign environment while still maintaining a foothold in my own world, my own sanity. It is a time that calls for even greater attunement to the patient's reality, without surrendering my own. "No, Alyce," I say, "I don't hear the voice. I suspect that voice is coming from inside you."

"It can't be. It's so clear. It's a woman's voice. She's telling me I'm bad. Maybe it's my mother, my real mother. Maybe she's in heaven. Maybe she's telling me I was bad and that's why she gave me away." She startles and looks at me fearfully. "She just said I'm not supposed to talk to you, I'm not supposed to tell you about her! Maybe she's trying to protect me. Maybe I can't trust you. I hardly know you. What if it's wrong to talk to you!"

"It's not wrong to talk to me, Alyce, and it isn't your mother speaking. It's a part of you. A part of you that feels you're bad, a part of you that's afraid to trust me," I say softly and soothingly.

She looks repeatedly at me and away from me, as if listening to two conflicting dialogues.

"That's not the only voice I hear. Sometimes I hear another voice. I think it's Jesus. I know that we're Jewish – or at least THEY are – but I still think it's Jesus. He tells me to come to him, that he'll take care of me. Maybe he's telling me to kill myself – but Jesus wouldn't do that, would he?"

I lean forward, my brow knitted. Struggling to keep my fear at bay, I say, "I don't want you to kill yourself, Alyce."

"But what about that voice? What if Jesus really would take care of me?"

"That voice is a part of you too, Alyce. It's the part of you that wants to be taken care of, the part that wants someone to protect you."

"I don't know. I'm so confused. I'm so mixed up."

"Alyce," I say tentatively, "I am here for you and I do want to help you, but I wonder if it wouldn't be helpful for you to see the psychiatrist who's…"

"No! No!' she screams. "You're trying to send me away. You're trying to get rid of me again!"

"No, Alyce, I'm not trying to get rid of you. I'm going to continue seeing you. This is a psychiatrist who's in this same suite of offices. She could see you and perhaps give you some medication that would help with the voices, that would help you be less afraid."

"So you think I'm crazy! That it's all in my head."

"I don't think you're crazy, but I do think it is in your head. What I think is that you've been holding yourself together for a very long time and now that you've decided to work with me, to trust me, you're letting yourself relax and many of the demons that you've kept down for so long are coming to the surface. It might be helpful for you, for us, to have a little help for the moment."

"I want you! I want you to help me. Why aren't you enough? Why do you need help?"

"We all need help sometimes, Alyce."

"I don't need help! I don't need help from anyone! Not from you. Not from some stupid person who needs help!!"

Despite Alyce's protestations, she did see the psychiatrist who prescribed an anti-psychotic medication. I never believed Alyce took the medication as directed, but rather that she took it sporadically, especially when she became particularly frightened. In time, this was a battle I stopped fighting, especially as she settled into the treatment, feeling more securely held by our relationship and more able to own her feelings rather than expressing them through psychotic symptoms.

Early on, however, the chaotic nature of the treatment made it very difficult for me to get much coherent information about Alyce's background. Initially I therefore welcomed the meeting with Alyce's parents, the meeting Alyce had told me about in our first session. Mrs. Carhart was tall and thin, heavily made-up and bedecked in jewelry, with hair teased high above her head. She seemed cold and distant and rarely smiled. Mr. Carhart was initially overly friendly and ingratiating, as if trying to impress me with his charm. That demeanor was not long lasting. But at least I was able to gather some history. As Alyce had told me, she was adopted. Three years prior to the adoption, Mrs. Carhart gave birth to a stillborn child, a girl, whom she still mourned. After that trauma she was unwilling to attempt to have another biological child and they began the process of adoption. Mr. Carhart thought his wife "silly" for not wanting to "try again," but succumbed to her wishes and "pulled strings" to expedite the adoption.

Alyce was adopted at two months. They knew nothing of her biological mother and did not seem clear as to where Alyce had been for the first two months of her life. They described a difficult infant from the beginning – colicky, clingy, hard to satisfy or console. They gave up the idea of adopting a second infant. The mother, a stay-at-home mom, was tearful as she described the early battles between herself and Alyce. Alyce just wouldn't listen, she wouldn't obey, she didn't seem to do anything right.

Mrs. Carhart was both relieved and heartbroken when Alyce went off to school. But Alyce had difficulty there too. She couldn't concentrate. She couldn't keep friends. Although never explicitly stated, the message was that Alyce was a disappointment, someone who was never as good as the stillborn child would have been. As for Mr. Carhart, underneath his charm, his anger seethed. He was furious at his wife for insisting upon the adoption in the first place and furious at Alyce for bringing such disruption into his home.

Mr. and Mrs. Carhart wanted to meet with me again and again and yet again. Although I certainly understood their concern and fear for their daughter, I found them almost as demanding as my patient. They continually questioned my competence and intruded themselves into the treatment. They seemed determined that I label Alyce schizophrenic, a diagnosis I resisted. With her quick anger, terror over separation, and her need to maintain a clear split between good and bad, between love and hate, I saw Alyce more as a borderline patient who was – I hoped – only temporarily displaying psychotic features. Besides, I was loath to diagnose Alyce as a schizophrenic and to have her bear that stigma for the rest of her life. As it turned out, I was correct. Alyce's psychosis disappeared completely within the first six months of treatment with one noticeable exception, her conviction that I was her biological mother.

"Why won't you just admit it!" she would rage. "Why are you rejecting me again? Why did you reject me the first time? I hate you! I hate you!! I hate you!!!"

Or she'd try a gentler approach. "Please just tell me you're my mother. I won't tell anyone. I understand. You don't want your husband to know you had a child before him. I won't tell. I promise. Just make me feel complete. Just tell me you're my mother."

My reaction to these exhortations varied, both internally and verbally. There were times I wanted to yell, "Enough already, you know I'm not you're mother." At other times I wanted to take her in my arms and tell her that everything would be all right; that she didn't need me to be her mother, that I would protect her and take care of her as if she were my child. Needless to say, I did neither of these things. At times I would just sit and listen to her rail at me. At other times I would try, fruitlessly of course, to argue her out of her conviction. And many times, feeling intense empathy, I would tell her that I understood her wish that I be her mother, that I cared about her a great deal and that I would try my very best to help her and protect her.

"You know," Alyce says defiantly one day, arms crossed in front of her chest, "Sometimes when I call you at home it's actually your husband I want to talk to. I try to figure out when he's more likely to pick up the phone and call then. I can't always predict it though. Sometimes I just get you. But I like it better when he answers, even if he just ends up handing you the phone."

My concern about Alyce's potential for suicide, her constant crises, and the unreliability of my then answering service, led me to give Alyce my home phone number. It was a decision I was to regret many times during the course of the treatment.

"And why is it you want to speak to my husband, Alyce?"

"I don't know. Do you have a problem with it?"

When I don't respond Alyce continues. "He has a soft voice, gentle. I imagine him smiling at me, almost like he's asking me to come in. He's way friendlier than you! Okay, yes, you're right! You don't have to sit there like you know all the answers and like I'm so easy to read! I imagine he's my father!!" She softens. "It would be so great. You're my mother and he's my father and we live together as a family. It would be a wonderful family. And he is gentle, I know it, I can hear it in his voice. He'd like me as his daughter. He'd encourage me. He'd tell me it was great that I wanted to be a writer. He'd read everything I wrote and I'd write lots more because I'd want to please him. And you'd like it too, of course, but I'd really be writing for Daddy."

"Do you write for your Daddy now?" I ask.

"Why'd you have to bring him up! You're always spoiling it!! You're always taking away my happy family!!"

"I'm sorry, Alyce. I know it's nice to have a fantasy of the perfect family, but just like when I 'spoil it,' when I show you there's no perfect Mom, there's also no perfect family. And I think it is helpful to stay with the reality of your present-day family."

"My fake father is an ass. You know that already! And, no, he's certainly not supportive of my writing, not that I show him any of it. But he says there's no way to make a living as a writer. He wants a daughter who's a doctor or a lawyer, or at least a teacher. He doesn't want someone he'll have to support for the rest of his life. That's what he says. Big help he is!"

I'm twelve, reading an autobiography of Joseph Alsop in my couch-bed in Gram's and Gramps' living room. Everyone has been asleep for ages. But not me. I can't put the book down. Alsop had such an interesting life, going all over the world, writing amazing stories about the war and Roosevelt and Churchill and all kinds of famous people. Getting to know all these people, really knowing them, and then being able to write it down and have it read by millions of people. That's what I want to do! What I really, really want to do. I don't want to be a scientist. I know that's what Daddy wants. But that's not what I want.

I get up and walk back and forth in the living room. I twirl my long braids between my fingers. I have to tell Daddy. I have to make him see. I have to make him let me do what I want to do. I walk into the kitchen to check the wall clock. It's only 3 a.m. Daddy won't be at the office for a long time. I have to tell him. But I'll have to wait.

I call the office at 9:30. No Daddy. At 9:45. No Daddy.

A little after 10 I finally get him on the phone. I tell him I need to talk to him about something really, really important. I want to do it in person. I want to do it alone. He tells me to come whenever I want. I hurriedly rush off to the subway. I've made this trip many times by myself – 167th Street in the Bronx to the Broadway station in Manhattan. This time I'm really scared. I can't even concentrate to read. I bite my nails. Mommy is always telling me to stop biting my nails, but I can't. I think it's because I'm nervous. I'm nervous a lot. Like when I'm studying for tests. Or when I'm reading some of the books Daddy wants me to read that I can't really understand. Or when he's asking me all kinds of questions I don't know the answers to. But that's just normal nervous. Now I'm really, really nervous. I wish the train would go faster.

I get to the office at 321 Broadway and take the elevator to the third floor. I say, "Hi," to Diane, the receptionist, and start towards Daddy's enclosed office on the right. Mommy's at her desk in the back and calls to me. She wants to know what's going on, if I'm all right. I can tell she's hurt that I said I wanted to talk to Daddy alone, so I tell her it's okay for her to come in. We walk together to Daddy's office.

For a second I can't say anything. I start crying and angrily wipe the tears from my face. I'm being a baby. I just need to say it. So I do. I tell Daddy what I rehearsed over and over in my head.

"I read this great autobiography of Joseph Alsop. I love it. It made me see that I want to be a journalist, not a scientist. It's you who wanted to be the scientist, not me. I can't live your life over for you."

There, I've said it! I hold my breath waiting for the reaction. There is no explosion. I exhale. First Daddy tells me that of course I need to do whatever will make me happy. Then he tells me I mustn't believe everything I read. Alsop is a very conservative columnist and if I'm going to be a journalist, I need to be a discriminating reader who can analyze and understand what's really being communicated. I can tell Daddy is going into one of his lectures, but that's okay, at least he heard me and didn't explode. And then he tells me I have to remember that I'm very young and that a lot could change for me. But if it turns out I do want to be a journalist, perhaps I could write for Science magazine.

I say nothing. But I feel really, really disappointed. He doesn't want me to become who I want to be. He still wants me to be who he wants me to be. And he wants me to be him!!! I just know that I'm never, ever going to please him. I need to stop trying. I need to stop trying and just do what I'm going to do.

But of course I didn't. Through high school and college I took a great deal of math and science. In high school it wasn't too bad. By college I was way out of my league. Calculus and physics were both killer courses for me. Each time I struggled through another test I'd say this is it, I'm not doing this again. But I did. Again and yet again.

"I'm going to major in psychology," I announce one day, my voice shaking with anxiety, knowing full well my father's reaction. This is even worse than being twelve and telling my father I wanted to be a journalist. That earlier goal had fallen by the wayside, the result of an angry, critical journalism teacher I had in high school. One angry, critical parent was enough.

My mother turns off the lamb chops she's making for dinner and sits down at the table. She also knows what's coming.

"Psychology! What idiocy!! How can you be so stupid?! That's not science, that's hogwash! What do you think you're going to do, listen to people and magically solve their problems? If you wanted to study the brain, the synaptic connection of the nervous system, that would be different. But psychology! I forbid it!"

Trying to keep the anger out of my voice, I reply, "You can't forbid it. That's what I'm going to do."

An even lengthier tirade follows, filled with adjectives such as "stupid," "idiot," "bitch," "ass," and so on.

My mother says nothing.

I, too, say nothing. My father's rage terrifies me, but it doesn't deter me. I made up my mind. Nothing my father said would change it.

We continue to argue as I work my way through graduate school and, even more so, through analytic training.

"Freud?! How ridiculous! He was a charlatan!! He pulled the wool over everyone's eyes. Children with sexual feelings, the Oedipal complex, dreams!! How can you be so stupid? How can you say I'm dreaming even if I don't remember it? That's nonsense, hocus-pocus, magic, like all that garbage Freud spouted. The unconscious! What idiocy!! It's all pure poppycock! If I can't see it, if it can't be measured in a laboratory, it's just stupidity!"

During one of my visits home from graduate school, I show my father the research on REM dreaming. Here are laboratory studies, here is science, here is something he could believe. And he does! I'm amazed. He reads the studies and agrees that he could be dreaming even if he doesn't remember the dreams. I'm ecstatic! I finally won!!

But the next time I come home it's as if this discussion never happened. He's back to his old position, dismissing the research as hogwash as well.

There were many times that both my unwillingness to accept Alyce as a daughter, as well as my inability to be the omnipotent, magical therapist, led Alyce to intense feelings of hatred that sometimes threatened the treatment. I couldn't count the number of times she would yell at me, telling me she was sorry that she had met me, that she made a huge mistake in asking me to be her therapist, that she never wanted to see me again, that she wouldn't ever see me again, etc., etc. She hated me for not being her mother and hated me for being the mother who had abandoned her. There was, however, no greater threat to the treatment than the day she made a startling confession.

She is unusually quiet, sitting with hands crossed in front of her, alternating between staring at me defiantly and looking sheepishly at the floor. I make repeated attempts to engage her and find myself increasingly frustrated.

"All right, Alyce," I say, "if you want to sit here in silence that's what we'll do."

Silence.

"I'd like to know why you're being silent, but if you won't tell me, there's really not much I can do."

Silence.

The hour drags along. Alyce looks at the clock.

"I have to tell you," she finally blurts out. "I have to tell you before this hour is over. I don't want to go through this again. But I can't! I know you'll be mad at me."

My mind races. What could she have possibly done? Has she begun cutting herself? Did she attack one of her parents? No, that's ridiculous. I hold my breath, my anxiety increasing.

"I'm seeing another therapist."

I look at her, stunned, not even quite sure what she has just told me.

"My father wanted me to try seeing someone besides you, so I've been seeing this man – just once a week."

I stare at Alyce, unsure what to say. I feel hurt, angry, and betrayed. I have been giving Alice all that I could possibly give and it has not been enough.

"Say something," she demands.

"How long have you been seeing this other therapist?" I ask lamely.

"I don't know. Maybe… two months. Well," she says after a brief period of silence, "what are you going to do about it?"

"What do you want me to do? And what do you want to do?"

"I don't know what you mean," she says defiantly.

"Alyce, our time is almost up. Why don't we both go home and think about what would be best for us to do, what would be best for you."

"Are you going to stop seeing me?" she asks, a slight tremor in her voice.

"I don't want to stop seeing you. But it doesn't seem like a good idea for you to see two therapists. So again, why don't we stop for today and both think about what we want to do."

Alyce's revelation led me to think carefully about the intensity of our relationship and the possible problems it created in the treatment. Although Alyce looked to me to be the all-perfect, all-giving mother, she also could not allow me to fulfill that role – even assuming it were possible – because to do so would be to fuse with me, to be engulfed by me in a way that would mean the destruction of her identity (Adler, 1985; Giovacchini, 1986; Searles, 1986). Although, on the one hand, my love for Alyce provided her with a feeling of safety and security, on the other hand, it frightened her, threatening her sense of self. She then moved outside the bounds of the treatment in order to protect herself.

I am five years old. I am lying on Mommy's lap in the back seat. I love it here. Grandma's up front and Mr. Ment is driving. He always drives. He's Gram's and Gramps' really good friend. We're going away, to Vermont. Mommy tells me we've been there before but I don't remember. Gramps is away for the summer working as a baker. And Daddy doesn't come. He stays home to work. Besides, he and Gram don't get along too good. I don't care. I like it just the way it is. I love being here in Mommy's lap. It's warm. It's safe. I wish it could stay like this for always. I wish I could stay little, little like I am right now and stay right here forever and ever.

I ask, pleadingly, "But why can't I stay at Marshe's. She lives right upstairs. Why can't I sleep over? All my friends will be there. Their mothers don't mind them sleeping over."

"I've told you again and again, Linda," my mother replies sternly. "You have your own bed to sleep in. There's no reason for you to sleep at anyone else's house."

"Everyone does it!"

"If everyone was going to jump off a bridge you wouldn't have to do it too," she adds as I turn away.

She's never going to let me sleep over at my friends'. There's no point in asking and asking.

She doesn't let me do lots of things. She thinks bike riding and roller skating are too dangerous, especially in the city. I don't care about that. I know all my friends can do those things, but it really doesn't bother me. Who wants to ride a stupid bike anyway? I just wish that just once she'd let me sleep over at a friend's.

I come home from school. I call Mommy at work as soon as I walk in the door. "I got a D on my arithmetic test," I say, trying not to cry. "I just don't understand fractions! I know we worked on it and worked on it but I still can't do it!"

"It's all right, Linda," Mommy says kindly. "You tried the best you could. We'll just have to work on it a little more and I'm sure you'll be able to master it."

"But it will ruin my grade! Maybe it's because I've been sick so much, missed so much school."

"That's certainly possible," she agrees. "I tell you what. Why don't I go to school and talk to Miss Feldman? I'll explain to her that you've missed so much school and that you have been trying hard to catch up. Maybe that way she won't count the test."

"Oh thank you, Mommy. That's a great idea. I feel so, so much better. I knew you'd be able to think of something."

For many, many years I was cocooned in the comfort of my mother's embrace. It was welcoming, consuming, all-inclusive. I did not wish to move beyond her; I did not know that she could strangle me; I did not know that I had to separate before I could find my own self.

In ruminating about Alyce, it occurred to me that her seeing another therapist was probably a healthier response than her becoming even more childlike and succumbing to the regressive pull of what she experienced as my loving maternal responsiveness. She could have reacted and, in fact, sometimes did react to my excessive caretaking by becoming more and more needy and demanding in what Balint (1968) referred to as a malignant regression. In such a regression, the patient can never be sated. The analyst ends up feeling helpless and depleted as her best efforts fail to satisfy an increasingly demanding and regressed patient.

Had I been loving Alyce too much? Had I been needing her too much? Had I been trying too hard to hold onto her? I needed to be able to let her go in order to assure her that I could not and would not swallow her up. This need to be sensitive to Alyce's need for space and distance is particularly important with patients such as Alyce whose mother seemed to alternate between hostility and rejection on the one hand, and intrusion and clinginess on the other. As the child of such a mother, Alyce internalized these splits and vacillated from being the needy child to being the rejecting mother. And, not surprisingly, these splits were re-enacted in the treatment. These two parts of Alyce – the rejected child and the rejecting parent – were alternatively projected onto me and taken as her own. In other words, Alyce would project her rejecting parent onto me and experience herself as the rejected child or, as when she was seeing a second therapist, project the needy child onto me and herself be the rejecting parent.

And then there was my part in this interactive enactment, the part that did perhaps need Alyce too much.

I met George, the man who was to become my husband, four years prior to Alyce entering my life. The day I met him I was looking for a contractor to remodel my barely livable home on a small lake outside of Ann Arbor, Michigan. There he was on a typically cold, blustery day with his sparkling blue eyes, graying goatee, and a warm, engaging smile. I liked him immediately. So far I had two other estimates. One was from a large company – Sherlock Homes – that was way over my budget. The second was from the brother of a colleague. I didn't much trust the colleague and I trusted his brother even less. Before George even walked into my house, I hoped that I would like what he had to offer and that I would be able to afford him.

To say the least, the house needed a considerable amount of work. I had bought it the year before. It was the first time I had ever lived in a house, let alone owned one. At the time I was involved with David, a man who embodied the essence of every narcissistic, emotionally unavailable man with whom I had ever been involved, and with whom I fantasized living in this idyllic setting. The house had previously belonged to a friend. From the first time I visited Sally I felt an incredible sense of peace looking out at the lake through the cascading leaves of the large elm tree that stood in front of the house. The lake, about a half-mile across, made the homes on the other side visible, but not intrusive. I felt simultaneously cradled and set free, immediately safe and at home. When Sally married and began making plans to move to Virginia, I made an impulsive decision to buy the house. I did look at three other lakefront properties, but didn't feel the same sense of connectedness. I wanted that house. I paid $36,500 for it. George was later to tell me I paid too much. It wasn't the house I was buying, it was the feeling of peace I experienced being there.

The house – more a cottage really – had once been a boat house. It had been haphazardly transformed into a small, two-bedroom house with no dining room, no garage, no laundry room, no septic system, and, most importantly, no central heating! There was a gas heater built into the wall that warmed both the kitchen and the living room. Closing the bedroom door in the winter was impossible as you could end up with hypothermia. Now I was planning a major renovation and was looking for a professional contractor. I wanted central heating, a septic system, a garage, a laundry room, a guest room, a remodeled kitchen, and two walls removed – the one between the kitchen and the second bedroom that would now be a dining room and the one between the master bedroom and the porch so that the lake could be seen from the bedroom. George's estimate came in at $12,000. I hired him. He was to begin work in late spring, early summer.

George came to lay the foundation for the addition early one Saturday morning. He came with one other man, a man who looked both odd and uncomfortable. In fact, he reminded me of the schizophrenic patients I had worked with at the Forensic Center before starting in private practice. It was the job that originally brought me to Ann Arbor since I was, at that point, very interested in psychology and the law. George introduced the man as his son, Mark.

"When's your crew arriving?" I asked.

He laughed. "This is it."

George did all the work himself – the drywall, the electrical, the plumbing, everything. I was amazed by George's ability to create anything and everything with his hands –

strong, powerful, workman's hands. His physical stamina was astounding. He was a fifty-two-year-old man who could work twelve hour days, easily carry a hundred pound bag of shingles, and be totally unfazed by the summer's heat. What I didn't yet know was that George had broken his back in his early thirties when a building he was working on collapsed. He had been told that he would never walk again. But after extensive back surgery he was to fool them all and walk on roofs for years to come.

While George worked on my house, I was often away seeing patients. But I tried to be home as much as possible, both because summer on a lake in Michigan is all too short and because I so enjoyed admiring George's work and talking to this most interesting man. George and I talked endlessly. We were fascinated by the radical differences in our backgrounds and the startling similarities in our interests and values. I was incredibly impressed by what George had been able to accomplish in his life, given his early hardships. His mother, Betty, was sixteen when he was born, and went on to have eleven more children by two husbands. George's father was a philanderer who contracted tuberculosis but refused to stay in a sanitarium. As a result, he passed on the TB to both Betty and George, to Betty in her lungs, to George is his lymph glands. Betty spent much of George's childhood cloistered in a sanitarium; George spent two years of his childhood in the same facility although he was barred from seeing his mother. He was raised primarily by his grandparents, a kind, loving grandmother and a strict, harsh, religious grandfather. They were extremely poor. George called them – and himself – "Michigan hillbillies." He was raised on a farm as a Seventh Day Adventist in a home where education and intellectual pursuits were largely ignored. His grandfather hired himself out as a handyman/builder but, according to George, had little skill. He would take George along with him and, even as early as nine years old, George was often the more competent. George's grandmother took to saying, "Let George do it," a refrain George was to hear from many people, including me, during the course of his life.

Wanting to get away from his family, George lived a large part of his adult life in southern California with his first wife and their three children. After finishing college and trying his hand at teaching, he went back to what he knew best, construction. With two other men he started a construction company that sold and built cookie-cutter homes. Then he was a boss, an administrator. He supervised the work, hired out to subcontractors, but did none of the work himself. For a while he made lots of money. But he hated the work. And, as he told me, he hated what he became. He felt that he was empty, unfeeling, that he became dishonest, scheming, and too preoccupied with making the dollar. And he felt that his children were coming apart, too influenced by money and the loose California lifestyle, as well as by his absence. About fifteen years before I met him, George literally decided to cash it all in. He sold his part of the business for ten cents on the dollar, packed up his family and returned home to Michigan. He never regretted his decision. Both of his business partners were dead of heart attacks within five years after George left. Once he returned to Michigan he decided that he would build only by himself and only what he wanted to build. And right now I was more than happy that it was my house he wanted to build.

Among our many conversations, George and I talked about psychology, the mind and the unconscious, as well as my work that brought me profound pleasure and fulfillment. He listened, fascinated, apparently interested in my every word. He was intrigued by my *constant introspection and found it refreshing. He hadn't ever known anyone who thought so much about their own mind.*

George is on a ladder putting finish molding in my new dining room. I'm painting the drywall he's already completed. We've been talking about how each of us so enjoys working for ourselves, not having to be accountable to anyone else.

"I'm sure for me," I say, "it's at least partially a result of my not wanting to answer to my father, not wanting to bow to a capricious authority."

He looks at me quizzically, as if not clear of the connection.

"You know," I continue, "if you have a boss who tells you what to do, it's partly like being a child again, having to do what he says, having to obey, whether you agree or not."

"That certainly fits for me. I was only a kid and I knew a lot more than my grandfather, but he was the one with the strap."

"That's it exactly," I reply. "My father didn't use a strap, but his trigger-happy temper, his explosiveness scared me to death. I'm sure that's one of the reasons I worked at the Forensic Center, trying to cure or control violent men."

George looks at me thoughtfully. "Do you always think this much about why you do what you do?"

"Definitely," I say laughing. "I can never get out of my head."

"And that's what you do with your patients too?"

"Um hmm. I help them to look at themselves and understand themselves so they can hopefully not repeat the same mistakes again and again."

"I certainly know all therapists aren't like you. All those VA psychiatrists ever wanted to do for Mark was push medication at him, and none of it ever worked."

I had, unfortunately, been correct in my initial assessment of Mark. He was a paranoid schizophrenic. Mark had become psychotic in Vietnam, although he had been a troubled child and an acting-out adolescent. In Vietnam he chopped off the index finger of his right hand – he was left-handed – and was discharged from the service with one hundred percent disability. Since that time, despite medication, he was continually psychotic, sometimes violent, and a terrible responsibility, chore, and heartache to George.

"I have worked with schizophrenics," I say, "sometimes quite successfully. Truthfully, though, I wouldn't work with someone like Mark on an outpatient basis. I'd be too scared of his potential for violence. Another legacy from my father. But I do know some therapists who probably would take Mark on if you – or he – ever wanted to go that route. I don't know if he could be helped with therapy, but it might be worth a shot."

George gets down from the ladder and walks over to me. "You know," he says, "you're an amazing woman. You're smart, independent, thoughtful, and caring to boot. I admire who you are and what you do."

How could I not find such words intoxicating? This man I so esteemed actually respected me and what I did. So different from my father who had nothing but contempt for my life's work. And now here was this smart, strong, accomplished man who liked to listen to me and admired me and my ideas. How could I not start to fall in love with him?

George finished all the work on my house, a house that looked truly beautiful. I could see the lake from my large bedroom windows. I had my own laundry room. There was no ugly heater embedded in the wall of my living room. And George had even built a tiny enclosed porch where I put a small table so that I could sit and eat and look out at the lake. It was perfect.

Except that it was over.

I told George that I would miss him. He told me he'd miss me too. I suggested that we have lunch sometimes during the week. He said he'd be messy, that he'd have to come in his work suit. I told him that didn't bother me at all. He reminded me that he was a vegetarian. I hadn't forgotten. George stopped eating any sort of animal at age twelve when, as he said, his "friend the chicken" ended up on his plate. We met at the Blind Pig, a funky Ann Arbor landmark not far from my office. It evolved into weekly lunches, then dinners, then invitations to my house and then to a passionate love affair. I marveled at George's capacity to love and to constantly express that love in both words and actions. He said repeatedly that he couldn't believe his good fortune. He couldn't believe I could love a man so much older than myself.

George's age was a problem for me. He would most likely die before me and leave me a grieving widow, especially given the longevity in my family. I already knew I didn't handle death well. I was twenty-four when my beloved grandmother died of a heart attack. Even though she was eighty-one, the news of her death came as a tremendous shock to me. It was as if I had never expected her to die. Almost, in fact, as if I didn't believe in death itself. I couldn't take in that this strong woman, this pillar of my childhood, was gone from me forever. When my grandfather died three years later, I was again heartbroken, but the shock and reality of his death was not as stark. I grieved for them both for many, many years and still felt their loss acutely when I met George.

The other problem for me was that I could not have children with George, at least not biological children. He had had a vasectomy many years previously when he found himself the father of three by his fourth anniversary. I had always pictured myself being a mother. In fact, as I went into my early thirties, I even considered becoming a single parent but had never quite gotten up the nerve to attempt such a huge undertaking on my own. George and I talked about the question of children. He would have agreed to my conceiving if I felt I had to be a mother. But I knew that he didn't really want the responsibility of more children. Death and childlessness. Death and childlessness. Two big problems. Two big losses. In the end I chose George. I loved him more than I would have thought possible and there were, after all, no guarantees in life. If I had him for twenty years that would be better than not having him at all. I told a friend that I saw my life as existing in thirds: one-third before George, one-third with George and one-third after George. As for children, there was my cousin, Danielle. Her mother was killed in a car accident when she was ten, just as George and I were getting involved. I hoped that eventually she and I would become closer and that I would be able to assume the role of a surrogate mother. But she was, not surprisingly, an angry, depressed child who wasn't that easy to get close to, especially since she lived first in North Carolina with her adoptive father and then with her grandparents in New York. And there were always my patients. Perhaps they too could help satisfy my longing to have children.

Alyce walked right into this maternal need. She was a scared, needy child–woman who desperately wanted me to be her mother. For my part in the enactment that led Alyce to see a second therapist, I did perhaps need Alyce too much. Although I did not understand this at the time, I now wonder if Alyce had become the biological child I could not have with George. And, even further, a child who I could nurture and heal, unlike Mark who seemed forever broken. So it is quite likely that I was holding onto Alyce too tightly. I needed to be able to let her go. I could let her go. She could not have two therapists. She needed to choose. She decided to stay. My willingness to let go helped strengthen her boundary and her sense of self. Our work together could continue.

My out of awareness desire to have Alyce be George's and my child may have intensified the needy, clingy part of myself. On the other hand, I believe that my relationship with George also helped me to create the necessary boundary with Alyce at this juncture of the treatment. Although there may have been times I felt like the needy child with Alyce, I mostly felt neither needy nor childlike. Quite the contrary. I was sated. I was with a man who saw me for myself, loved me, stood by me, and would take care of me in whatever way he could. I could love Alyce and want to help her, but I did not need her to feel whole myself. I was not like her mother who may have indeed felt helpless and projected her needy self onto Alyce. I was not, at this point in my life, coming from such a needy place. It is interesting to wonder whether Alyce's treatment would have taken a different turn were I not with George. Or, assuming I had been willing to take her on as a patient, whether there would have been a different treatment outcome if I was seeing Alyce during George's declining health or immediately after his death. These are of course unanswerable questions, but speak to the question of how an analyst's current life circumstances can affect a treatment for better or for worse.

2

THE LOVE STORIES CONTINUE

Alyce chose me. She now intended to prove me worthy of her choice.

"You don't understand how much of a witch she is! She's not my real mother, she's not, she's not! I couldn't have a mother who cared so little about me. Aren't all kids loveable? Aren't we supposed to be loved?! What about me? Don't I deserve to be loved? All she cares about is herself – looking pretty, caring what the neighbors think, hoping my idiot father will bring her another piece of jewelry she doesn't need! Answer me, don't I deserve something in all of this?"

"Of course you do, Alyce," I say. Then, futilely attempting to interject a more reasoned and reasonable voice I add, "Maybe it's possible that your mother does love you, Alyce, that she's just not very good at showing it and that you're so angry with her you can't ever take in anything positive she does."

Silence. Alyce glares at me. Then the glare disappears, replaced by a look of abject despair. "You're right, I probably don't deserve to be loved. I'm just bad, bad through and through. I should just kill myself. I have these fantasies of how I'd do it. Or more like how it gets done. I just see it. All the blood and gore. They just come to me. Like I see myself dangling from a rope, my head half off my neck, blood oozing down. And there's a knife too, a knife sticking out of my stomach and blood oozing from there as well. I like the picture. I see it. It's soothing."

I can barely keep myself from shuddering. And from kicking myself as well. My comment about her mother was way off the mark, an unempathic, unattuned response that has fueled her rage and turned it inward. "Alyce," I say more strongly than I feel, "I think you're angry with me, angry that I defended your mother rather than supporting your feelings. I'm sorry. I understand. It's okay for you to be angry with me."

She looks at me skeptically. "I don't get you. When I'm angry you say I need to look at my sadness, or my neediness, or some other shit like that. And when I'm sad you say I need to look at my anger. I'm not angry now. I just want to die."

"It's true I do say that, Alyce. And this time I think you are angry with me and have every right to be. But often when we're angry we need to find the sadness underneath and when we're sad or vulnerable we need to look at what's underneath that and perhaps find the anger. Often they're two sides of the same coin. Right now I think you're turning the anger you feel towards me inward and taking it out on yourself."

"I FUCKING HATE YOU!!!"

Silence.

"I HATE YOU! I HATE YOU! I HATE YOU! You're so fucking reasonable!!! Just get mad at me sometimes! Yell at me! Tell me how bad I am."

"I do get mad at you sometimes, Alyce. But not this time. This time I'm more mad at myself. And I think you're mad at me too."

Alyce sat silent for the rest of the session. She called me frantically that night at home. "Are you all right? Are you mad at me? Will you still work with me?"

I reassured her. Her anger hadn't killed me. She wasn't bad. It was all right to be angry. I would see her again tomorrow.

Alyce was making plans to return to school for the winter semester. Neither her parents nor I thought she was ready, but I did not want to stand in her way and her parents were tired of the constant battles at home. Alyce told me that once upon a time she had thought that her father could do no wrong, but that now she saw him as almost as evil as her mother. All he cared about was money. He didn't love her; he never had. She had to get away and school seemed like the only way out. Unfortunately, almost as soon as Alyce arrived at school she started panicking. Her anxiety soared. She was too far from home, home being both her parents and me. She returned to her parents, defeated and depressed. In many ways this was a calmer time in Alyce's treatment. Although she was quite clingy and demanding, and her rages certainly did not disappear, she was more able to work from a place of knowing and accepting her need for me. The bond between us grew. Her underlying fragility was all the more apparent, although still covered by a defensive, defiant toughness that came and went. I could easily see the vulnerable little bird and felt my love for her deepen. I was back in the kitchen defending Sunshine. I was back in the kitchen, attempting to protect both Sunshine and my own little girl self.

It was, therefore, with both great trepidation and some guilt, that in March I told Alyce – and all my patients – that I would be taking a five-week vacation starting in May. It was the longest vacation I had ever taken since starting private practice. George and I were planning a trip to New Zealand, Australia, and Tahiti. For two weeks of the time in Australia we would be staying with friends of mine from graduate school. I told Alyce she could write to me at their address and assured her that I would send her postcards along the way. Much to my surprise, Alyce did not seem as distressed by my planned departure as I anticipated. Although understandably experiencing it as an abandonment, she expressed more fear and sadness than rage. There were no threats of suicide or termination. She seemed appreciative of my willingness to give her my friends' address and to write to her. I worried that she was either blocking her feelings or feeling too unsafe to voice them. I don't mean to imply that all went smoothly, but rather that my planned leaving-taking did not result in either a severe regression or constant emotional upheavals. I now wonder if my offer to write was also a way for me to keep in contact with Alyce, as if she were indeed my child, the child I would send postcards to at "home." If Alyce sensed that she served this function for me, she might well have experienced it as both reassuring and gratifying, thus curtailing her regression and acting out.

George and I have a wonderful five weeks, totally enmeshed in each other's company. On the plane ride home I cry. I don't want to go home. We were so close, so intensely involved. I find it hard to accept that we have to return to our regular lives.

Although Alyce tolerated the five-week separation without decompensating, I returned to find her even more enraged at her parents and more determined than ever that I fulfill her fantasy of being her biological mother.

Once again, Alyce had decided that she wanted to return to college, but this time to a school that was closer to both me and her parents. Her father was adamantly opposed to the idea. They fought constantly. I was supportive of her feelings, but clear that I was powerless to influence or change her father's decision. She then began to threaten to terminate. I was useless, no good. Why should she see me if I couldn't help her? Why didn't I just admit I was her mother and get custody of her? Then I would truly be able to help her. And if I wouldn't, then she might as well leave. After enduring several of these struggles, out of anger or fatigue or both, I finally gave in. I told her we would terminate in two months if, after a month, she still wanted to.

That night she had a huge fight with her father. She asked if he wanted her to move out. When he said that it was up to her she took that to mean that he wanted her to leave and felt horribly rejected. She called me at home extremely distraught and unsure of what to do. I tried to interpret the similarity between what had occurred between us earlier in the day and what occurred with her father. She totally denied any connection and was angry with me for being insufficiently supportive, for not being "on her side."

The next session Alyce is silent, arms crossed in front of her, a scowl on her face. I feel the rage exuding from her. I make one comment after another, never knowing whether they're relevant, never knowing if she takes them in.

"You're wanting me to make everything all right," I say. Silence. "You'd like me to wave a magic wand." Silence. "You want me to take care of you." Silence. "You want me to say you can live with me." More silence.

I feel myself getting more and more angry. I finally stop trying. I too sit in silence. Her anger erupts.

"I FUCKING HATE YOU!!! I CAN'T WAIT TO LEAVE YOU! YOU'RE TOTALLY WORTHLESS. I HAVE NOTHING TO SAY TO YOU. I'M NOT COMING BACK. I HATE YOU. I HATE YOU. YOU'RE JUST LIKE MY DAD! I'M NOT WAITING TWO MONTHS TO LEAVE YOU. WHY SHOULD I? I'M LEAVING RIGHT NOW! RIGHT THIS MINUTE!!"

With that, Alyce starts to get up. Feeling intense rage myself, I act without thinking. I get up and sit on Alyce to prevent her from leaving. We're both startled. I quickly resume my seat. But the rage has been broken. We both start to laugh uncomfortably.

"You sat on me," Alyce says incredulously.

"Yes, I did. I'm sorry."

"I guess you didn't want me to leave."

"No, I didn't want you to leave. I was also pretty angry," I admit.

"I don't want to leave either. I don't want to terminate. I just want you to be my mother."

Just as Alyce loved me and hated me, so too did I love and hate Alyce. Although I certainly do not recommend sitting on a patient as good therapeutic technique, I did and do forgive myself, knowing that patients such as Alyce often inspire their therapists to hateful reactions. As Winnicott (1949) said, "If the patient seeks objective or justified hate he must be able to reach it, else he cannot feel he can reach objective love." When Alyce behaved in a consistently attacking or provocative manner, had I always responded with warmth and understanding, she would have come to question my authenticity. And, if she could not be assured of my genuineness, she could never trust that my caring and concern was any more genuine. Alyce could never have taken in, internalized my positive image of her because she would always have doubted the authenticity of that image.

Additionally, if I always reacted to Alyce's vituperative attacks with patience and forbearance – assuming that were even possible – she could have even further idealized me, seeing me as the embodiment of "goodness" and feeling even worse about her own "badness." The contrast between her "badness" and my "goodness" could have become too much for her to tolerate, leading to greater feelings of hate directed at either herself or me.

I also think that Alyce's rage is yet another piece of the puzzle that helps explain my intense connection to her. Although I was no longer attempting to heal violent men such as those in the Forensic Center, Alyce may have provided a similar challenge. Perhaps I could transform this angry young woman into someone who could contain her rage and learn to express her anger more appropriately. Perhaps I could succeed with Alyce in a way I never could with my father.

The following session Alyce is silent again. But this time the room feels full of sadness, not rage.

"Something you said last time really got to me."

Silence.

"I don't want to tell you what it was," she says, sounding almost childlike.

"Can you tell me even if you don't want to?" I ask.

There's a brief silence. "It was your saying that I hoped you'd say I could live with you. I hadn't realized that myself. But when you said it, it was like you took it away from me, like you were saying it couldn't happen. I'm not ready to know that yet." Alyce begins crying. The vulnerable little bird has reappeared.

"You can hold onto whatever fantasy you need, Alyce. Your feelings and fantasies are always all right. You still think you need the perfect mother. You don't know yet that you don't need her and that she doesn't exist."

"I do need her! I do need you!"

"I'm here, Alyce. I'm here for you. You can keep me with you always. You don't have to live with me to be able to have me with you."

As Alyce became more convinced that I neither could nor would wrench her fantasy away from her, she relaxed more into the treatment. Gradually she was better able to hold an internal image of me between sessions, to have a sense of my supportive presence even when she wasn't in the room with me.

Alyce did get her way with her parents. They allowed her to return to college and go to the school of her choice. The compromise was that she would live at home and commute to school. This time around Alyce fared much better. Although not an outstanding student, she was able to concentrate and performed adequately. She was also transforming herself into a beautiful young woman. She lost weight, was attentive to her appearance and became more interested in dating. All of this was, of course, fraught with difficulty. Alyce had tremendous ambivalence about growing up, for to do so meant giving up on ever having the mothering she so desperately wanted. There were sessions in which she again felt young to me, helpless, vulnerable, needing to be taken care of. And then there would be times she'd declare, "I don't need you." She fell in love with one man after another, each a fleeting romance as love turned to hate, before turning back to love and then again back to hate. Despite these real life issues and concerns, a major focus of the treatment remained the relationship between us, including her fantasy that I was her biological mother.

While Alyce and I continued to struggle with our relationship, I was engaged in a struggle of my own.

As I cry on our way back from Tahiti, George is following a different track. Inspired by the incredible variety of tropical fish, but less than enamored with snorkeling, George is determined to learn to scuba dive. So we do! Here I am, the same unathletic me – the person who can't ride a bike or roller skate – learning to scuba dive. I figure if a man twenty years my senior can learn to dive, I certainly can too. So I take the plunge, just as I did in my relationship with George.

The book work is easy for me; the pool lessons far more challenging. I am anxious, uncoordinated, and unsure of myself. But even the pool work is a piece of cake compared to the open water dive we need for our certification. We want to be certified before January when we plan to go to Grand Cayman for our first diving vacation. Our two-day test – torture is a better word – is in a quarry in Ohio in November. The air and the water temperature are bitter cold; the underwater visibility is terrible. I'm freezing despite the extra-heavy wet suit. I am definitely not happy. At one point the instructor tells us to go to the ledge and wait for him. I never see a ledge. I just keep on going. George comes after me. He later tells me that he watched me sink right past him. After the first day we're both exhausted, George from trying to help not only me but another woman with all the heavy equipment; me from both the cold and the anxiety. But we persevere. We become certified divers.

As January of 1984 arrived and George and I planned to take our trip, Alyce was enraged and inconsolable. I was to be gone for one week. She had tolerated my five-week vacation. This was just too much. She railed against me, accusing me of being cruel, insensitive, indifferent to her suffering. She couldn't understand how I could leave her again. What gave me the right to go? Wasn't she my child? Didn't she deserve first consideration? I was choosing George over her. That wasn't fair. Not fair at all.

I was puzzled by Alyce's intense reaction to my upcoming one-week vacation since she had done fairly well when I was absent for five weeks. In fact, she had been proud of her ability to cope. But, at the time, I reasoned that this additional week was just too much for her to bear, a terrible reminder of her dependence on me, while I felt no similar dependency and was free to come and go as I pleased. In retrospect, being now more aware of the exquisite and often unconscious interaction between patient and analyst, I wonder if Alyce sensed my anxiety about this trip – our first experience diving in an ocean – and that her loud protestations reflected my own underlying fears. Would I return from this trip? Would George? Did some catastrophe await us? As always, there is no way of knowing definitively whether my anxiety fed Alyce's, but it does seem worthy of consideration. And, although nothing catastrophic happened on the trip, I certainly had more than enough to be anxious about.

George and I are staying in a small resort on the East End of Grand Cayman, an example of our preference for more out-of-the-way places. Unfortunately, we arrive to discover that earlier that week the diving boat had ploughed into the dock, rendering both the dock and the boat unusable. The boat is being repaired with no time line as to when it will again be available. No one is working on the damaged dock. The extremely unhelpful staff has no suggestions as to how to solve this major difficulty. They make no plans to rent another boat or to arrange for another diving facility to accommodate us. Fortunately for us there is a businessman from California who brought his sales staff to Grand Cayman to celebrate the outstanding year they had just enjoyed. He rents a boat and generously offers to have George and I join them.

So, after figuring out how to get in the dive boat without benefit of a dock, after dealing with extremely rough seas and George's seasickness, and after my making innumerable trips to the bathroom, we are ready to jump into the ocean! To say that I am anxious is putting it mildly. I don't even see any fish on our first several dives. I'm too busy figuring out how to adjust my buoyancy, how not to suck up enormous amounts of air, how not to constantly flap my arms or legs but rather glide seamlessly through the water, and how to keep George in sight without swimming on top of him. He, of course, loves it as soon as he hits the water, despite his still being seasick. In fact, he's so nauseous that he has to take out his regulator to throw up. He later says, "I wasn't going to vomit into a brand new regulator. Besides, I got to see fish no one else saw. They loved eating what I threw up!" Nothing deters him. Being his usual daredevil self, at one point the dive master has to tug on his hose, showing him that he is going below the permitted 100 feet.

Although repeated trips to the bathroom before the first dive of the morning remains a constant during this trip – and, in fact, many trips to follow – I do get better at managing the mechanics and actually begin to enjoy the incredible sensation of floating through the water – as close to flying as possible. I love the colorful parrot fish, the graceful angel fish, and the friendly groupers. There is a whole new world to explore, and explore it we do, as we go on to dive Palau and Yap in the South Pacific, the Red Sea in Egypt, the three Cayman Islands, Cozumel, the Turks and the Caicos, Honduras, Belize, Baja, and the Florida Keys.

Not surprisingly, I returned to find Alyce still enraged with me, but also relieved to have me back. Again, I wonder if she had sensed my own anxiety about the trip and was now reassured that I had returned safely. It's not that I consciously feared some catastrophic ending, but I wonder if I had somehow communicated my more unconscious terrors.

One week after my return, Alyce wrote me a letter. I quote from portions of it.

> After much thought and consideration I had decided that seeing you again would probably be the worst thing I could do. After thinking it over a second time I thought that not seeing you again could possibly be the worst mistake I have or could ever make.

In the first two sentences of this letter, Alyce's splitting – her tendency to experience herself and the world in black and white terms – is evident. She hates me and never wants to see me again. She loves me and cannot possibly let me go. The conflicting feelings switch from one side to the other, exacerbated by my recent vacation. During the course of her treatment, I repeatedly pointed out to Alyce her tendency to split, to think and feel in extremes. In time, she was able to recognize and understand her splitting, but being able to feel different emotionally and to respond less extremely remained an issue throughout Alyce's treatment. On one occasion Alyce told me that she understood that she was only black and white and that she needed to become more "mulatto."

The letter continues:

> If I just stopped coming it would mean that I would give in to the biggest problem I have, the realization that I have only the mother that adopted me. That is hard for me to write, because I still don't fully understand or accept that. It's so much easier for me to believe that I was stolen away from my mother at birth and till this day she is still looking for me. I can't begin to explain the sorrow, hurt and rage I feel towards her when I think that maybe she really did give me up...
>
> When you stated my rage at you was for your not being my mother I was sure there had to be a better reason for my anger. Careful analysis has proved to me that you were indeed right. My mother in my mind had come to bare a lot of resemblance to you... I have made up a glorified version of her in my mind and she somehow came out like you. And when I knew that I could never have you in the maternal sense it pissed me off!! It just didn't seem fair that God could take away my original mother and give me a shitty one, then give me my idea of the perfect mother and then you took that away from me too...

To say I fully believe that you are not my mother would be lying and as I understand it, we are supposed to be honest with each other. In the back of my mind lies a fantasy about you being my mother ready to spring up when I am vulnerable.

Since Alyce was adopted, it was particularly easy for her to see me as her idealized biological mother from whom she had been stolen. However, at this point in the treatment at least part of her did know that she had not been stolen, but voluntarily surrendered, thereby resulting in her rage at both me and her biological mother. It is possible that any unconscious desire on my part that Alyce be George's and my child might well have contributed both to the intensity and the tenacity of her conviction. It is apparent that Alyce also experienced me as her omnipotent protector, ready to "spring up" whenever she felt vulnerable. Here again, it is interesting to speculate whether the feeling of protection I experienced with George made me more able and willing to assume this role for Alyce.

She continues:

I am full of jealous rage at the people that get your love and attention. I feel like that love should be given to me full force.

Here is a clear indication of Alyce's sense of entitlement and demandingness, with the corresponding rage when the unrealistic demand goes unmet. Whether this rage results from excessive inborn aggression (Kernberg, 1975) or because of the feelings that arise with the threat of aloneness and, hence, annihilation (Adler, 1985), patients such as Alyce are often rageful, and the analyst must be prepared to withstand the assaults.

The letter goes on:

I have always dreamed of showing a child the love, support, and caring that I never got. I have the power within me to destroy my dreams before they become reality. That lurking, black power within me is the same power that exhibits itself when I am angry. It is that same destructive force that wants to take me. No, it's my good side that wants to take me so I can spare the pain of others on my account. My unhappiness deepens when I feel like I am losing control of the good side and am letting this bad side take over.

This portion of the letter captures the torture, the constant battle between the internal forces of good and evil, that so besets Alyce and other borderline patients. There is the constant terror that the bad self will take over. Here, too, is one of the justifications for suicide: I will destroy the bad-me so that the good-you and, magically, the good-me, can survive. Analysts understand this suicidal behavior as a desire to kill the hated introject, the hated person who feels as though he or she exists as a whole and separate being within the patient's mind. But patients such as Alyce often think about or experience suicide as an act of goodness or salvation. Similarly, self-mutilation can be seen as the desire to exorcise the "black power within," as Alyce so aptly states.

Here is the last, brief paragraph:

> I just wanted to let you know how I was feeling, because I can never seem to hang on to my feelings long enough to tell them to you. I hope you had a nice weekend. Love, Alyce.

After all the soul-searching, self-analysis and insight, Alyce still needs to express her anger through sarcasm. She hopes I enjoyed myself while she suffered.

The concrete question of where Alyce and I sat in my office was one of the threads that wove throughout the treatment. Initially, seated on the far side of the Victorian love seat, Alyce pleaded with me to sit beside her, saying she needed me to be close to her, that she needed the support of my presence. At first I resisted, unsure if agreeing would open the floodgates and lead to requests that felt more and more uncomfortable to me – hand holding, touching, hugging, or even kissing. Our discussions of where I would sit and what it meant went on for weeks. I finally capitulated, but also made clear that I would move back to my chair as her need for me decreased. Just shy of two years into the treatment, I suggested that it was time for me to resume my regular chair.

"See, I was right," Alyce says petulantly. "As soon as I get a little better you want to reject me. You only like me when I'm sick."

Rather than replying to this provocative and patently untrue statement, I look at Alyce over the top of my glasses.

"What?" she demands. "Don't roll your eyes at me! Aren't you rejecting me? Aren't you trying to get away from me?"

"No, Alyce," I reply, more patiently than I feel. "Our understanding was that I would move back to my chair when you didn't need me to sit so close, when you could feel my presence when I was sitting a few feet away in my usual chair. I'm bringing it up for discussion today, to see if we can figure out how to best negotiate my return to the chair."

"If you're going to move back, just move back! I don't care. Who needs you anyway?"

"I want us to negotiate this change, Alyce, not do it impulsively, not have it be all or nothing and not have it be something we have to fight about for however long."

Stony silence.

"How about if we agree that I'll move back to my chair in a month? That way we can talk about it and see how it feels to you."

"What if you spend half of each session next to me and half in the chair," Alyce suggests.

"And that we do that for a month?"

"For two months."

34

"All right," I reply. "Starting today I'll spend the first half of each session on the couch next to you and then I'll move to my chair. And we'll do that for two months when I'll move back to the chair permanently."

"Do what you want! I told you, I don't care what you do! … No! I do care. I want you back in your chair today! This will feel like Chinese water torture. I won't be able to stand this back and forth, this sometimes here, sometimes there."

"The half and half was your suggestion, Alyce. We could try it for a few sessions and see how it feels to you. If it feels too uncomfortable we could fall back on my suggestion of my moving to the chair in a month."

"I notice you didn't give me the option of your staying next to me," she says petulantly.

"No, I didn't give you that option, Alyce. I think you'll be fine without my sitting next to you and I think it's important that you be able to learn that about yourself."

"I should just quit! You always get your way. Just like my parents. I have nothing more to say."

Obviously, my move back to the chair was not seamless, and involved much negotiation and renegotiation. At times I would revert to sitting next to her; at other times I remained in my chair. This concretizing of the issues involved in separation proved very helpful to both Alyce and the treatment. Eventually, however, I decided that Alyce would be better served if she could move beyond the concrete and put into words her conflicts over closeness and distancing. I made the decision to remain in my chair. I was not abandoning Alyce. I did not care for her any less. We could talk about her wanting more of me. We did not have to enact it.

About three years into the treatment, I thought we might progress further if Alyce moved to the analytic couch. She was sufficiently stable for me not to fear a return of her psychotic symptoms and I believed that the couch might provide her with greater access to her unconscious. Alyce thought the idea was a good one, but immediately felt frightened and feared that I was abandoning her. Our agreement was that she could try the couch and if she felt too overwhelmed by feelings of aloneness she could return to the chair, either permanently or temporarily. The move to the couch was surprisingly easy. Alyce seemed able to relax and free associate with little difficulty. She reported more dreams, often of lost, frightened, or damaged children on the one hand, or huge conflagrations of warring armies battling to the death, on the other. Themes of wishing me to be the savior appeared again and again.

"I start out being my age and wandering through downtown Detroit. That would be a stupid thing to do. I'd never go wandering in downtown Detroit by myself, not in the middle of the day, not ever. But that's my dream and I'm wandering through downtown Detroit. It starts getting darker and as it gets darker it seems like I'm getting smaller. Not just smaller in size, but younger, like I'm moving backwards in time. I'm not sure where I am. I don't know how to get home. I'm not even sure where home is. I'm really, really scared. I think that maybe I can call home. I can call and they'll come get me. I guess I mean my Mom or Dad. I see a phone booth at the corner. But then I realize I don't have any money. I thought I had a purse, but I must have lost it or it disappeared, you know, however it happens in dreams. But however it happens, I don't have a purse so I don't have any money. I think maybe I'll call the operator and tell her my name and she'll figure out how to contact my parents. The phone booth stinks of pee. There's graffiti all over it. You know, the disgusting things they write all over phone booths or bathrooms or whatever. Anyway, I pick up the receiver and realize the wire's been cut. Then I'm even more scared. There doesn't seem to be any people around. It's not like I'm afraid somebody is going to hurt me. It's that I'm all alone. I'm all alone and I don't know how I'm going to get home. Then I think of Judy Garland, of Judy Garland in the *Wizard of Oz*. I think of how she clicked the heels of her magic shoes together and how she got taken home to Kansas. I think maybe that can happen for me too. If I close my eyes and wish real hard and tap my heels together maybe I'll get to go home. So that's what I do. I close my eyes, but I don't tap my heels together. Instead, I start screaming your name over and over again. I keep screaming and screaming your name, so loud that I eventually wake myself up."

The question of how she chose me as her therapist came up once again.

"I know you always wanted to understand why I was so sure I wanted you to be my therapist," she begins one day. "You know, it was perfectly clear to me then, it made complete sense. But now I no longer know what I was thinking, how I could have been so sure I wanted you."

"What brings the question up for you now?" I ask.

"I don't know. I think I saw your book on my bookcase and took it out to look at it. I do that sometimes. It makes me feel closer to you. I know I shouldn't need to do that, that I should be able to feel you with me, to have you in my head, but I still like to see it, to hold the book in my hands. It feels good. And I always look at your name. Your name, right there in the middle. Maybe it was something about your being in the middle."

"What about my being in the middle?"

"I don't know. It's certainly hard for me to be in the middle. We sure know that by now! How I always have to be black or white, how hard it is for me to be 'mulatto.' But I doubt I would have known that then. I didn't know anything about extremes or middles or anything like that. It would be hard to imagine that even my unconscious would have known that," she says laughing.

Laughing with her I say, "Well, it is hard to imagine that your unconscious would have known about both your desire to be in the middle and your difficulty with it, but then again it's hard to know what the unconscious knows. Does anything else come to mind?"

"Maybe one other thing, but I don't think I was thinking about that when I was holding the book. And I don't know why it makes me uncomfortable to talk about, but I was thinking about being second. I'm my mother's second child, you know, after the stillborn baby. And she's my second mother. So maybe I have a thing about seconds."

"That's a really interesting thought. Do you have any idea why it would make you uncomfortable to talk about?"

"I don't know. Maybe it makes me seem needy, like I want there to be some similarity between us, that that makes me feel comfortable, safe. I don't want to still need you in that way, in that way like we're joined, like we're the same."

Several months after Alyce's transition to the couch, she graduated from college and began work. Her life change made it necessary for us to change her treatment times. During the first week, Alyce became extremely distressed, reverting to her earlier behavior of switching rapidly from being clingy and demanding to being angry and rejecting. Since she was no longer a student and had joined the adult workforce, I assumed the regression was due to Alyce's ambivalence about "growing up." Although this issue may have contributed to Alyce's backward slide, she soon informed me that this was not her primary concern.

"You don't get it, do you? After all this time and you still don't know me. I don't know why I bother coming here. I don't know why I want to come here. You should know me by now. You should know what's bothering me!"

Feeling myself getting more than a little annoyed I say, "This isn't a guessing game, Alyce. As you know by now, I can't read your mind. If you know what's bothering you, it would be best if you tell me."

She sits up from the couch and glares at me. "I can't see you anymore," she says gesturing to the floor.

I look at her totally perplexed.

She bursts into tears. "I can't see you anymore," she says between sobs. "Even your shadow is gone from me."

Alyce had lost me yet again. Her previous appointment times frequently allowed her to see my shadow as I sat behind her in my chair. The new times made that impossible. Now she could not see me at all, now she felt truly alone. Fortunately, Alyce was far enough along in her treatment that her distress proved only temporary. We could talk it through. We could work it out. She could even entertain my earlier interpretation that perhaps her greatest fear was more about growing up and that the absence of my shadow was merely a symbol of that. Regardless of the reason, Alyce settled back into our work and the new schedule.

Alice continued to work productively. Her rages decreased; her splitting diminished; she felt more self-reliant. Yet problems remained. Feeling settled in work, in friendships, or in love relationships was difficult. She would flit from job to job. She discarded friends too easily. She continued to fall in and out of love too quickly. It was as though Alyce had to keep moving; settling in evoked too many feelings of both wanting more and fighting against that wanting. Given how Alyce was handling closeness and distancing, I should not have been surprised when, soon after the end of the fourth year of treatment, she began to talk about termination. In actuality, I was shocked. This wasn't like her earlier threats to terminate. This time she meant it. She really wanted to go.

"I'm always going to have issues! Everyone has issues! Remember, you always told me there was no such thing as perfection. No perfect mother. No perfect therapist. No perfect person. Well, that's who I am, a not perfect person and I don't want to be in therapy for the rest of my life!"

"I'm not talking about perfection, I'm talking about your getting to the point of being able to be more comfortable in a relationship, including in a relationship with me."

"I've been in a relationship with you. For a long time. I don't want to be in a relationship with you anymore. It's time for me to leave. I want to be free. I want to see how I'll do on my own."

I couldn't believe that Alyce actually wanted to leave me. So here I was again, enacting one side of Alyce's conflict. I was now the needy child and she was the rejecting mother. I was again fighting to have her stay, while she fought to separate, to leave. I truly did believe that Alyce was not yet ready to end treatment, but I also understood our enactment. We disagreed for many months. I finally decided that I had to respect Alyce's wishes and let her go.

In retrospect, I wonder both what led to Alyce's determination to leave right at that time and my willingness to accept her decision. Did she sense the ever-increasing intimacy between me and George? Did she find my twice-yearly vacations more and more unbearable, as she experienced me and George as "the couple" and herself as the excluded child? As for me, perhaps my feeling of continuing safety and contentment in my relationship with George made me yearn less for Alyce as the substitute child. I also had additional "children." I had begun analytic training and was heavily engrossed in both my own mind and those of others. Perhaps Alyce sensed a shift in my attention. Perhaps there was a shift in my attention. Again, these are all unanswerable speculations, but ones worthy of posing and considering.

Alyce and I finally set a termination date for four months in the future. She worked hard to leave in a healthy manner – not enraged, not withdrawn, not indifferent.

"It's going to be very sad to leave you," Alyce says a few weeks before our last session. "I keep imagining what it will be like to walk out that door for the last time. I keep imagining what it will feel like to not come here three times a week. I keep imagining how I'll feel when I have a problem and don't have you to talk it over with."

"It will be sad for both of us, Alyce. But I'm very proud of you, you've come such a long way. Here you are actually thinking about – imagining as you say – how something will feel. You're anticipating, you're letting yourself rehearse, rather than being blindsided, caught off-guard, rather than being buffeted about by overwhelming feelings."

"You're right. I am doing that. You see, I told you I was ready to terminate."

To respond or not respond to the last provocative statement. Is she looking for a fight? Has she again thrown down the gauntlet? Or is she more unsure of herself and asking me to validate her decision to leave? Should I bring up my uncertainty about her statement? I say nothing. I don't want to fight with her and I'm unable to agree with her decision. Am I being the less than perfect therapist? Perhaps. But at the moment I'm content to let her be, to avoid any contentiousness and to know that I have truly accepted Alyce's decision to terminate.

When Alyce left I found myself sad and depressed. I thought about her and missed her. George's presence did not make up for Alyce's absence. Nor should it have, for one person does not substitute for another. Alyce was gone. It was fitting that I should mourn her. Still, her loss was not devastating to me. I continued to love my life, my husband, my work with other patients. My internal and external foundations were sufficiently secure that the loss of the intense bond that Alyce and I shared did not destroy my sense of myself or my connection with others. And George and I were planning another adventure.

George's youngest son, John, was getting married in August. He lived in Oregon. We had always wanted to go to China. We reasoned that since we were already on the West coast, we might as well go! So off we went on another great, memorable trip.

When I returned, I came back to a practice without Alyce. I wasn't bereft. I didn't suffer her loss every day. I did think about her and wonder how she was doing. I hoped that she might return to treatment one day, but I was fulfilled in my life without her. Again, I can only wonder if Alyce's loss had come at a different time in my life, a time of George's illness or his death, whether I would have reacted differently. Would I have fought harder to keep her in treatment? Would I have felt more abandoned by her leave-taking? Her loss at that vulnerable time in my life might well have left me feeling more depressed and less resilient, less able to resume the necessary parts of my life both within and outside the consulting room.

3

THE EROTIC
COUNTERTRANSFERENCE
Exploring an Analyst's Sexual Feelings

Today I'll be seeing a new patient, a man by the name of Dr. Harry Davis, a medical researcher he told me in his initial phone call, not a practicing physician. I walk to the waiting room to greet him. As he rises to shake my hand I am instantly aware that I am sexually attracted to him, a relatively short, stocky man with curly black hair and a slender moustache. I've never experienced this before, this immediate attraction to a patient, and find myself distinctly uncomfortable. I also know that I've just completed the quickest diagnostic assessment of my career. Beyond a shadow of a doubt, this man will prove to be a narcissist. Although George is definitely the exception to my rule, I spent too many years involved with narcissistic men, trying to win or change the father of my childhood, to expect Dr. Davis to be anything but a continuation of my old pattern. He even has a moustache like my father. What do I find so attractive about this man? What is it that so captures me? Certainly there is nothing particularly distinctive in his appearance. He's not that handsome. He doesn't have rugged good looks. Perhaps it is the self-assurance he projects, an aura that declares his feeling of being at the top of his game.

There have been many changes in my life since George and I first met, fell in love, and married. For one, I ended my analysis. Although I am sad about the loss of a man who had been with me through so many ups and downs and who had so positively affected my life, I feel as though the analysis came to a comfortable conclusion and do not feel an overwhelming sense of loss. Besides, there is always George to talk to, to rely on. He is, however, in a different phase of his life. When he reached sixty-two, he retired. His old back injury and his arthritis made carrying and bending and lugging increasingly difficult. We both decided that enough was enough. He still spends his time working on projects for us and can often be found in his two-story, three-car garage involved with various projects. Now, though, George has a new hobby. He has taken over the entire running of our household, including becoming a gourmet cook. That's quite an accomplishment for a man who could hardly boil water when we first started living together. Now we rarely meet for lunch, but he always has dinner waiting for me when I return home, always eager to see me, always eager to hear about my day.

I gesture Harry Davis into the chair opposite me. "What brings you here?" I ask in my most stilted therapeutic mode. I'm going to have to be careful. I don't want my attraction to drive me in the other direction, towards an artificial coldness and distance.

"I've never been in therapy before, but that sounds like a typical therapist question," he says smiling at me.

I smile back, but say nothing.

"I guess I'm a little uncomfortable," he says, laughing nervously.

He's not the only one who's uncomfortable. My office has never felt so small. Suddenly there isn't enough distance between our two chairs. It's as though our knees could brush one another, as though he could reach out and touch me. I have been in this office in downtown Ann Arbor for several years now, an old, two-story house that my friend and colleague, Ann, and I purchased and which George renovated for us, making it into five therapy offices and two waiting rooms. I chose this office on the second floor despite its being small and compact. The office is divided into two parts. In the first part, where Dr. Davis and I now sit, there are two chairs, a file cabinet and bookshelves. The analytic space requires a small step downward – both literally and figuratively – to a long, rectangular area with enough room for my analytic couch, the chair behind, and a table that once stood in my grandparent's foyer. What is most wonderful about this space is that it is like a tree house, with greenery on three sides that seems to suspend the office while keeping it safe and cushioned. It is another space in which I feel held and comforted. Usually. At the moment, I feel cramped and confined, more aware of the too small distance between myself and my patient.

Dr. Davis continues, "I'm not even sure I believe in therapy. But my friend sees your colleague and he says she's been very helpful to him." He inhales, apparently ready to take the plunge. "I've just broken off my fifth engagement." He looks at me waiting for my response. When I say nothing he continues. "I'm forty-one, I'm well established in my field, I want to have a family. I want a wife and kids and all that stuff. Besides, I'm Jewish and my parents are constantly on my case about getting married. Both my sisters have been married for a long time and have kids and the whole nine yards. My parents are constantly visiting them and telling me they want to live to see my kids. At this point they'd even be willing to accept someone who's not Jewish! But I can't do it. I mean, I have no difficulty finding women and they're great looking women, but I can't stay faithful to them. I don't stay faithful to them. I don't think I've been faithful to one woman ever. I'm not proud of that. In fact, I feel terribly guilty about it, but I can't seem to help myself. No, that's not right, it's more like being in a relationship with one woman drives me to find someone else."

"Can you say more about that?" I ask. "Can you say what it is you feel in your primary relationship when you feel driven to find someone else?"

"That's hard. I don't know. It's like I feel suffocated, like I have to get away."

I wonder about the similarity of my patient's feeling "suffocated" and my experience of feeling "too close" in this room with him. Does he also feel too close here? Perhaps this is a projective identification, an unconscious process involving the projection of his feelings into me, thereby enabling me to feel what he feels (Ogden, 1982).

"And when I feel the need to get away," he continues, "I start finding all these things wrong with the first woman – she's too much this or too little that or whatever."

"Could you be a little more specific?"

He flashes me another of his engaging smiles. It is a smile that seems inviting while, at the same time, suggesting that perhaps he has a secret, a secret that he's not yet willing to share. It is a smile that I will come to identify with Harry Davis and one that will stay with me and taunt me in my mind.

He continues. "You're tough! You know, I wasn't sure I wanted to see a woman therapist. I thought it would be easier to talk about these things with a man. But when my friend's therapist recommended you I thought, hey, since all my problems are about women, maybe a woman therapist would be best."

"Do you feel uncomfortable talking with me?"

"No, not really, at least not yet, but I think some of it may be harder to talk about, like sexual stuff, or my attraction to certain kinds of women. Like all the women I'm attracted to have big breasts. That's a requirement for me. I don't like that about myself, but it's true. But I'm not ready to deal with that yet."

"That's okay, we'll have plenty of time. Why don't you tell me a little about your background."

"Well, I grew up in Flint, Michigan. You know what Flint's like, even before it totally began to go to pieces. All that was ever there was General Motors. That's where my father worked, at the plant. But other than that it's a wasteland. There's nothing there. Including almost no Jewish families. As I said my father worked for GM. My mother was a stay-at-home Mom. I guess you'd say we were middle class. There weren't too many extras, but we weren't going hungry. I always hated the town. I knew I was going to get out of there. I know this sounds conceited, but I always felt better than most of the people there. I was good in school, especially in math and science, so medicine seemed like a logical choice. But I was more interested in how and why the body worked, especially gene research, rather than the day-to-day grind of seeing patients. I love what I do. The University of Michigan Medical School is tops in the country. I could have gone anywhere. Some of the big Ivy Leagues wanted me, but I knew that I'd be able to get to the top at the U. I knew I'd make a name for myself. I'm a very talented grant writer so they let me do whatever I want as long as I bring in the money and I do that with no problem."

I register his enjoyment in talking about his accomplishments, in wanting to come out ahead, in wanting to stand out from the pack.

"Can you tell me a little about your parents?" I ask. "And did you say you had two sisters?"

"Yeah, my sisters are older than me – three and six years older. I was the long-awaited son. We were never close. We still aren't. My father? He was a hard worker, strict, critical. I don't think I was ever tough enough for him. My mother, what can I say? She loved me. Maybe too much. She could also get nuts about every little thing. I don't know… I guess I have a hard time describing the people in my family…"

It strikes me as interesting that he described me as "tough" and now says that he was not "tough enough" for his father. Does he see me as an idealized version of himself? Or is this the beginning of a father transference, where he experiences me as similar to his own father? These are questions I ask myself and file away for future consideration.

"You know," he says, "I find this awkward, but I don't know what I'm supposed to call you. If I'm going to be telling you all my life's secrets, Dr. Sherby seems way too formal," he adds, again flashing his captivating smile.

I almost say nothing and then realize that would be deviating from my usual response to this line of inquiry. "You can call me anything you feel comfortable with," I say.

"Fine, that's settled. I'll call you Linda and you'll call me Harry."

Harry has taken charge. He has assumed control of the session. Is it that he needs to prove that he's "tough enough" for me? For his father? For himself?

Like my office, this treatment exists on two levels. It progresses from a once-a-week therapy, down the step to the couch and a more intensive, analytic process. It also exists on two levels for me. There is what goes on in the sessions themselves and what goes on in my mind outside the treatment room. As is apparent in the first session, Harry is a self-involved man who wants and needs to be the center of attention. He is smart, charming and enjoys proving himself and winning, whatever the competition happens to be. He relishes talking about his professional success, the grants he's procured and the kudos he's received.

In terms of his family, Harry speaks most easily about the conflictual relationship with his father, a blue-collar worker, who loves sports, fishing and hunting and hanging out with his buddies. Although apparently supportive of his son's academic achievements – "my son the doctor" – Harry feels that his father is envious of his success and still takes any opportunity to put him down. Harry says that his father could never understand his disinterest in sports – worrying in childhood he might be one of those "queers" – and making fun of his distaste for killing animals as recreation. His sisters seem tangential to both the family and the treatment. They are both married, moved away from Michigan and have families of their own. My understanding of their apparent insignificance is that Harry is indeed the anointed prince and that his siblings are irrelevant, certainly to him, perhaps also to his father, and almost assuredly to his mother.

Harry describes himself as the apple of his mother's eye. She had desperately wanted a son and planned to keep having children until her need was fulfilled. From the first she fussed over him, never wanting him to cry or be out of her sight. As an infant and then a toddler who was afraid of being alone, he felt welcomed into the parental bed. He experienced his mother as terrified whenever he became ill and all too ready to take him to doctors or even to the emergency room. Harry remembers her crying his first day of kindergarten and driving him to and from school for many years, despite the fact that the school bus stopped in front of their house. Unlike her husband, she was ecstatic that Harry was uninterested in sports. At least then she didn't have to worry about his being injured on the playing field.

"So how do you feel as you describe your mother's feelings towards you?" I ask.

"I guess it makes me kind of embarrassed to actually be telling it all to you. I sound like such a wimp. And so pampered. But, I don't know, at the time, I guess at the time it felt pretty good. Like she was there for me. She'd protect me from my father. And she wouldn't let me be alone. I didn't like to be alone. Being alone in my room at night was very scary to me. My sisters got to share a room, but my room was at the top of the house, all alone. I didn't like it. I think I only started liking that room when I became a teenager and my friends and I could hang out there and we could sneak cigarettes or pot – as long as we kept the window open. And then when I could sneak girls up there, well, that was the best," he says flashing me his broad smile. "But as a kid I hated it. Lots of times I'd have bad dreams, or I wouldn't be able to fall asleep at all and I'd go into my parent's bedroom. My father didn't like that at all. But my mother always let me stay. I'd sleep curled up next to her."

"Next to her breasts?"

"Yeah, next to her breasts… I know, I know what you're thinking," he says flashing another of his smiles. "You think that's why I like big-breasted women."

"What do you think?"

"I don't know. I suppose you're right. I know I loved the feel of their softness. They offered such comfort, such solace. And I did like to peek a look at them. I think my mother liked that too. I think she liked offering me up her breasts. I think she liked my fascination with them."

"And how does that make you feel?"

"I don't know. Right now when I was telling you, I felt special, like this was a special relationship and she was offering me something she wouldn't offer anyone else. I mean I know my father saw them… I don't know. I guess it's kind of weird, like sort of gross, almost sick. Like why would a mother do that?"

"Have any guesses?"

"No, not really."

In the silence, I sense that Harry is thinking.

"What comes to mind?" I ask.

"Well, I don't know if this is true, but I wonder if it was her way of getting back at my father. Like she could tease him with me or get back at him or something like that. Like she had two people admiring her breasts, not just him."

I feel a flash of anger at this woman who may have used her son as a tool against her husband. I wonder if my patient feels the anger too or whether, again through the process of projective identification, my patient is inducing in me the feeling he cannot yet permit himself to know.

"Do you have any feelings about her…" I start to say, "using you in that way" and quickly decide that a more neutral question is called for. "About her doing that?"

44

"Her relationship with my father certainly isn't great. Of course, I don't know how anyone could have a great relationship with him. He's always been such a bastard. He used to tear her down just like he tore me down. Dinner wasn't hot enough, she didn't buy the right soap, she didn't iron his shirt the way he liked it. He was an ass. He is an ass. But I always knew I'd do better than him. I knew that I was smarter than him. I knew that I'd get out of that town and I did. He is proud of me, but he's jealous too. I can see it in his eyes."

"That seems to give you a feeling of satisfaction," I say.

"Yes. Yes it does," he says, his hostility more than apparent in his voice.

So Harry has his parents split – father as the bad guy, mother as the good. As such he is unable to recognize his mother's manipulativeness or narcissism. He sees her as a victim like himself, forced to endure his father's criticalness. Harry's anger at his father is apparent. His anger at his mother – the anger that I experienced – is out of his awareness. In my mind I hypothesize that his unconscious anger at his mother is generalized to all women and is at least one reason he is unfaithful again and again. A second reason, despite his obvious delight at outdoing his father, is his fear of being the Oedipal victor, of literally winning his mother and having to deal with his father's wrath.

I am driving down the road to have dinner with a friend in Manchester, Michigan, a trip that involves taking some sparsely traveled two-lane roads. Suddenly a deer scampers in front of me and I veer onto the berm and down into a ditch. My car is stuck. My right front tire is flat. I look around helplessly. Several cars pass me by. It will be dark soon. Would it even be safe if someone stopped and offered to help me? How far is my friend's house? Just then a man in a black pick-up-truck pulls onto the berm and stops in front of me. I'm apprehensive. Then I realize it's Dr. Harry Davis! I'm shocked. What is he doing here? What is he doing in a black pick-up-truck? I thought he told me he drove some little sports car. He smiles at me and walks around the car. "Looks like maybe I can help you for a change," he says. "Thank you," I stammer. "I swerved to miss a deer." At his instruction, I get into the car, put it in reverse and, after several tries, he pushes me out. He offers to put on my spare, but that too is flat. I'm mortified. "No problem," he says, "Just get in the truck and I'll get the spare and we'll bring it to a gas station." I do as I'm told. "I'm so sorry to put you through all this," I say uncomfortably, as he gets back into the truck. "I don't know how to thank you." As he looks at me, his hand immobile on the gear shift, I hear the implication of what I have just said. The tension in the truck builds. My heart pounds. He holds my gaze. He leans over and kisses me.

Such are the fantasies that occupy my mind when I'm not with Harry. Although I know I will never act on them, they make me extremely uncomfortable, both because of their obvious sexual nature and because I often, although not always, place myself in a submissive, helpless role with Harry as my savior. They never progress beyond the stage of passionate kissing or tentative fondling. We never end up nude or actually having intercourse. It is as though there is the possibility or promise that more might occur, but never the actuality.

At the time I understood these fantasies to be the result of my still trying to both win and change my father. All my years of analysis still did not negate my wish that my father could have been a kinder, gentler man who saw me and loved me for the person I was, as opposed to the person he wanted me to be or the person he himself wanted to be.

That Harry represents my father is clear to me. Each is one of three children and the only, very much prized, boy. Each sees himself as smarter than everyone else in his family and determined to break away and be different. Each craves being the center of attention and never feels satiated. I am also aware that there is both a childlike and adolescent feel to many of my fantasies. I am the helpless, dependent child who needs rescuing by the bigger, stronger, smarter man. The fantasy reflects my wish that my father be understanding and helpful, rather than angry, critical, and demanding. And the lack of consummated sexual intercourse in my fantasies demonstrates both their adolescent quality, as well as my discomfort at moving too close to being the Oedipal victor.

The other factor that does not escape me is that Harry's family dynamics are similar to my own. Like me he experienced his mother as intrusive, although his description of her includes someone who is more overtly and inappropriately sexual, while also being more protective of her son. And his father was as critical and aggressive as mine, but less explosive. Does this mean that I am attracted to a male version of myself? Do my feelings imply a desire to be one with that male part? Would that give me a sense of greater power? Of completeness? The similarity of our early experience has undoubtedly created a similarity in our internal worlds, in the self and other representations we carry around in our minds. Does this mean that I am experiencing a regression, a pull back to a time of idyllic merger? And, at an Oedipal level, what does it mean that we both share the desire to win with the opposite sex parent, while fearing that "win" at the very same time? So many questions. So many unknowns.

Although these musings and fantasies occupy a considerable amount of my internal thoughts, I never share them with George. He knows that I'm working with a man I find extremely interesting, but giving more information feels too uncomfortable to me, as well as potentially hurtful. I know that my fantasies in no way threaten our relationship and, at the time, I give little thought to how they may be related to George. It is true that the intense passion of the early years of our relationship has diminished, but that does not seem unreasonable or unexpected to me. We still love each other as deeply as always. We enjoy making love and basking in our closeness. We remain the best of friends and would rather spend time with each other than anyone else. Besides, as far as I am concerned, my fantasies are all about my life well before George and have nothing whatsoever to do with the present.

In retrospect, I now wonder whether George's retirement added fuel to what would anyway have been an intense fire. When I was first attracted to George I was attracted to a powerful man, to a builder, to a man who could do anything with his hands. Although these capabilities haven't disappeared, they are waning and George has less opportunity to show off his manly prowess. Instead, he has become the homemaker, the househusband, the man who has turned his creativity into gourmet cooking. My conscious mind and my feminist sensibilities applaud George's skill and his ability to transform himself and to continue to be creative and fulfilled. But I now wonder if my unconscious "damsel in distress rescue fantasies" are left unsatisfied by this turn of events, just waiting for a successful man like Dr. Harry Davis to make his appearance. If this is true and if I had been aware of it at the time, would it have changed the pull I felt towards my patient? Perhaps. But perhaps not, for the unconscious is a powerful force not always overcome by insight.

Harry has been dating Debbie for six months, a top administrator at Domino Pizza's corporate headquarters in Ann Arbor. He's seen other women during that time, but now she wants an exclusive relationship.

"She's good in bed," Harry is saying. "She's willing to try most anything – at least anything I'd be interested in trying. But I don't know. I'm starting to get bored. I've been noticing this really cute nurse at the hospital. She has a perfect body, full breasts, a small behind, she's blonde."

"Isn't that pretty much how you described Debbie not too long ago?" I ask.

"I guess," he says, sighing. "I suppose I'm back in the same place I always am. I'm interested in a woman for a while and then as soon as she starts asking anything of me I want to run the other way. I can't help it. I just feel suffocated."

"And you're feeling suffocated by Debbie?"

"Yeah, I suppose I am."

"Can you talk more about the feeling of being suffocated? Can you try to be more specific?"

He laughs. "Even trying to describe the feeling makes me feel like I want to run away."

"From me?"

"Not from you exactly, from the feeling… Okay, I'll try. It's like there's not enough air in the room. Almost like I'm claustrophobic. And besides, there are always so many other women out there. Women who might be prettier or smarter or have the potential to be better mothers. I mean, do I really want a pizza executive as my child's mother?"

This is not Harry at his most endearing. I find myself annoyed by his cavalier assessment of women and his inability to focus on himself. I say nothing.

"I just can't give her what she wants! I know I'm only going to disappoint her, I'm only going to get involved with someone else, so why bother even trying?"

I hear a difference in Harry's tone of voice. There's almost a beseeching quality. I listen carefully.

He sighs. "I'm so tired of this. I'm weary."

"The feeling that you're going to disappoint her, does that remind you of anything?"

"Yeah, every woman I've ever been involved with. Every woman I've left. Every woman who found out I was cheating. Every woman I broke off with. You name it!"

"You sound very angry," I venture to say.

"I'm just angry with myself."

"Are you sure?"

"What do you mean?"

"Well, first I was wondering if you're angry at me and at all the other women who ask you for what you cannot possibly give. Like my asking you to describe a feeling that makes you uncomfortable. And I was also wondering if all those other women include your mother."

"Wow! There's a lot in there. I'm not angry at you. You're just trying to help me. And you listen to me go on and on about this shit. At some of the other women, I suppose. Like sometimes I'm straight from the beginning. I tell them I don't have a good track record. I tell them I have a problem with commitment. But they think they'll make me different. And maybe I hope they will. But I just can't stand it when they want me to do things for them – like take care of their dog for the weekend or pick up a prescription on my way home from work. I know they're not big things, but it implies something to me. It implies we're in a relationship and we're not! I'm not ready to be in a relationship! Wow! Did I say that? Am I really not ready to be in a relationship? I think I'm ready. I'm past forty. If I'm not ready now when will I be ready?"

"Maybe you still feel like a child, a child who's not ready to be in a big person relationship."

Silence.

"When you said that, I thought about myself as a kid in my room alone at night. I was really scared. I don't even know what I was scared of. The aloneness I guess. Then I'd think about whether I should go to my parent's room. I'd want to go and I knew my mother would welcome me with open arms – literally – but I also knew that my father would make fun of me, call me a sissy. If I got scared enough I'd go. I'd always feel safe cradled in my mother's arms."

"Did your mother ever want anything in return?"

"What do you mean?"

"Well, I was thinking about your saying that women always wanted more from you than you could give. I was wondering if you felt that from your mother too."

"I never thought of that. That was certainly true when I got older, when she'd want me to stay home with her if my father was working and I'd want to go play with my friends."

"And when you were younger?"

"I guess sometimes. Sometimes I'd be watching TV or reading a book or playing with my toy trains and she'd want me to come sit with her, to come cuddle with her. If I didn't want to she'd make a pouty face, like she was hurt, or say something like, 'Doesn't Harry baby love his Mommy anymore? Mommy loves her Harry baby. Won't Harry baby come be with Mommy like he is at night.' Ugh!! I can almost hear her sickeningly sweet baby talk voice. It's disgusting! ... I hadn't thought of that for a long, long time. And I never realized how mad it made me. It's like she wanted me for her, to comfort her. She couldn't let me be."

This session brings Harry considerable insight. We can now begin to explore his reaction to his mother's intrusiveness and her use of him as a narcissistic extension of herself. Left unsaid in this session is my hypothesis that Harry also feels unable to be in an adult relationship because of the sexual inadequacy he felt in relation to his mother. In other words, from Harry's perspective, although his mother may have indirectly offered herself to him, he was indeed only a child and could not have performed in a competently adult manner. Thus, it is not only that Harry fears breaking the incest taboo and encountering his father's dreaded response, but also fears being faced with the too harsh reality of not being good enough himself.

As Harry's greater vulnerability comes to the fore, my fantasies are further fueled. I have succeeded in having some effect on this man. I have succeeded in softening him, in making him more aware of himself. I have succeeded with him in a way I never had with my father. Simultaneously, changes are occurring in my life as well.

We walk through a ramshackle two-bedroom house on a dirty canal in Key Largo.

"If we buy this house you'll have to come visit me on the weekends," I say to George jokingly.

We have been in Key Largo diving, as we had been many times previously. This time, however, we are also looking to buy a small home. It is our plan to have George spend the winters in Key Largo and to have me fly weekly between Detroit and Miami. I know it will be a hectic schedule for me, but the winters are becoming increasingly difficult for George. The cold adversely affects his arthritis and particularly his old back injury, leaving him housebound and in continual pain. He wants me to move to Florida, preferably to the Keys, although he understands that having a psychoanalytic practice in the Keys would be virtually impossible. Besides, the reality is that I don't want to move. Despite the horrible weather, I love my life in Ann Arbor. I love my home, my practice and my friends and cannot imagine being separated from any of them. So this is the compromise we've come up with. Assuming, of course, we can find something halfway decent at a price we can afford.

Eventually, we do. It's a small two-bedroom, one-bath house in pristine condition. It has a large screened porch with an enormous banyan tree that cradles the house. Although not on the water, the property comes with what is called a homeowner's park, an area on the bay that only two square blocks of residents can use. It's less than two short blocks away and is incredibly serene and quiet, with small islands out in the distance to break up the expanse of ocean.

I settle into a stressful but tolerable routine. I see thirty-six patients from 1 p.m. on Monday to 5 p.m. on Thursday. It's doable as long as no other problems arise – like falling on the ice and breaking my glasses or having the pipes in our house freeze. Still, I manage. I leave my car at the airport and fly out of Detroit on Thursday evening. George picks me up in Miami and we make the hour and a half drive to Key Largo. On Monday we get up at 5:30 a.m. and reverse the process. If all goes well I'm in my office with time to spare before my first patient. I miss George during the week. I talk to him multiple times a day, but it's not the same. I yearn for Thursday nights when I'll once again be in the warmth of both his embrace and the Florida sunshine. I sleep little on Sunday nights, feeling anxious about our impending separation, as well as the possibility of weather or airline snafus that might disrupt my carefully planned schedule.

I'm sitting in the window seat of the plane, staring nervously at my watch, hoping they'll finish loading and get on their way. If we land too much after 11 a.m. I feel overly pressured to get to my office. "Well, hello," a familiar voice says, startling me out of my reverie. I look up to see Dr. Harry Davis settling into the seat next to me. "Fancy meeting you here," he says. I'm speechless. None of my patients know I make this weekly trek to and from Florida. He's sitting right next to me! What are we going to talk about for three hours?! What are we going to do? "Well, what do we do now?" he asks mirroring my thoughts. "What were you doing in Florida?" I finally manage to ask. "A medical convention at the University of Miami. ... And you?" "I spent the weekend in the Keys." The plane takes off. Our conversation continues. I ask him about his conference; he asks me about the Keys. We talk about other places we've traveled, restaurants we've eaten at. I'm struck by how normal the conversation seems, how ordinary. But I'm reluctant to continue it indefinitely and make an excuse about having to catch up on some reading for a class I'm teaching. I escape into my book, but find it impossible to concentrate. All I'm aware of is his sitting there, his thigh practically touching mine. I feel as though I can hear him breathing. I feel his eyes on me. I turn slowly to look at him. He's smiling at me. "You know," he says, "You don't have to be afraid of me." I sit transfixed. He leans over and kisses me on the forehead, on my eyes, on my lips.

Long and frequent plane rides are fertile ground for fantasies. Does Harry keep me company during the times I miss George most? Or are the fantasies an unconscious expression of my anger at George for separating himself from me? Or for his aging? For his physical difficulties? Perhaps they are even my way of punishing George for what I assume will be our inevitable parting, when he dies and leaves me for good. Again, these are not thoughts and questions I raise at the time. I consider the fantasies only in relation to my history with my father. I do wonder if they are exacerbated by the absence of my analyst from my life. Do I feel the loss of a strong male figure, a void into which my patient can easily fall? Perhaps. But mostly what I remember feeling is regret, regret that I can't turn to my analyst as someone with whom to discuss my fantasies, someone who might relieve me of the burden, the guilt of carrying them all on my own.

Meanwhile Harry's treatment progresses.

"I had an interesting experience with Rachael the other night. We'd just finished having sex. I feel as though she can't get enough of my body, like she wants me further and further inside her. It's a turn-on."

"Yes it is," I think to myself.

"But that's not what I wanted to talk about," he continues. "I wanted to talk about how I felt afterwards. I was cuddled up next to her breasts and I felt this strange swing of emotions. You know how you ask me to think about what I'm feeling when I start to feel suffocated? Well, that's what I was trying to do. And it was weird. Like one minute I wanted to pull away and the next moment it was like I couldn't get enough.

50

I thought maybe it was like with my mother, like I wanted her breasts but found the whole idea too weird."

"And when you thought of that, did anything change?" I ask.

"I don't know. Maybe. Maybe I could tolerate staying a bit closer."

"You know, Harry, I find myself wondering something else here, in addition to what you're suggesting. You notice how you said she couldn't get enough of your body and you couldn't get enough of her breasts? Well I wonder if that's exactly true, if in addition to the sexual pull there's something else going on here. I wonder if there's the child you who feels a tremendous neediness – just like the aloneness and desperation you felt when you were young – the child who wants and wants and never wants to let go and that this neediness is very frightening to you."

"I always see the woman as the needy one, as the clingy one, as the one I have to get away from. Are you saying that that could be me too?"

"Yes, that's what I'm suggesting. I'm suggesting that you either pick women who have dependency issues similar to your own or see them as dependent rather than experiencing your own scared, needy child feelings."

"I don't know. I know I don't like it. It makes me feel weak. I want to disagree with you, but I don't know, there just might be something there."

In this session I shift the focus of the treatment from Harry's sexual issues to a perspective more embraced by Fairbairn (1952). It is not that I discount Harry's sexual conflicts as influencing his difficulties with commitment, but rather that I wish to add an additional component. For Fairbairn (1941), the goal of development is to move from a state of infantile dependency to an adult state of mutual interdependence. To accomplish this developmental task the child needs to know that he is "genuinely loved… by his parents and … that the parents genuinely accept his love" (p. 38). "In the absence of such assurance his relationship to … [others] is fraught with too much *anxiety over separation* to enable him to renounce the attitude of infantile dependence; for such a renunciation would be equivalent in his eyes of forfeiting all hope of ever obtaining the satisfaction of his unsatisfied emotional needs" (p. 39, italics in original). Although Harry was presumably the heir apparent and the anointed prince, neither of his parents was able to love Harry for who he was. His father wanted Harry to be a jock, a tough guy, who could hunt and fish with the best of them. His mother saw him as her plaything, an object to meet her own needs and desires, a narcissistic extension of herself. Because Harry did not feel genuinely loved for himself, he developed "a sense of painful craving, and a longing to get total control and complete possession of … [his] love-object so that … [he could not] be left to starve" (Guntrip, 1968, p. 24).

This love grown hungry is the dynamic I am attempting to address in the above session. Because Harry feels that his own love is too big, too dangerous, too devouring he has to pull back from it and, therefore, from the woman with whom he is involved. Even becoming involved with more than one woman can be seen as Harry's attempt to dilute his neediness across more than one person. And when he still feels too needy he then projects his neediness onto the woman and feels that he has to escape from what he then experiences as her attempt to swallow him up.

The treatment enters a period of us dealing more and more with Harry as the needy, dependent child. Contrary to what I might have expected – or hoped – this does not lead to a diminution of my fantasies. On the contrary, now I can be attracted to the successful, strong man who also has a weak, vulnerable side. I can take care of him, just as he takes care of me.

I've stopped to pick up a few items at the grocery store. On my way out I see a group of people standing looking down. Unlike my usual propensity, I walk towards the crowd. Harry is lying on the ground, his bicycle twisted beside him. A driver backed up, didn't see Harry and accidentally hit him. He is assuring everyone that he is quite all right despite a few cuts and scrapes. I go up to him, bend down and dab his forehead with a tissue. He smiles at me. "I'm fine," he tells me, "but I'm not so sure about my bike." I tell him that I have a convertible, that we can put the bike in my car and that I would be happy to drive him home. He readily agrees, but insists on driving. In a few moments we are in front of his house. I help him carry the damaged bike to his garage. He invites me in to thank me. I hesitate. I agree. I walk up the steep, open garage steps. I stumble briefly. He catches me by the arm. We continue up the stairs. The door shuts behind us.

In this scenario I find Harry's neediness appealing. We are both helpless, dependent children. But, as is true for him, I am quick to disclaim my own need. We are both "fine." We only have easily healed scrapes and bruises. This fantasy encourages me to look more deeply at myself, at my need to disown my own neediness and dependency. Like Harry, my neediness makes me uncomfortable; like Harry I want to move away from it, to declare my competence and independence.

It is only with George that my neediness is glaringly apparent and impossible to hide. Even the few days I spend without him each week I am more anxious. And the thought of his eventual death fills me with an all-consuming dread. Are my fantasies of Harry partially a way for me to protect myself from my overwhelming need for George? Are they a wall that seeks to shield me from fully acknowledging my need for this man who will one day die and leave me? Am I doing what I suggested to my patient, dispersing my need across more than one person? Again, these thoughts occur to me now, many years after the fact, not actively at the time of the treatment. Then I saw them only as a resurgence of my earlier wish to win with my father. I didn't think to connect them to George or to my present day life. In addition to not being accustomed to looking at the immediate, I may also have needed to keep these fantasies separate and apart from all other aspects of my life. Although I knew I would never act on them, I also felt ashamed of them and needed to keep them secret, as much as possible, even from myself.

Around the beginning of his fourth year of treatment, Harry becomes interested in a new woman, an associate professor of sociology who doesn't quite fit his usual body type. We spend session after session dealing, on the one hand, with his wish to make this relationship work and his fear of failing yet again and, on the other hand, with his fault-finding and desire to withdraw.

"I know that Karen loves me. I know she'd be good for me. I couldn't ask for anything more in a wife or mother. Well that's not true. She could have bigger breasts. And she could be more punctual. But that shouldn't be any reason to stop seeing her. So far I haven't been unfaithful to her. I'm pretty proud of myself about that. I could be. Well, I always could be so that's not saying anything. But I haven't. That's what's important."

"And what do you think has made that possible?"

"I don't know. I guess the work we've done here the last three or four years or whatever it is."

"You sound kind of dismissive of our work."

"No, it's not that, it's just that… I don't know."

"I actually was asking more specifically what you think might have resulted in your being faithful to Karen, but your reaction to what you thought I asked was interesting. I think you put me in the role of the mother, asking for gratification, asking to be told what a great job I was doing."

"I didn't think of that, but I think you're right. I can see how I did hear it that way and then needed to back away from it immediately."

"I also wonder if it made you uncomfortable to acknowledge that our work here has been helpful, like that would imply you're dependent on me."

"I don't know. I don't know if that's true. I do realize that our work here has been helpful and I am appreciative of all your help. No, that doesn't seem to fit… But I was thinking about your original question, about what has made it possible for me to be faithful to Karen – at least so far. I don't know why this came to mind but it did. I was thinking about the last time we slept together. I was snuggled next to her breasts and I felt terribly sad. I couldn't figure that out. I've read where sometimes people cry after they've come, but it wasn't like that. It was later. Maybe almost just before we fell asleep. I felt overcome by this sadness. It was so intense I thought about getting out of bed and reading or something, but it passed and I fell asleep. But I can feel it now, just talking about it."

I remain silent.

"I was thinking about the obvious thing, but it seems too ridiculous to say. Was I feeling sad because her breasts were too small? That seems impossible."

"Well, what might being with someone with small breasts…

"They're not small," he interrupts, "just smaller than I like."

I continue. "What might being with someone with breasts smaller than you like mean to you?"

"Well, I get the obvious. It means giving up on my mother," he says matter-of-factly.

Some time goes by in silence. I encourage him. "When you just said that, giving up on your mother, what did you feel?"

"Nothing, really."

"And if you allow yourself to feel, like you did that night with Karen?"

The feeling tone in the room changes.

"I guess I feel sad. … I sound like a stereotype. Like all this is about having to give up my mother."

"By saying you sound like a stereotype, I imagine that you're again moving away from your feelings. But I think this is very important. What do you think of if you think of giving up your mother? What do you feel?"

"Sad. Really sad. It feels like a big loss. … But is this possible? Is this really all about not being able to sleep with my mother?"

"I suspect it's not that simple. I think that may be a factor in it – your overstimulation as a child – your wanting what was right there but that you couldn't have. But I think there's more, I think there's your wanting your mother to have loved you for you, not for her own needs. To have really seen you as the precious little person you were, rather than as a toy she could play with and discard as she wished."

"This is all sad. I don't like it."

Harry gets engaged to Karen. His sixth engagement, but his first since beginning our work together. They don't set a wedding date. She knows his track record. Although she is obviously willing to take a chance for whatever reasons of her own, she also isn't foolhardy.

Harry and I continue to work. His sexual longing for his mother, his anger at women, his fear of his own neediness, his sadness at not being genuinely loved by either of his parents, remain ongoing topics.

Six months after his engagement Harry says that he wants to think about ending therapy. He has remained faithful to Karen and they are now thinking of setting a wedding date. He is optimistic. I think termination is a good decision for him. It will give him the chance to work through the loss of his therapist/mother while he works through the actual letting go of his mother and his true commitment to a new woman. We set a termination date. And we continue to work. His issues around loss and mourning intensify. He is angry at both his parents for not being the parents he needed. Now more conscious of his anger at his mother, his anger at his father diminishes. Although he recognizes that they are not evil people and can only be who they are, his interactions with them continue to be difficult. He strives to accept their limitations and tries to relinquish some of his anger. When the anger abates, however, he is left with his sadness, sadness for the child who he was, who did not and could never have the parents he needed and deserved. I am pleased with how termination is progressing. I am pleased with what seems like a successful treatment.

As for my feelings, I am more ambivalent. On the one hand, I fear I might experience Harry's leaving as a major loss. On the other hand, I wonder if it might not be a relief and a precursor to the end of my fantasies. In fact, all proves to be true. Our last session is sad, but not particularly painful. He acknowledges that we did good work together and that he appreciates me for helping him move his life forward in the direction he wanted to go. He hopes that he and Karen will marry before too long, that they will have children and that he will remain faithful to her. I tell him that it was a pleasure to work with him and watch him grow and that I would always be available to him if he wanted to come back, even for a few sessions. Like him, I worry about whether he will be able to remain faithful in the long run and what problems and feelings may be restimulated for him if and when they have children. We hug good-bye, a very platonic, non-arousing hug.

Still, his leave-taking makes me sadder than I hoped and for a while I have more than my usual share of fantasies about him, fantasies that again have us meeting accidentally and moving towards the promise of something more. In time, however, the fantasies recede and then stop completely. Harry becomes another analytic patient who I enjoyed working with and who responded well to the treatment.

Then, two years after the termination of Harry's treatment, an extraordinary event occurs. George and I are sitting in the Detroit airport waiting to board a plane for a brief visit to New York. Harry, and a woman I assume is Karen, enter the same boarding area and take seats not far from us. As is my custom when meeting patients or ex-patients outside my office, I wait for the patient to acknowledge or not acknowledge me. The plane is delayed. Some time goes by. I think about my previous airline fantasies involving Harry and think how strange it is that I feel so little. A bit awkward, but nothing more. Then Harry rises and comes over to me. He leans towards me and I assume that he is going to shake my hand. Instead, he kisses me on the mouth! I am stunned! I stammer through the rest of the greeting, the rest of the pleasantries, but am totally immersed in my own thoughts, in my instantaneous, all-too-obvious awareness.

In that one moment I realize that of course not all the sexual feelings in the treatment room were mine! How could I have not seen that? How could I have not explored the possibility of Harry's sexual feelings towards me? My answer is that because I had been so immediately attracted to Harry and because his similarities to my father were so obvious, I always assumed that the sexual feelings in the room were all mine. The immediacy and intensity of my feelings had led me to forget that both countertransference – the therapist's feelings toward her patient – and transference – the patient's feelings towards his analyst – are always a co-creation of the two subjectivities, the two individuals, in the room. I took all the feelings as my own and never looked further. I had analyzed other feelings as possible joint creations – the anger I felt at his mother, his discomfort with his dependency on me – but I had never, ever explored the possibility of Harry having sexual feelings towards me. This lapse now seems ludicrous to me. Here was a womanizer who sexualized most relationships, who had sexual and dependency issues towards his mother, and yet I never looked at his sexual transference. I can hardly believe my own blindness. Perhaps I felt more guilty or frightened than I realized about my own sexual fantasies and had therefore been unwilling to risk raising the sexual tension in the consulting room by directly asking Harry about his sexual feelings towards me. Regardless, I consider it a major shortcoming of the treatment, what Gabbard (1996) called a countertransference enactment when talking about the case of a woman he supervised who had similar sexual feelings towards a male patient. It was an enactment in that my feelings toward my patient led to my inability to adequately interpret my patient's feelings towards me.

But, it is done. There is no going back. There is nothing to do but forgive myself and hope to remember and learn from the experience for a future occasion. And it does seem as though Harry hasn't fared too badly. It was Karen he was with and they were married. I obviously couldn't know if he was being faithful to her.

George and I board the plane for our New York getaway. Harry and Karen board as well. Harry and I aren't seated next to each other. I am going on with my life; Harry is going on with his.

4

FORCED TERMINATION

When Pain is Shared[1]

It is January of 1993, the fourth year I am commuting weekly between Ann Arbor and Key Largo. I am on the plane to Miami, the one I typically take on a Thursday evening. But this is by no means my usual plane ride. Tonight I am so anxious I am barely able to keep myself from shaking; tears flow intermittently. George has had what he calls a "heart episode," pain and constriction in his chest. His doctor wants him in the hospital. Instead, he is picking me up at the Miami airport. I am beyond terrified. Will this be it? Will this be the time that my worst fears are realized? Will this be the time that George leaves me for good?

One decision becomes clear to me on this trip. If George is seriously ill he will have to move back to Ann Arbor permanently. If what he has is more easily fixable, I will move to Florida. I have spent the last four years agonizing about this decision, about whether or not to move, for I knew that I could not keep commuting indefinitely. Asking George to move back to Michigan year-round seemed heartless since he clearly felt so much better in the warmth. And I too began to love Florida winters and hated to return to Michigan's cold bleakness. To move or not to move became my obsession. And, as with all good obsessions, I could change my mind ten times in a day. The warmth of George and Florida called to me, as did the safety and familiarity of home, my practice and my friends. My mind was like a ping-pong ball, moving from one side to the other and back again. I hated the indecision, but could not move beyond it. On this plane ride my decision is made. It is clearer to me than ever that George and I have only a finite number of years together. I don't want to squander the years with unnecessary distance. Besides, I can't imagine being apart from him. My anxiety would be intolerable. George's health will determine our path, my path. I know I will abide by what I have decided tonight.

George meets me at the airport, his usual cheery, upbeat self. I hug him and burst into tears. I never, ever want to let go. He's reassuring. It will be nothing. He felt some chest pain while riding his bicycle and thought it best that he take himself to the emergency room. He had had an abnormal EEG in December that the doctors had yet to understand. I know George would never have taken himself to the hospital were it not for the abnormality on that test. Now he is scheduled for tests at Miami Heart Institute tomorrow. We will drive there in the morning. I will drive I tell him. I want him doing as little as possible until we know what's going on.

And so began my first real foray into the medical system. Looking back I marvel at both my naiveté and the intensity of my anxiety that often made it difficult to hear and understand what the doctors were saying.

Snapshots from that day: I sit forlornly in a dark corridor while George is having a thallium stress test. A nurse passes by and asks if there is anything she can get me. I tell her, "A miracle."

The hospital is frigid. I can't warm up. The thin sweater I brought is worthless. George offers me his sweater. I burst into tears.

And then there's Dr. Juan Garcia, George's Miami Heart cardiologist. He is tall and thin with a dark, bushy beard and piercing brown eyes. Even at the time I recognize he is an extraordinary physician – kind, caring, concerned not only about George's heart, but about both our well-being. The test shows that George does have some heart blockages. He will need an angiogram to determine more specific information, their extent and their exact location. The question is whether to have the procedure in Miami or to return to Michigan. At the moment it is impossible to know whether George will need angioplasties – a relatively simple procedure that requires little recuperation time – or open heart surgery – a much more invasive surgery that requires weeks or months of recuperation. If it turns out to be the latter do we want to be in Miami or Michigan? It's clear to me the answer is Michigan. That's where my support system is. That's where my life is. Besides, commuting daily between Miami and Key Largo would be quite a chore. And what would we do with Kali, our cat? Dr. Garcia spends time with me looking through the phone book to see where there might be a nearby pet store to buy an airline carrying case for Kali. He sits with me as I call a physician friend in Ann Arbor to find a local cardiologist. He calls the physician himself to tell him about George's condition. I tell him I will never forget his kindness. I haven't.

Two angioplasties later, George feels as good as new. "You see," he tells me, "I told you everything would be all right."

We are moving. I am going to leave that which is known and safe and embark on a new and frightening journey.

It is the above events that eventually led to my writing the following:

On August 23, 1993 I saw the last seven of my 14 patients, said good-bye to each of them, packed up my office, and waited, tears flowing, for my husband and friends to carry my furniture to the rented U-Haul waiting below. I was closing an 18 year practice in Ann Arbor, Michigan and preparing to begin again in Boca Raton, Florida. Even after all these years I find I cannot write these simple lines without weeping.

I, of course, was not the only one who wept. Through the seven months of the termination process, patients sobbed about losing me, railed against me for abandoning them, and questioned their ability to survive without me. They felt alone, adrift in a world that seemed suddenly unsafe and unprotected. In this, my patients and I felt very much alike. Each of my patients was losing me and

58

the potential safety and security afforded by the therapeutic setting. Each was losing me as a stable, dependable figure; each was losing me as a foundation on which to build. I, too, was suffering many losses. In addition to losing all my patients, I was losing the security of a well-established practice, the comfort of a close circle of friends, and the safety of a home I cherished. Like my patients, I was losing my foundation and felt vulnerable and alone. It is this confluence of experience between myself and my patients that I will address … for I believe that it profoundly affected the therapeutic process by leading to shared identifications which in turn created a more porous boundary, a lack of clear distinction, between my feelings and those of my patients.

(Sherby, 2004)

The decision to move was made. I now had to decide on a termination date and begin telling friends and patients. I felt both anxious and withdrawn, carrying this "secret" I was not yet ready to share. In addition, George had returned to Key Largo. My days away from him were almost unbearable. I worried constantly about his health, calling him multiple times a day to make sure he was still alive, to make sure he hadn't had any more "heart episodes." I began keeping a journal, both as therapy for myself, as well as a way to chronicle the process of termination. I kept copious process notes, thinking that I might one day write about the experience. It took me six years to open those notebooks, another two to begin the process of writing. My notebooks hold a tremendous amount of pain, both mine and my patients. They also hold stories of struggle, and courage, and growth, and change. They are a testament to the resilience and capability of individuals to grow despite hardship and trauma. The notebooks also capture the experience of a forced termination, in which patient and analyst are going through a similar, although not identical, traumatic event at the same time. The parallel circumstance blurs the boundary between patient and analyst and fosters shared identifications and fantasies, making it difficult to know, "Whose feeling is this anyway?" In all human interactions we communicate with each other in complex ways that go on outside of our awareness. Or, as Loewald says, "we are less individual than we realize, that the sharp boundedness of intrapsychic life is an illusion" (cited in Winer, 1994). In forced termination, the similarity of the patient's and the analyst's experience can make this boundary even more porous, placing both a tremendous burden and an expanded opportunity on the therapeutic process.

The journal begins with my telling my first patient, Richard, a somber, serious, removed man I have seen in twice weekly psychotherapy for four years. I hadn't planned to tell him today, but he begins the session by saying that he thinks he's ready to cut back to once a week. I'm torn. Before he makes a definite decision I think he should know that we have only seven more months to work together. But I'm not sure I'm ready to say out loud that I'm actually leaving, thereby making it feel all the more real. At the time, I think that my therapeutic concern wins out. I tell Richard the news. He becomes teary.

"It's been so helpful for me to talk with you," he says. "When I needed you more, I didn't know that I needed you. Now that I need you less, I know I'm attached to you and need you."

Listening to my patient, I'm overwhelmed by sadness and fight back tears. But I am also relieved. I feel more pain, but less anxiety; more sadness, but less aloneness. I feel as though I have broken through a defensive wall and am more connected to both Richard and myself.

Seven months later, near the end of the journal, there is an excerpt from the last session with William, a man I had seen in analysis for seven years.

"While I was cutting the grass this week-end," he says, "I heard crickets and they made me think about my grandparent's house. So I lay down in the hammock and talked aloud to myself. I was able to recall my grandparent's entire house. It felt a little sad, but mostly I was glad to be able to recall it all. I thought that although a lot of it was gone, a lot of it remained as well – the summers are still hot and the grass still grows by their house."

Tears stream down my face.

Tears stream down my face. I am in a taxi with my mother, sobbing. We are leaving my grandparent's apartment for what I know will be the last time. My grandfather died a week ago. My grandmother has been dead for three years. Her potted geraniums and avocado plants lie carefully at our feet. I cannot believe that they are both gone. I loved them so much. They loved me so much. And their apartment! The safe haven of my childhood, a place where I was free to dance in front of their bedroom mirror pretending to be a great ballerina, a place where I read The Yearling, sobbing on my grandfather's bed, a place where we ate my grandmother's home-cooked matzo ball soup and gefilte fish, and where my grandfather baked me elaborate birthday cakes. It's all gone. And it will live forever. Some of my grandparent's possessions are already in my parent's home: pictures that hung above my sofa bed in their living room, an art-deco bookcase and floor lamp, a Queen Ann-looking table that stood in their foyer. The one object I especially wanted we don't have, my grandparent's samovar, brought from Russia. My grandfather had asked me to take it many times, but I couldn't. Not while he was still alive. Even in my mid-twenties I wasn't ready to face the reality of his eventual death. I refused to take the samovar. Now my uncle has it, lost in a coin toss with my mother. It's a bitter loss for me. It's only a thing, I tell myself, but it feels like more, a symbol of the past, both theirs and ours together. It is all gone. It will live forever.

Remembering that taxi ride, I feel both the pain I had felt twenty plus years ago, and anticipate the agony I will feel when I leave my Michigan home for the last time. I can't bear to think of it. I can't imagine that I will really, of my own free will, walk out of that house for the last time. With difficulty, I bring myself back to my patient.

"Is the something gone and the something remaining true of me as well?" I ask.

"Definitely," he replies. "I know I'll imagine you as being somewhere, wherever that might be and I know when I walk by your building it will still be here and that will comfort me a great deal."

Much of the past is gone and over, but some things do remain. Life is not all brief and illusory. My patient and I grieved together, joined in the experience of mourning past and present losses, while struggling to hold on to that which still remained.

Under the best of conditions, patients often describe termination as an experience akin to graduation. There is a sense of ending a significant chapter in one's life, of leaving a safe, protected environment, of moving out into the world. It is a time of hope and possibilities; a time to change one's focus and see what lies ahead. But it is also a time of loss and mourning, for both the patient and the analyst. If the analysis has been successful and both parties have come together in the decision to terminate, both will have to deal with the ending of a relationship that has brought growth and fulfillment to each of them, in different ways and to different degrees. The patient will be losing a unique relationship where he has potentially been able to say anything that came to mind without fear of being judged or criticized, where he hopefully has felt more understood and supported than he ever thought possible, and where he has ideally been free to explore himself while his analyst carefully listened to his every word. Such a blissful environment is indeed difficult to relinquish. As in all mourning, termination involves a giving up, a disconnection from the analyst, the relationship, and the unique space they established between them. But it also involves a taking in, an internalization of the person of and experience with the analyst so that there is a capacity for what Gaines (1997) calls "maintaining continuity."

The analyst, too, suffers a loss (Balint, 1950; Firestein, 1978; Gorkin, 1987; Novick, 1997; Searles, 1979; Viorst, 1982; Weigert, 1952). She must leave a human being she has come to know intimately over many years, as well as a person who has gratified her in her role as a helper. She, too, must both detach from and take in her patient. In addition, the analyst may have identified with the needing, longing, wanting parts of her patients and, in giving to them, may have nurtured herself as well.

> ... termination involves many different kinds of loss – the loss of a whole, real object; the loss of some identified part of the object; the loss of a healing symbiotic relatedness; the loss of some especially pleasing role; the loss of a host of professional and therapeutic ambitions; and the loss of the analyst's dream of his or her own perfection.
>
> (Viorst, 1982, p. 416)

But what of forced termination? What happens when the analyst makes a unilateral decision to end the treatment, regardless of the patient's needs, wishes, or readiness to terminate? Such endings are certainly not uncommon, particularly in the early or later years of an analyst's career. Early on, forced terminations are the norm for the novice therapist as she moves through various internships, residencies, and initial therapeutic settings. These terminations may not be as painful as ending an eighteen-year practice, but they are still difficult and complicate the termination process. Retirement or semi-retirement can bring more wrenching terminations as the analyst ends her practice entirely or moves to a different part of the country. Whenever a therapist on her own makes the decision to terminate the treatment, the process of mourning and working through becomes more difficult for both patient and analyst. A patient's anger can make internalization of the positive aspects of the therapeutic experience more difficult, leading to an even greater sense of loss and bereftness. And an analyst's guilt about her leave-taking might result in a defensive withdrawal, making connection with the patient more difficult, and leaving the patient feeling alone and left before the actual date of termination.

Commentaries on analyst/therapist's forced terminations have indicated a wide range of patient reactions depending upon the patient's history and dynamics, as well as where he or she was in the treatment process (Beatrice, 1982–1983; Dewald, 1965, 1966, 1982; Limentani, 1982; Martinez, 1989; Schwartz, 1974; Weiss, 1972). The patient may justifiably feel betrayed and abandoned, as if everything the analyst had explicitly or implicitly promised – security, safety, consistency, trust – has now been destroyed. As exquisitely captured by one patient, "When you said you were leaving, you lost your right to remain a therapist" (Beatrice, 1982–1983, p. 323).

The analyst certainly cannot claim a similar betrayal since she is the one making the choice, she is the one doing the leaving. Still, "In many ways the position of the departing therapist resembles that of his patient. He, too, sustains a loss. He, too experiences the anxiety of separation. Perhaps for him, it is harder to claim abandonment and desertion, but he may feel equally adrift in the therapeutic world..." (Scher, 1970, p.281). Both patient and therapist are losing their safety net, their foundation, a place where they feel secure and "held." While the patient is losing a person in his life he has come to depend on, the analyst is facing multiple losses of her own. She is about to give up all that is familiar and venture off into a new life. Both patient and analyst must say good-bye to that which is comfortable and safe. Unlike the toddler who can venture away from mother while keeping her safely within his sight, there is no mother to return to. Each party of this therapeutic dyad must face the unknown on his or her own.

This similarity of experience between patient and analyst makes forced termination a powerful therapeutic experience fraught with both danger and opportunity. Gone is any remnant of the analyst's conviction that the feelings generated in the consulting room are solely a product of the patient's internal conflicts, fantasy elaboration, and projective identification. The words transference and countertransference are no longer sufficient, for in a forced termination, when the analyst and the patient are feeling much the same things, even perhaps with equal intensity, the boundary between patient and analyst blurs. How does this blurring of boundaries manifest itself in the clinical situation? Did my patients know the angst I was experiencing? If so, how was it communicated and what did it mean to them? Had I curtailed their freedom to be angry with me because they knew the pain that I, too, was experiencing? Or did my immersion in my own pain free them to deal with theirs? Was the therapeutic process forestalled or enhanced? My answer is both, in differing degrees, with different patients. Scher (1970) describes losing his empathic capacity in two directions – over-identifying with patients in a way that led him to assume they were feeling what he felt or numbing himself to the patient's pain so as to protect himself from an overwhelming identification. I, too, could fall victim to these empathic failures. On the other hand, I found that the parallel experience between me and my patients could also enhance identification, connection, and attunement in a way that provided a sense of being "held" and was thus able to promote therapeutic growth.

Seven months prior to termination, I told all my patients about my decision to end my practice and relocate. The most difficult patient for me to tell was Allison, a woman I had seen in analysis for fourteen years. I was literally the most important person in Allison's life, a life with few if any other significant relationships or attachments.

Allison is the sixth patient I will be telling today. I feel my anxiety build as I walk towards the waiting room. What am I afraid of? My guilt that Allison will be devastated and that it is all my fault? Definitely. Allison's rage? Perhaps. Although Allison is not a large woman her seething rage can fill the room, almost as though it is sucking out the air and making it difficult to breathe. I smile my usual smile, perhaps a little more weakly than usual. She lies down on the couch.

"Allison," I say, my voice shaking, "I need to start today. I need to tell you something. I need to tell you that George has developed some heart difficulties. You knew there were a few times I had to cancel our appointments, well that's because he was having some procedures done to his heart. He's all right, but we're going to be moving to Florida because of his health. And of course that means I'm going to be ending my practice. My last day, our last day together will be August 23rd."

"Oh, Linda," she responds, "I'm so sorry. How terrible for you. You must be so scared. You must be out of your mind with worry. I don't know how you've even been able to work."

"Thank you, I appreciate your concern, but seeing people has actually been helpful for me. But what about you? How do you feel about what this will mean for you, for us?"

Silence.

A prolonged silence. I can feel the air leaving the room.

"You can say it Allison. Whatever it is you can say it."

"He should have just died!!" she says, her rage both constrained and vitriolic. "If he'd just died, you'd have it over with! You wouldn't have to worry any more. And you wouldn't have to leave!! I always knew it," she continues, the force of her anger building. "I knew that as soon as you married him that he'd take you away from me. I remember that first time I realized you were wearing a wedding ring. I knew it! I Goddamn knew that he'd take you away from me!"

"It's fine for you to be angry, but you need to allow yourself to be angry with me too. I'm the one who's made the decision to move. Yes, it's because of George's health problems, but the decision to leave is mine."

"It's him! It's him!! If it weren't for him you wouldn't be going any place."

Silence.

I feel the rage leave the room.

"I'm sorry, Linda. Of course I don't wish him dead. I'm just so scared. I just don't know if I'll be able to survive without you. I can't imagine what it will be like. I don't know if I'll be able to go on without you."

Although Allison's reaction was more intense and dramatic than most of my patients, they all, to varying degrees, struggled with feelings of sadness, anger, rejection, and loss. All of them had to deal with both my leaving and with the information I had given them about my leaving. I basically told all my patients what I told Allison, that my husband had developed some heart problems, that he was all right, but that we had decided to move to Florida for his health. There is of course the question of why I told my patients what I did, why I told them about my husband's illness and how that affected my decision to relocate. My answer is that this communication captured my *subjective* experience of feeling compelled to leave because of George's health, of the decision not being entirely under my volitional control. Even though I made the final decision, and repeatedly told patients that I made the decision, I felt that life circumstances pushed me in the direction of moving. I did, of course, have other reasons for my self-disclosure, some of which I realized at the time, others that I did not understand until years later. I presented patients with what I considered to be a "good" or "legitimate" reason for leaving. The idea of giving my patients no reason for my leaving was never an option for me. I had long believed that to not speak or, by extension, to respond in the most minimal manner, was not necessarily therapeutic. I knew that my patients would feel dismissed, discarded, and betrayed by my forced termination. To make my leave-taking seem like a decision that I had come to easily, without some compelling reason, felt both untrue and unnecessarily hurtful.

Additionally, at this juncture of my life, I needed to be seen as more of a human being, as a person with my own struggles and difficulties. I would have been unable to contain all my patients' projected rage, envy, and jealousy unless those projections were mitigated by some degree of reality. I needed to be seen as a person who was hurting, in ways that were similar, albeit not identical, to how my patients were hurting. I told patients for them and for me. I told them because I felt I had no choice, much as I felt I had no choice about leaving. I told them because I felt to not tell them would leave me removed and distracted, too involved in my own thoughts and feelings to be fully present with them in the moment. I told them because to not tell them would have left me feeling too alone and despairing in the consulting room. In retrospect I believe that my patients would have known anyway, not the specific reason for my leaving, but certainly the angst that I felt underneath. We were connected in this process of mourning and it is difficult for me to imagine that they would not have sensed my pain resonating with their own.

About a month prior to termination I had lunch with a colleague who asked if my patients had begun to disconnect from me and the treatment. I looked at him in amazement and replied, "Not at all." With the exception of one patient who had been struggling with her relationship with me for some time and who left as soon as I told her I was moving, every one of my patients stayed engaged with me to the very end, often increasing the frequency of their sessions and, in most instances, doing an incredible amount of productive work through the last day. I believe that my patients' ability to remain intensely involved with me was fostered by the degree of pain and vulnerability they consciously or unconsciously knew I too was experiencing.

I am going to look at the ways in which my patients and I were exquisitely intertwined, both consciously and unconsciously, by returning to the two bookends of my notebooks, Richard, the first patient I told about my leaving, and, William, who talked about what remained after a relationship was over, as well as by focusing on the intensity of the relationship between Allison and myself.

Richard was a detached, remote man who had improved greatly over the course of treatment. My decision to tell Richard about my move was not planned and was ostensibly stimulated by his beginning the session by telling me he wanted to cut down on the frequency of his sessions. Consciously I thought he should know that we had only seven months left to work together before he decided whether or not to reduce the frequency of his sessions. In retrospect I think my motivation was far more complex.

At the time that I told Richard about my leaving, I felt very much as he had early in the treatment. I was removed, cut-off, defending against feelings of neediness and sadness by keeping myself behind a wall that resulted in my feeling distanced from everyone, including George. I told myself it was the only way I could get through my days in some semblance of normalcy; it was the only way I could tolerate my separations from George; it was the only way I could keep myself from panicking about the possibility of his death. I couldn't allow myself to feel needy. I just couldn't. Instead, I identified with the harsh, rejecting part of myself that had little tolerance for any childlike neediness. This, in fact, was a very familiar stance for Richard, particularly in the early years of treatment. It was what he meant when he said that when he needed me most, he didn't know he needed me. Now, here I was, being like Richard and unconsciously choosing him as the first patient I told.

I now wonder if in telling Richard first I was hoping that he would "cure" me, just as I had "cured" him. In other words, I hoped that he would identify with my needy self and rescue me from my isolation, just as I had done for him. And, in fact, that is what happened. In tearing up and speaking the words that acknowledged his need, he was declaring his comfort with needing without being reduced to a helpless infant. His identification with the needy part of himself enabled me to reconnect with that part of myself, particularly since our ability to be sad and teary together meant that neither of us had to feel alone or unsafe. Our ability to feel sad together enabled both of us to know that sadness could be survived and endured without reverting to a childlike helplessness. Additionally, I was comforted by the knowledge that this had been a successful treatment in which both Richard and I had been "cured."

In the session with Richard, I began it knowing that I felt removed and withdrawn. These were *my* feelings, not the projection of his feelings that I was experiencing. In this instance the distinction between my feelings and his feelings was clear to me. Such is not always the case.

William was another patient who struggled with extreme discomfort about his own neediness and tended to project those feelings unto others and then experience himself as empty and despairing, feeling only "nothingness." An example of the porous boundary and shared pain between me and William can be seen in a session that occurred shortly after I had to cancel several appointments because George had another medical emergency.

William looks at me quizzically out of the corner of his eyes as he comes into my office. "How are things?" he asks tentatively.

How are things? That is indeed a very good question. I had to cancel patients for part of last week and take an emergency flight to Miami. This time I rented a car and made my own way to Key Largo. George was back in the emergency room with weakness and chest pains and was again to be transferred to Miami Heart the morning after my arrival. Just when I think I can't get any more anxious, any more terrified of losing George, there's another incident and my terror rises. Will this be it? Will this be the time I lose George forever?

George is transferred by ambulance to Miami Heart. After an interminable eight-hour wait in a room with another patient who has clearly lost his mental capacities and moans constantly, along with his continually arguing adult children, Dr. Garcia performs an angiogram. One of the angioplasties has closed. It's only a small artery. Dr. Garcia is surprised that this apparently insignificant artery is causing all George's difficulties. He again recommends that we return to Ann Arbor in case they are unable to open the artery with an angioplasty and need to fall back on open heart surgery.

This time George feels so weak that he needs to be in a wheelchair. This time George is terribly depressed. I've never seen him react in this manner. His depression scares me. We have friends visiting Key Largo from Ann Arbor. They were supposed to stay with us. They opt for a hotel. I try to be sociable. George stays at home while I visit some of the tourist sites with our friends. I'm anxious the whole time. Will he survive my absence? Will I survive his?

I make arrangements for our return to Ann Arbor, this time with George in a wheelchair. He is beyond demoralized. At the Detroit airport I park the car by the curb and go in to collect George and our cat from inside the terminal. Way before 9/11, a security guard tells me I can't leave the car parked there. I explain that my husband is just inside the terminal in a wheelchair. He doesn't care. I can't leave the car there. I tell him I'm leaving the car there and getting my husband. A bystander cheers me on. There is no further argument.

We are back in our Michigan home. George remains despondent. We are waiting for the cardiologist to schedule the angioplasty.

How shall I answer William's question? I have decided that I will not volunteer information, but will answer patients' questions honestly.

"Not great," I reply. "One of my husband's angioplasties closed and is going to be redone next week."

"I'm sorry," he says, "I know this must be a terribly difficult time for you."

"Yes, it is," I say truthfully. "And I appreciate your concern, but we're here to deal with you and it's actually helpful for me to have someone else to focus on."

"It's so horrible that nothing is forever, that nothing is permanent," he continues. "I wish I could be immortal, above death. I wish I could feel that there was something sure, something that carried on. The impermanence is so all encompassing. Sometimes I wonder what it all means, if anything matters, why we bother at all."

Feeling as though I am beginning to be drawn into quicksand by the heaviness and despair in the room, I ask, "What about your grandparents? They influenced and affected you. Doesn't that mean that they're still with you, that they have some permanence?"

"It's made them immortal for me," he replies, "but not for them." He pauses. "I remember thinking about my grandmother rotting in the ground and how horrible that thought is. Too horrible to think of at all," he adds, his voice entirely devoid of emotion.

My anxiety begins to skyrocket as thoughts about both George and my grandmother fill my mind. Suspecting that I am feeling both my own pain as well as William's I ask, "What did you feel when your grandmother died?"

"I felt profound grief," he says. "Then I put it away. Then I felt it again about a month later at her grave. I can feel it now when I think of it. But I don't want to think about it anymore."

William goes on to talk about a topic he presents as unrelated, namely his not getting to see his daughter, Peggy, for the second weekend in a row – the first week because of her illness, the second because of a snowstorm. He wonders, however, if he gave up too soon, if he should have tried to figure out some alternative. "I'm afraid she will feel disappointed and abandoned."

"Are you possibly talking about your disappointment at not getting to see me because of the canceled appointments?" I ask.

"Oh no," he replies, "I could never feel that. You had no choice but to cancel. I'm much more worried about you. I know this shouldn't be my concern, but I worry about your being left and abandoned by your husband."

Although this is, of course, my constant terror, I say, "I don't mean to dismiss your empathy towards me, but what you're saying is so much a part of who you are. Here you are dealing with your intense feelings of mourning about your grandmother and about death in general and rather than owning those feelings of loss and abandonment, you project them outward and put them into me or Peggy or whomever, and then feel bad for us rather than for you."

There is a brief pause, then William says, "I know you've made similar statements in the past, but something about the way you just said that was like a revelation. I always thought that the reason I identified with other people was to feel something and to avoid the emptiness I feel. But it suddenly makes sense to me that I have these feelings and find them so intolerable that I have to rid myself of the feelings by putting them in other people. That feels entirely new to me." He smiles at me as he leaves the session and I realize that I feel both lighter and less anxious.

So what happened in this session that allowed William to finally hear and take in an interpretation that I had in fact made many times previously? First of all, the entire session is suffused with intense feelings about death and loss. The specter of George's illness and possible death haunts the session. Additionally, the patient is dealing with the loss of me – both in the canceled sessions and in the eventual termination – while I am dealing with a host of losses of my own. I bring up his grandparents in an effort to dispel some of the hopelessness, only to find that we become further mired in despair. I suspect that the issue with his daughter is related to the overall topic of the session and make an interpretation that returns him to the question of losing me. He denies it emphatically – he could not possibly be concerned with his own feelings, only with mine. Although I do not doubt or deny the intensity of my sadness, I say that I am not the only one in the room with these feelings and suggest that he needs to take back and own those feelings which originate from within him. This is also a session in which I have said that although I am "not great," I am consciously choosing to focus on him rather than myself. I am not denying my feelings, but rather putting them on the back burner. William has spent his life unconsciously ridding himself of feelings because they felt too painful to bear. I offer an alternative; it is possible to own your own feelings without drowning in them.

So this has been a helpful session for William. And it has been helpful for me as well. In helping him to take back his projections, I have not had to carry his feelings of sadness as well as my own. Additionally, in helping him to deal with feelings of loss I have also helped myself, teaching us both that it is possible to feel and endure the pain of separation, and even death, without being destroyed by the grief.

Six months later, during our termination session, William's growth is obvious, for he now feels and expresses that there is something that remains, that not all is impermanence. Although profoundly sad, the session also provides a feeling of connectedness and hope stemming both from our years together, as well as from our memories and identifications with our grandparents. For both this patient and me, our relationship with our grandparents was a life-sustaining part of our childhoods. Although I had never told my patient of this similarity between us, it would not surprise me if he knew of it. And now, in this last session, we are both focused on our grandparents, on our grief for their loss, but also on what remains. Although my patient focuses on the concrete – the summers that are still hot and the grass that still grows – I understand this as an internalization, as taking his grandparents inside himself so as to remain connected to them and to continue to feel their continuing comfort and solace. The reminder that there is a continuity, that people and things do remain with us in our minds, is soothing to us both as we prepare to say our final good-byes and venture off into our respective lives.

George's angioplasty has been successfully redone. He has returned to his usual, upbeat self. He will not, however, return to Key Largo for what is left of this winter. I'm not letting him out of my sight. Besides, there's much to be done in preparation for our move. George's two-story, three-car garage packed with tools is in itself a chore demanding many weeks of work. We haven't even definitively decided where we're living. I had previously ruled out Key Largo. I knew there was no was way I could have an analytic practice there or, for that matter, much of a therapy practice at all. A physician who worked there suggested that I'd have better luck opening a bar.

My practice will be in Boca Raton. Where our home will be still remains to be decided. I can't really think about it. To think of any home besides the one in Michigan is incomprehensible; to think of any home besides this one envelops me in sadness.

The most mutually heartrending termination process occurred between myself and Allison. The level of Allison's dependency, rage, and despair can be seen in a session that occurred about three months into the termination process.

Allison enters my office and lies down on the couch without ever meeting my eyes. I feel both the brick wall that shields her as well as the seething anger underneath. I make several attempts to ask her about her anger and to help her express her feelings. I am met with nothing. I decide to wait to see what develops.

Finally, Allison says, "I don't feel angry. I know I'm being silent, but I'm not angry."

"Are you sure your silence isn't covering your anger?" I ask.

"I'm not eating. And I'm smoking dope. And I'm not eating even though I'm smoking dope. I know those are signs of anger. I know I'm trying to hurt you by hurting myself. I even smoked pot during the day and I haven't done that for years."

"Sounds like anger to me," I say.

She is silent for a few seconds and then says, "I guess there's anger there, like I want to get back at you, to hurt you."

"It would be better if you could express your anger directly."

"Well," she responds, "I've been having fantasies of yanking the blinds off the windows and beating you with them."

"How do you feel about telling me that fantasy?" I ask.

"Okay," she says, "But I think there's something more. I think it's like, if I go back to the way I was years ago, maybe you won't leave. Like with my mother, you'll know that I need you and you won't go."

A palpable sadness fills the room.

"I saw the movie, *Hook*," she says. "It's based on Peter Pan. You know how I've always loved Peter Pan, always wanted to be him. Well, I was thinking, maybe if I believe hard enough you won't go. I can make time stand still and you can be with me forever."

I am instantly overwhelmed by pain, both Allison's and my own and, like my patient, I'm aware of the desire to distance myself from that pain. The childlike wish Allison has articulated is very much like my own. I, too, want time to stand still. I don't want to deal with the possibility of George's increasing health problems and eventual death. I don't want to deal with driving away from my home for the last time. Having everything stay as it is right now would be fine with me too. But, of course, that is impossible. Allison and I are both powerless to change the inevitable movement of time. August will arrive and Allison will be have to deal with my leaving just as I will have to deal with leaving her, as well as my home, my friends, and my other patients. We are joined in our feelings of pain, despair, and hopelessness from which, at this moment, I can provide no escape. I want to comfort and protect Allison, but feel as powerless as she does. We have both descended to a level of infantile helplessness.

Despite these days of agony, there are times that the intensely primitive and strong connection between us feels comforting and that we both take solace in the bond that exists between us. In caring for the early, infantile parts of Allison, I am tending to both Allison and to myself. This caring becomes symbolized through a hanging plant I have in my office. At some point I begin thinking about giving Allison this plant. It seems a concrete way for her to hold on to me, as well as a way for me to expiate some of my guilt about leaving her.

I am still considering whether to broach the topic of the plant when, one day, Allison says, "I'm going to miss your plant. The plant is you. I know sometimes I've thought the plant is me and that your taking care of the plant is taking care of me, but not now. Now it's you."

I hesitate for a moment and then say, "It's interesting that you say that because I've thought about giving you the plant, but wasn't sure how it would feel to you."

"You have?" she exclaims, excitedly. "I've been wanting to ask you if I could buy the plant from you, but I was afraid you'd say no."

We discuss her difficulty in asking for what she wants, as well as her problem with taking and accepting and feeling grateful.

Then I add, "One of my concerns about giving you the plant is how you'd feel if it died."

"I thought about that, too," she says. "I don't think I could survive the plant dying."

This is the beginning of many sessions in which Allison and I deal with the plant which we now both care about a great deal, hoping that it will grow and prosper. Some days Allison sees the plant as looking healthy and hearty, at other times she sees it as sick and on the verge of death. The plant sometimes symbolizes Allison, sometimes me, and sometimes our relationship. Mostly, however, it represents the needy, infantile part of us both, the part we try to nurture, more or less successfully. Sometimes Allison treats the plant with loving care, at other times she destroys it with her anger or neglect.

It is our next to last session.

"How are you doing?" Allison asks.

I reply truthfully, "Not great."

"That doesn't make me feel any better," she responds petulantly. "I'm angry that you're leaving. I'm scared. I'm sure I'm going to die. When I write down an appointment for next week, I feel better, I feel like I'll be here. But mostly I feel

70

overwhelmed by the pain and frightened by it. It feels like a big wave that will just overwhelm me and take me under."

I am again struck by how closely Allison's feelings resemble my own, for I too have been fearful of being engulfed by waves of sadness.

Allison continues. "I don't think I can take the plant. It's too much of a risk."

"You're afraid your anger would destroy it?" I ask.

"I don't think I can trust myself," she says. "I know how angry I can get and if it died I'd never forgive myself."

In the end, however, in the last few minutes of the last hour, Allison asks, "Can I have the plant?"

I'm thrilled. I feel uplifted. But I remain wary. "Are you sure?" I ask.

"Yes," she says. "I want something of you to take with me."

Allison's decision to take the plant feels like a triumph to me. It seems to indicate that she has enough faith in her ability to take over where I left off and to be the caretaker for the dependent, helpless part of herself. I feel extremely sad at our parting. But more hopeful than I had anticipated. Perhaps I am indeed the plant and Allison is indicating her willingness to take care of me, as well as herself.

I am terminating with Fred, a patient in my Boca Raton office, almost nine years to the day since I left my practice in Ann Arbor. Fred is an analytic patient I have seen for only a year and a half who is now leaving because of a job relocation. Throughout the termination process I have made repeated attempts to encourage him to deal with his feelings of loss of myself and the treatment, as well as friends, family, and other people and things of importance to him. Again and again I have come up against a brick wall. He "can't wait to get out of here" and looks forward to having greater flexibility in his schedule. Rather than deal with his sad, vulnerable, needy feelings, Fred has defensively identified with his rejecting, abandoning father and is only contemptuous of his underlying dependency.

I have felt discarded and frustrated by Fred, but I myself am not awash in my own angst. My infantile self is safely underground. I do not need this patient to connect with me in order to feel secure in my role as an analyst or to feel safe in the world. Although I have made frequent interpretations about his defensiveness, I have begun to feel that I am working too hard and can sense myself withdrawing, much as Fred himself has done. Such withdrawal on my part would have been impossible during the months before leaving Ann Arbor, for I was far too consumed with feelings of loss and separation, far too needy myself. Additionally, I have not communicated to Fred – either consciously or unconsciously – that I am struggling with issues similar to his for, indeed, I am not. Although I feel sad about his leaving, I am not overwhelmed by that sadness. This time, only he is going off to a new, unfamiliar place. I am staying in what has now become my home. He has to deal with feeling frightened and unsure, while I do not. The absence of shared feelings may increase Fred's sense of aloneness, as well as his discomfort with his vulnerable, dependent feelings. As a result, he may experience me more as the one rejecting him, rather than being able to identify with me as a similarly abandoned child. His response is then to identify with the abandoning other and to become rejecting himself.

We are now in our last session. It begins awkwardly, with meaningless chatter and long silences. In one of the silences my mind wanders. Soon I am thinking about leaving Ann Arbor and the intervening nine years. George has thrived in the warmth of Florida's sun and my constant presence. It has been a wonderful move for him, a more difficult move for me. I have struggled to complete the process of mourning. Despite my new friends, my new patients, and my new house, despite the pond and the birds and the always-green trees, I have continued to yearn for my Michigan house by the lake and that yearning has made it difficult for me to let go and fully connect to my new life. Interestingly, it is only within the last few weeks that I have begun to sense a change in myself, of reaching an emotional awareness of the true richness of my current life and beauty of my surroundings.

Now, though, as I sit with my patient, thinking about past and present losses, I am back into my sadness, feeling that not-so-old yearning for "home." Soon I am aware of sadness filling the room and realize that Fred can sense it as well. When he resumes speaking the sarcasm is gone from his tone; he is gentler, more connected. He begins talking about the insights he has gained from our sessions, while acknowledging that he has always kept me at bay.

"Why get close if you know the relationship is only going to end?" He pauses. "But then again, why not? Why not get the most out of a relationship while you have it?"

The termination process has turned to a place of greater connectedness, so that our final good-bye is indeed more meaningful.

I am reminded of what I learned during the tortuous months of terminating my Ann Arbor practice: that shared pain can facilitate the therapeutic process by creating mutual identifications which lead to a greater sense of closeness and connectedness. Despite the anguish and the trauma, some positive results did emerge during the process of forced termination. I believe that knowing, both consciously and unconsciously, that my struggle with pain and loss was similar to their own, helped patients to find the strength both to feel their own pain and to grow beyond it. Some of my frightened, dependent patients found they were not as helpless as they felt. They were able to identify with and take in the stronger, more competent parts of myself and deal with the upcoming loss from a place of hope and strength, rather than despair. Some withdrawn, defended patients found themselves surprisingly awash in the pain in the room, able to break through their defensiveness without drowning in their neediness. Although my forced termination re-stimulated many patients' childhood traumas, in many cases patients' awareness of my pain and difficulty with the leave-taking helped to reduce the fantasy of being left because of their own insignificance, shortcomings, or badness.

I, too, found comfort in the therapeutic process. My identification with my patients as they experienced losing me, helped me to feel less alone and less frightened as I went through my own mourning process. And, my role as analyst allowed me to feel grounded in the competent part of myself, while giving to my patients also enabled me to give to my needy, vulnerable self.

Perhaps what I learned during those painful months of termination is both the inevitability and the value of being human in the consulting room. Although I may have revealed more than some analysts might have been comfortable with, it is my belief that patients could not help but have known about the pain that I experienced during the termination process. I further believe that this place of shared identifications and mutual connection was helpful for both my patients and me in that it enhanced our feelings of connectedness, of importance, of significance and that it is the internalization of these feelings that remain as we say our final good-byes and continue on in our lives.

5

SELF-DISCLOSURE

Seeking Connection and Protection[1]

As discussed in the previous chapter, seven months prior to closing my eighteen-year practice in Michigan and relocating to Florida, I began the torturous process of telling patients about my leaving-taking. In this chapter I look at what I disclosed to patients about my move, and what I knowingly or unknowingly kept to myself. At the time, I gave considerable thought to what I would say. When I looked back at the telling from a distance of ten years, I realized I gave much less thought to what I omitted and why. In exploring the motivations behind both the spoken and the hidden, I came to understand that my disclosure was an unconscious expression of my need to feel connected without feeling overly exposed, to feel close without feeling too revealed.

Since some extraordinary life circumstance, be it relocation, illness, pregnancy, or the death of a significant other, is likely to occur during the course of an analyst's career, it is important to consider how much we reveal and why we reveal it. In many such circumstances, patients must clearly be told something, but what they are told falls to the discretion of the analyst. During times of great stress, the analyst may well have a greater need for human connectedness. She may have less tolerance for feeling alone in the consulting room and may therefore reveal more than she might in other circumstances. Conversely, these same times of stress may lead the analyst to yearn for greater privacy. Already feeling vulnerable, she may wish to withdraw and expose herself even less than usual to the scrutiny of her patients. This need to protect herself will also impact what she is willing to reveal or, more likely, not to reveal to her patients.

Although this chapter focuses primarily on the disclosure of events that occur outside the treatment, it does raise the question of whether all types of self-disclosure and, in fact, analysis as a whole, can be looked at as an analyst's struggle to feel neither too alone nor too exposed. Psychoanalysis as a profession provides an excellent compromise between the need for connection on the one hand and the need for privacy on the other. It allows for intense involvement with another human being, while remaining the aloof, silent, hidden observer. Different historical times, different theoretical persuasions, different personalities, different life circumstances all affect how an analyst deals with these conflicting needs both in her psyche and in the treatment room. What is important is that, as much as possible, these needs be brought into conscious awareness so that they can be reflected upon so as to best serve the needs of both patient and analyst.

When Freud (1912) wrote, over ninety years ago, "The doctor should be opaque to his patient and, like a mirror, should show nothing but what is shown to him" (p. 118), psychoanalysis was not yet established as a legitimate medical treatment. Freud's theories carried more than enough ideas to shock the average Victorian. A neutral, anonymous physician, who resembled all other physicians, was consistent with both nineteenth and early twentieth century ideas of science, as well as necessary to provide psychoanalysis with legitimacy and respectability. Theoretically Freud maintained that an anonymous analyst was necessary to allow both free association and the elaboration and interpretation of transference. In other words, an anonymous analyst made it easier for the patient to say whatever came to mind without censoring his words, as well as fostering the development of transference, of the analyst becoming whatever significant person in the patient's past the patient needed the analyst to become. In addition to his theoretical reasoning, however, Freud needed to protect the anonymity of the analyst in order to enhance the status of psychoanalysis both within the medical profession and society at large. He needed the analyst as a "blank screen" so as to protect him from excessive scrutiny or intrusion. In so doing he created an analyst prone to isolation and aloneness.

Within recent years much has changed, both within psychoanalysis and the culture at large. One only has to turn on TV to see that personal disclosure has become the norm rather than the exception, as people reveal their "secrets" to an audience of millions. That this zeitgeist has affected psychoanalysis can be seen in a moving paper by Schwaber (1998) that she delivered as a plenary address to the American Psychoanalytic Association. In that paper, Schwaber discusses her own struggles with the treatment of a non-invasive breast cancer and what she should or should not reveal to one particular patient. She says, "I am here going to share things about myself, my personhood, that I believe I would not have told at an earlier time" (p. 1045). She does question whether it is totally the times that have changed – "self-disclosure, to colleagues or to patients, has become acceptable if not de rigueur, even while still controversial" (p. 1046) – or whether it is more her inner need to disclose, but concludes that the inner and outer are not so easily separated.

On a more immediate, personal level, it is clear that I would not have been willing to write this book in a time where greater openness was not accepted and encouraged. There is indeed much of me in this book: my history, my feelings, my hopes, my terrors. And within this time of greater permissiveness, I expose myself to gain a greater connection to both the past and the future. As I write this sentence, my husband has been dead for almost three years. This book has provided me with a way to stay connected to George, as well as a way of moving beyond him. In writing of our joint history I can remember the pleasure of our meeting and the excitement and joy of our explorations of both each other and the world. This connection is bittersweet, but mostly sweet. The connection is also to the future. Although George will never read these words, never see this book in print, writing it enables me to capture forever the incredible man he was and the intensity of the bond we shared. In writing this book I seek to connect with you, the reader, as my audience, to immortalize part of George and my history. On the other hand, I do not reveal all. Not all my secrets are laid bare on these pages for I crave not only connection, but privacy and protection as well.

This zeitgeist of greater openness, and an increasing awareness of the impossibility of scientific objectivity on either side of the analytic couch, has led to the growth of the relational school of psychoanalysis and a corresponding exploration of the question of the possibility or desirability of analysts' anonymity (Aron, 1996; Bromberg, 1998, 2006, 2011; Cooper, 2000, 2010; Davies, 1994, 1998, 2001, 2006; Ehrenberg, 1992; Hoffman, 1998; Maroda, 1991, 1999, 2009; Mitchell, 1988, 1993, 1997, 2003; Pizer, 1998; Slochower, 1996, 2006; Stern, 2003, 2009). In the course of these explorations it has become clear that analysts are not nearly as anonymous as they believed. Therapists show themselves in how they dress, in how they greet patients, and in how they decorate their offices. Even interpretations can be seen as self-disclosures in that empathy is predicated on the analyst having "been there" at some point in her life (Singer, 1977). No matter what therapists do they cannot remain completely hidden and unknown.

Such inadvertent disclosures can be differentiated from a deliberate intervention, a therapeutic technique, in which the analyst reveals what she is thinking or feeling as a way of facilitating the therapeutic process. Many analysts refer to this as countertransference disclosure (Ehrenberg, 1992, 1995; Ginot, 1997; Gorkin, 1987; Maroda, 1991, 1999). "... the picture presented here is not of an analyst revealing external information about the analysts' self or own life, but of an analyst who is lending his or her participatory powers to an experiential and reciprocal process..." (Ginot, 1997, p. 366). In this form of self-disclosure, the patient becomes privy to more of the analyst's thoughts and feelings, albeit always in relation to the patient himself.

Broadening this approach, Renik (1995) concludes that it is impossible to isolate countertransference from other aspects of the analyst's mental life and advocates that the analyst "communicate everything that, in the analyst's view, will help the patient understand where the analyst thinks he or she is coming from and trying to go with the patient" (p.485). He contends that not knowing what the analyst is thinking "makes the analyst into a mystery," and interferes with the therapeutic process by diverting the patient from himself and "implicitly inviting the patient to guess what is in the analyst's mind" (p. 483). Renik (1999) recommends "playing one's cards face up in analysis" (p. 521), so that the patient understands as much of what the analyst is thinking and feeling and doing as the analyst knows himself. With this approach, anonymity becomes a thing of the past, and the analyst stands revealed and exposed.

But that is not all, for, like patients, analysts also have an unconscious and cannot always know if what they are revealing is indeed "the truth," let alone the reasons for revealing it. "... inasmuch as an analyst's activity is always determined in part by unconscious motivations ... [n]o matter how hard an analyst tries to play his or her cards face up, some cards will remain face down – and the analyst cannot know which ones, or how many" (Renik, 1999, p. 536). Perhaps at times we reveal more than we know and more than we wish to be revealed. Perhaps there are times that our patients know and understand us better than we understand ourselves. Perhaps we are always more exposed, more known, than we dare to imagine.

What happens to this already muddied picture if we add the reality of an extraordinary event impinging upon the analyst's life, an event unrelated to the patient's internal conflicts or the dyad's interpersonal interaction? What happens if the analyst's child dies or she develops breast cancer? What happens if she decides to retire or relocate? What does the analyst tell or not tell her patients and how does she make this decision? Chances are she already feels overwhelmed and frightened, unexpectedly impinged upon by life's unforeseen tragedy. It is from this place of great vulnerability that the analyst must decide what to say or not to say to her patients.

There is by now a considerable literature regarding analysts' dealing with extraordinary life events ranging from relocation (Martinez, 1989; Sherby, 2004) to severe illness (Edwards, 2004; Kahn, 2003; Morrison, 1990, 1997; Silver, 1990) from divorce (Schlachet, 1996) to death (Chasen, 1996; Gerson, 1996; Mendelsohn, 1996). Each of these authors and others struggled with the issue of what they should or should not tell their patients about their life circumstances. Each made a considered decision depending upon the specific circumstances, their theoretical orientation, and who they are as people. It is my belief that each of them struggled, consciously or unconsciously, with the issue of wanting to feel both connected and protected, of wanting to feel neither too alone nor too exposed.

My own need for connection was painfully apparent to me during the period of my leaving Michigan and clearly influenced what I decided to tell my patients. As discussed previously, I told them that my husband had developed some heart problems, that he was all right, but that we had decided to relocate for his health. I gave a good deal of thought to why I revealed what I did. It was not my intent to burden patients with my problems or to change the focus of the treatment from them to me. But I was too in need of being known and connected to remain the anonymous analyst. As I understood it then, I told my patients the bare necessity for them to feel neither capriciously abandoned nor for me to feel totally alone and despairing. I told my patients for them and for me. I told them because I didn't think I could tolerate being raged at for a life event that felt out of my control. I told them because I wanted to feel more connected. I told them because I could not imagine not telling them and still continuing to relate to them in a meaningful way throughout the termination process.

During the time that I was preparing to leave Michigan, I lived in a state of constant anxiety. I was terrified of George's dying. I was terrified not only that he would die, but that he would die soon after our move to Florida and that I would be left without the safety of my friends, my home, and my familiar surroundings. Even if he survived, I had to deal with what I experienced as gut-wrenching separations. I had to deal with leaving my home on the lake where I found a level of peace and safety that I did not believe could ever be duplicated. I had to deal with leaving a secure, well-established practice and starting over again in an unknown, unfamiliar environment. I seemed to swing between only two feeling states: pain and terror.

Being with patients was helpful. Even as we dealt with their pain of losing me and even as I resonated with their feelings of loss and despair, I found great comfort both in my adult, professional role as analyst and in the depth of connection I felt with my patients. For me, to not have told my patients anything of my reason for leaving would have been to leave me so alone and isolated in the consulting room as to render me entirely ineffective. Had I revealed less, my anxiety would have filled the treatment room, resulting in my psychic energy being focused more on myself than my patients.

This state of anxiety and ineffectiveness had, in fact, been my experience during the month between my deciding to relocate and telling my first patient. In and of itself, that month was an extremely difficult period, as George and I waited to learn the extent of his heart difficulties. Additionally, sitting with patients knowing that I was carrying a secret that would so affect their lives made me feel fraudulent, disconnected, and anxious. I also believe that some of my patients unconsciously knew about my decision to leave. One patient said that he was not surprised when I told him, that he felt I had said something that gave him a clue, although he could not remember exactly what that was.

Most remarkable, however, was the session with a student therapist I was treating who came in and told me that a couple she was seeing had suddenly decided to move. "I wish I could see them for another eighteen months," she said. "Oh! That's how long we have left before I leave," she continued. "That will be awful. I remember how hard it was when Adam [her ex-boyfriend] and I broke up. How anxious I was all the time. But at least I had you to talk to… The couple's therapy has been so rich, I just wish we had more time." My note from that session indicates my internal reaction: "I'm instantly anxious. I feel that I'm lying by saying nothing."

This reaction is in stark contrast to my experience of the session in which I told my first patient, a session I have described in detail in my previous chapter. When that previously distanced and aloof man became teary and said, "When I needed you more I didn't know I needed you. Now that I need you less, I know I'm attached to you and need you," I myself became less anxious and felt very much more connected.

When I look back at my notes from the period in which I told all of my patients of my decision to relocate, it is clear that I needed an intense reaction on their part in order to feel connected and engaged. It did not matter if the reaction was sadness, anger, despair, or fear, as long as there was a genuine connectedness that kept me from feeling alone and abandoned. The following examples illustrate the difference in my experience of telling two patients.

Rhoda, a tall, thin, red-headed woman who was getting a Master's in Fine Arts, with a specialty in sculpture, had been in analysis with me for four years. We had a difficult relationship. She was often critical of me and complained that I was too intrusive. I experienced her as elusive, unconnected to me or to any significant others.

"Okay," she says, when I tell her of my leaving. She then sits up, looks at me and says, "I'm sorry about your husband," and lays back down. She continues: "My apartment is such a mess. I just don't know what I'm going to do about it. There's paper everywhere. I can't seem to organize myself. Any time I tell myself I'm going to tackle it, to get it done, I find a million other things to do. I talk on the phone to anyone I can think of. I sketch and re-sketch and re-sketch again the piece I have to do for my final thesis. But I can't get anywhere with that either. And then I put the sketches someplace and they get buried under the mass of paper and I promise myself I'm going to straighten it all up, but of course I don't do that either. Or I go into the kitchen and think about what I'm going to cook for dinner and realize that my kitchen pantry is a mess as well, so maybe I start fixing that up a little but I get distracted by something else and none of it gets done. I just can't understand why I can't get organized. I also have to decide if I'm going to go home for Spring break. I know my mother would be disappointed if I don't but I really should stay and work on my sculpture…"

Rhoda continues on and on, addressing anything and everything but my leaving. I feel as though I am slipping away, almost as though I no longer exist. In retrospect, I realize this is partially a projective identification. I am feeling dismissed and unimportant, just as Rhoda feels with the news of my leaving. At the time, however, I am only aware of my anxiety increasing and of feeling simultaneously intruded upon and alone.

Finally, near the end of the hour, feeling almost desperate, I say, "Do you have any thoughts about my leaving, about our having to end analysis?"

"I don't know what to say," she replies, "I don't know what would be appropriate. I can't be unpleasant. If you're going to leave, I don't want to leave you with unpleasant thoughts."

In contrast to my session with Rhoda in which I felt as though I was floating somewhere in space, there was my experience with Harriet, a woman I had seen in twice weekly therapy for over five years. Loss, abandonment, and separation had long been the focus of Harriet's treatment. Her father, the parent she adored, had died when she was nine leaving her and three younger siblings with a severely depressed mother who lost what little skill she previously had in raising children. With a horrible coincidence of timing, Harriet's mother died the week I was telling all my patients about my impending move. Although I delayed telling Harriet, I knew I couldn't postpone the inevitable and certainly did not want her to learn of my leaving from someone beside myself.

Despite my overwhelming guilt, I broke the news.

Harriet burst into tears. "It feels as if my parents' house suddenly stopped existing," she says. "The house made me feel safe and secure even though my parents were no longer there. And that's what it's like being here. It's a place where I feel safe and now it won't exist anymore."

Pain grips me. How can I leave my home? How will I ever be able to turn away, to shut the door for the last time, to drive out of the driveway forever, to know that I will never again travel the tree-lined, two-lane road to my sanctuary? I fall asleep at night thinking of these "lasts." I wake up in the morning wondering if I will truly be able to put myself through this torture. The questions keep going through my head. How will I manage the daunting task of packing up? How will I decide what to take and what to discard? How will I tolerate a garage sale in which people paw through what is only to my eye precious possessions? And worst of all, how will I tolerate people tromping through my home disparaging the spiral staircase or the atrium or the kitchen cabinets, trying to diminish in value that which I deem priceless? No money would be enough for this place of safety. I think about the possibility of keeping this home. Perhaps we could return here during the summer. But I recognize the impossibility. George is retired. I start out with zero patients, zero income. There's no way to keep my home and buy another one in Florida. And we must have a house in Florida – I can't yet call it a home – or I will never be able to build another life. I choose George. I must surrender my home.

I return to Harriet, filled with a multitude of feelings: sad for her losses and for my own, guilty for the added pain that I am causing her, angry at the unfairness of life that one can rail against but never change.

"I'm so, so sorry, Harriet," I say. "I know this is a terrible time for you. I know that my leaving is yet another loss for you to bear; yet another unreliable parent who abandons you when you are most in need. I'm sure you're really angry with me. You certainly have every right to be."

"Now I'm just sad," she says still crying. "I'm sad for you, too. This can't be an easy time for you. But you're not an unreliable parent. You've been here for me for years and years, always reliable, always here. I'm scared right now. I feel like a lost little girl. But we still have time. August is months away. I'm going to work harder at taking you with me. I'm going to try. I don't want to feel that all is lost."

"You're an amazing woman, Harriet. And you'll do it. You'll work really, really hard so you can get to a place where you'll grieve my loss, but not feel desolate, not feel like a helpless, powerless child, but rather like the strong, competent woman you are."

The intense connection between Harriet and me served us both well. It helped us to feel less alone and despairing. Experiencing intense, painful feelings together was definitely preferable to the anxiety of being out there, alone and disconnected.

The need for connection that I felt during the process of my leave-taking, is described by other analysts going through extraordinary life circumstances. In her paper on forced termination, Martinez (1989) reviews the literature that had been written on the topic prior to that time and concludes, "Certainly, nothing approaching the angst I felt in this task is mentioned in the literature" (p. 98). By her own description, Martinez was overwhelmed by guilt, not only because she was abandoning all her patients, but also because she was leaving clinical practice entirely which she understood as giving up her "lifelong project" of attempting to cure a depressed parent (p. 101). Interestingly, in contrast to the four previous authors whose work she summarizes, she disclosed far more information to her patients. Although Martinez certainly had her theoretical and clinical reasons for these disclosures, I suspect that she did feel more internal angst than the other authors she summarizes and, as a result, felt more of a need for connection, more need to be known in all her complexities, rather than remaining the aloof, anonymous analyst.

Illness in the analyst is an external life circumstance that places major stresses on both analyst and patient. In the previously mentioned paper, Schwaber (1998) had told no one besides her family and physicians about her disease. She had a non-invasive cancer, was not ill, was not missing sessions, and did not want to risk that her patients would find out and be unnecessarily burdened. As a result she felt isolated and alone, very much like her patient who described herself as "traveling affectively alone" (p. 1055). After consulting with a senior colleague who thought it would be best for her to tell the patient both "for her *and for me*" (p. 1058, italics in original), Schwaber revealed her condition and felt relieved and more able to be present in the analysis. "I had been burdened by the uncertainty of what to do – to say or not – burdened by holding back, and by my guilt about not being present with her as I might have been" (p. 1061). In addition to this relief, I suspect that in sharing her burden, Schwaber felt more connected and less hidden and therefore more able to reestablish her presence in the consulting room so that neither patient nor analyst were "traveling affectively alone."

The need to disclose an illness so as to be affectively alive and connected has been eloquently described by Morrison (1990, 1997) who struggled with breast cancer for eleven years. After the third reoccurrence of her illness she chose not to say anything to patients and found herself feeling increasingly alone in the room and less present for her patients. "The silence of my disease was, this time, deafening – for me. … There had been a 'need' to tell, and to 'help' people with their feelings of loss, including the loss of me! The preclusion of this opportunity was stultifying for me" (1997, p. 241).

In dealing with the death of his infant daughter, Mendelsohn (1996) found that "not revealing at least some information … would foster mutual alienation; I imagined I would feel I was keeping a secret and expected I would be more distracted if I did not acknowledge my circumstances than if I did" (p. 24). He adds that telling patients did help him to feel closer and more involved and, contrary to the usual expectations, he found that patients whom he told were more rather than less able to express their feelings and fantasies about his situation.

In the same article, Mendelsohn acknowledges that the desire for connection is not unambivalent. He writes, "Although my theoretical views and technical practice are identified most closely with interpersonal psychoanalysis and despite a belief in the therapeutic value of candor and directness, my ideological commitments involve an element of reaction formation. In ways that remain disconcerting to me, I can be quite formal and reserved" (1996, p. 25). It would seem that as much as therapists may wish to be close and involved, they often have a conflicting desire to remain safely hidden. Mendelsohn's theoretical persuasion reflects his desire for connectedness; his personality reflects more of his need for protection.

I have reached a different compromise. I present myself as warm, open, forthcoming and, to a point, I am all of these. There are, however, definite limits to my emotional openness. I will gladly tell you most facts about my life, but I will not easily share my innermost pains, particularly as they are occurring. It is this desire for closeness, without too much exposure, that makes psychoanalysis such an ideal profession for me. Even this book depicts these conflicting sides of me. Although open and revealing, it is being written after the fact: thirteen years following my move and relocation, six years since the time George's cancer took control of his body and our lives, and three years after his death. I have had some time to heal, to put my emotions into a more contained package that I am now willing to offer for inspection. This does not mean that I still don't cry for George or even grieve for the loss of my Michigan home, for indeed I do. And, in fact, the process of writing often immerses me into my feelings in a very powerful and sometimes overwhelming manner. But I can recover, I can draw myself back, I can write what I hope is a coherent sentence and express an understandable feeling.

I explore my reactions to George's illness and death in subsequent chapters. Returning now to the time of my leaving Ann Arbor, my emotions were so raw that I forgot that the wish to remain private was also a part of my psyche. As a result, I did not consciously think about what facts or feelings I was unwilling to divulge to my patients. I did not think about how my disclosure kept private my most intense vulnerabilities. To move because of my husband's health felt like a legitimate reason to leave and one that I was willing to share with my patients. To leave as a result of my own fears and dependencies felt weak and shameful and far too exposing to reveal.

Interestingly, I also gave no thought to the manner in which I told patients or to the fact that I told all my patients exactly the same thing. There is disagreement among analysts about whether the disclosure of extraordinary circumstances should be individualized for each patient (Dewald, 1990; Gerson, 1996; Mendolsohn, 1996), or whether it is impossible for the analyst to know what is best for each patient, particularly during times of such great stress (Abend, 1990; Lasky, 1990). For me, however, it was a question I never asked. I knew I was going to give all my patients the same information and, barring any unforeseen circumstances, I was going to tell them all the same week. What little thought I gave to this issue revolved only around my knowing that some of my patients could easily be connected through friends and colleagues in the field and that I would not want them to have different information or to hear about my leaving from anyone but me. I also wanted to be "fair," meaning I did not want to give preferential treatment to any patient by giving one more information than another.

In the course of writing the original paper on which this chapter is based, I gave further thought to this issue and received input from colleagues as well. These ruminations led me to conclude that my manner of telling was, in itself, a way to maintain distance. Giving all my patients the same information was a way of maintaining pseudoclinical objectivity, removing any excess feelings, treating everyone equally. I was also clearly the one in charge. I was revealing only that which I chose to reveal, foreclosing any further discussion. And, in fact, although some patients did ask me for additional details, by and large, they accepted what I said and did not press me for more. I was, therefore, exposing and protecting myself at the same moment.

Similarly, the specifics of what I told patients – and what I did not tell patients – both revealed and protected me. Thus, although it was true that George had developed heart problems and that we were moving for his health, it was not his heart difficulty itself that necessitated the move. I did not tell my patients that George was twenty-one years my senior and that his heart problems had only brought to the fore the difference in our ages and my constant terror about his mortality. In truth, the specter of his death kept me in a state of near panic, particularly when we were apart. And, in the end, I made the decision to move not because of his heart condition, but because I could not tolerate being separated from George, even for part of the week. Our years together now felt finite and I did not want to squander them with unnecessary distance.

An old friend from graduate school calls. Had I heard that Lou had died? I'm stunned. Lou was a fellow graduate student who was considerably older than the rest of us. He was also almost totally blind. Lou and I stayed in touch through the years and, in fact, George and I recently visited him in Chicago with his present wife. In addition to his greatly impaired vision, he had lost a considerable amount of his hearing and developed heart problems. And yet he still worked seeing patients at the Lighthouse for the Blind, fitted for a device that allowed him to hear somewhat better. And, sitting in the second row so that Lou might at least see something, we still went to the theater to see Lily Tomlin's one-woman show, "The Search for Signs of Intelligent Life in the Universe." Lou's a fighter. I can't take in his death. I call his wife. She tells me her best friend is with her. She tells me she has the dubious distinction of being the first of her friends to become a widow. Her words ring in my ears and echo louder and louder in my head. The first to be a widow. The first to be a widow. Will that be me? Will I be saying something similar? That night I cling to George in bed. That night I do not sleep.

It is February 1993. George has returned to our house in Key Largo after recuperating from his two angioplasties. It is a Thursday. I will be traveling down for the weekend later that night. I spoke with him in the morning. He's fine, he assures me. I try him again just before 1 p.m. No answer. I try again at 1:50. No answer. Again at 2:40. No answer. I'm starting to panic. Not even my patients can distract me. My hands are shaking. Again at 3:30. No answer. I call a neighbor couple who live around the corner. No, they haven't seen George. They weren't out in the morning when they often see him riding his bike. He wasn't at the beach. That's not a surprise. He never goes to the beach without me. Will they please go and check the house, I ask beseechingly. And call me back? No George. Allison is my last patient of the day. She eyes me warily and asks if everything's all right. I smile and nod my head. Am I lying? Am I trying to convince myself? My day is finally over. I try George one last time before I head for the airport. At least if I'm there I can know what is happening. At least if I'm there I can magically make everything all right. He answers the phone. I break down in tears. He was just running some errands. "From 1 to 5?" I ask. No, he'd been back to the house several times. Just not when I'd called. I can't stand this. I can't stand the uncertainty. I can't stand the unknowing. I can't stand the separation.

Now, all these years later, I still cannot know for sure why I revealed some facts and not others. Nonetheless, it seems clearer to me that I kept to myself that which made me feel most vulnerable, most exposed, and most ashamed. At the time, I told myself that my abbreviated version of "the truth" was an attempt to keep things simple, to intrude myself into the room as little as possible. It felt less like I was making the treatment about me if I could say what I had to say in relatively few words. Even today I believe there is some truth in that for I certainly would not have wanted to spend large parts of any hour dealing with my circumstances and my feelings.

Still, in retrospect, I realize I gave little or no thought to my own need for privacy, to what feelings I wanted to keep only for myself. Now, I see myself as wanting to keep out of the consulting room precisely the same feelings of desperation that had fueled my need for self-disclosure in the first place. On the one hand, I wanted to present a sympathetic enough picture so that patients would not become too angry with me, so that we could maintain a sense of closeness and connection that would help to diminish my feelings of aloneness. On the other hand, I did not want to present as too needy, too terrified, too dependent, for that would have laid me bare and left me feeling too exposed and frightened. Although my patients knew about my fears about my husband's health, they did not know the extent of those fears. They did not know I could not bear to be separated from him. They did not know that I was willing to give up everything – including them – to allay my terror by remaining close to him. I could tell patients I was leaving because of my husband's health. I could not tell them I was leaving because of my own neediness. Today I also wonder if my unconscious decision to tell only half the truth was yet another way for me to protect myself, to allow myself to begin the process of distancing from my patients before the time of my actual departure.

Although the reason for my leaving was the most significant of my partial truths, it was not the only one. Although my patients knew about my sadness about leaving them, my friends, and Michigan, they knew nothing about my gut-wrenching pain over the loss of my home. It is not that I should have told them what losing my home meant to me, but that I could not have told them. Partly I felt ashamed that I cared as much or more about the loss of my home than I did about all the people I was losing. Partly it was just too painful for me to speak. I could not talk about that pain and remain an analyst in the room with my patients. I could not expose that part of myself without feeling like a desperate, bereft child.

I return to Rhoda and to my last week in my Michigan office, a time of excruciating pain for both myself and my patients. Rhoda and I have come a long way from the time that I told her of my leave-taking. She has used the termination process well and has come to a place of far greater feeling and connection.

"I realize I'm thinking a lot about you these days," she says. "I suppose it's a way to hold onto you. I want to hold onto you, for I've learned how to feel with you. I'm afraid I'll forget how to miss you when you're gone, so I want to keep as much of you with me as possible. I wonder if you'll come back and visit your friends in Ann Arbor. I wonder if you'll be happy. I hope your husband will be all right, because as long as your husband is all right, it might be sad but it's not catastrophic."

Rhoda's words make me feel both sad that we have to end and proud of how far she has come.

She continues, "I wonder what rituals you'll miss, what you won't be able to do."

I am instantly transported to my home. Every morning George and I eat breakfast at our glass table looking out at the lake. Every season brings different pictures. The red and yellow of fall's diminishing colors give way to the barrenness of winter lightened by the white of the newly fallen snow as it hugs the trees; the budding hope of spring, and the glorious verdant greenness of summer with the squirrels that scamper, the blue jays with their raucous calls and the squeals of children as they make their first foray into the icy lake. I am overcome with feelings of loss, sadness, and despair. I struggle to manage my own pain and to refocus my wandering attention back to Rhoda.

"I love the leaves outside your office," Rhoda continues, almost as though she has read my mind. "I'll miss them. I think that's how I'll remember you."

I can't stay focused. I am swallowed up by my own grief. I am sitting under the large elm tree in front of my home. I always place my lounge chair so that it faces right. That's my favorite view. It captures the long view of the lake, providing a sense of freedom, with the holding feel of the tree. I am paralyzed by my pain. I say nothing.

"You don't have cardinals," Rhoda says. "When I grew up there was a family of cardinals. The cat got the mother cardinal. The father tried so hard to feed the baby cardinals. It was sad. The cat got the babies too."

Here Rhoda kills me off, expressing her anger at me, both for my self-preoccupation and withdrawal, as well as my imminent departure. But the result is devastating for her as well. Either as punishment for her own aggression or because she fears she cannot not survive without me, Rhoda too falls prey and dies.

Today, I wonder if this session would have been different if Rhoda had known about my intense feelings about losing my home. If this secret had been out there in the room, not hidden inside me surrounded by shame, would I have been less frozen and more able to deal with Rhoda's aggression, as well as her sadness? There is obviously no way to know for sure. What I do know is that I felt consumed by my secret grief and that I was not as present for Rhoda as I could have been.

When extraordinary life circumstances impinge upon an analyst's life, she must decide what she will and will not disclose to her patients. I believe that, consciously or unconsciously, every analyst who struggles with this issue is trying to find a compromise between too much isolation and too much exposure; trying to find a place to be both connected and safe. This place of comfort will be different for each analyst depending upon her personality, theoretical orientation, and the particular circumstance in which she finds herself. No one other than the analyst can decide what feels too isolating or too exposing. However, both patients and analysts are best served if the need for both connection and protection remains within the analyst's conscious awareness, that she knows, as much as possible, why she is revealing what she reveals and what she is keeping as hers alone.

Although the focus of this chapter is on the disclosure of events that occur outside the consulting room, any form of deliberate self-disclosure necessitates that the analyst be aware of the conflicting pulls between the need for connection and the need for protection. Theoretical orientation alone cannot account for the myriad of opinions regarding self-disclosure. "The resolution of the transference, too-one of the main tasks of the treatment-is made more difficult by an intimate attitude on the doctor's part..." (Freud, 1912, p. 118). "In this situation it is safe to say that remaining silent will lead to ambiguity and tension, while answering will tend to calm things down" (Greenberg, 1995, p. 202). By telling a patient "what he wants to know about us, we may be limiting his possibilities for imagining or even perceiving what he may *not* want to know about us..." (Epstein, 1995, pp. 231–232, italics in original). "Where we feel a sense of danger with a patient, articulating this feeling, as well as the ways in which we may experience a pull to be protective, or to walk on egg shells, can be a way to bring these important interactive issues under analytic scrutiny" (Ehrenberg, 1995, p. 226). "I decided to keep my sexual feelings to myself for the same kinds of reasons that would lead me not to express sexual feelings stimulated by, let's say, my teenage daughter or one of her friends" (Renik, 1999, p. 534). "Feeling that there was no other honest alternative, I said to the patient one day, 'But you know I have had sexual fantasizes about you, many times, sometimes when we're together and sometimes when I'm alone'" (Davies, 1994, p.166).

How is it possible that all these diverse positions might seem both reasonable and theoretically sound? How is it possible that the argument for allowing the maximum opportunity for patients to move unencumbered in the analysis can be as convincing as the need for authenticity and humanness? There is more to this debate than a difference in theoretical positions. There is more to this debate than advancing the treatment and acting in the best interest of the patient. And that more is every individual therapist. That more is each analyst as she sits in the room concerned not only with what is best for her patient, but also with what she can tolerate, with what makes her comfortable. I am not suggesting that therapists' comfort level should be the focus of treatment, but rather that it cannot be forgotten that analysts are human beings with their own needs for both connection and privacy.

An analyst who has the need to remain exceedingly private can embrace a theoretical position that advocates strict analytic anonymity and neutrality. She then has to come to terms with her feelings of isolation or loneliness, perhaps by being more aware of her attachment to the internalized image she carries of her own analyst or previous supervisors, perhaps by seeking a closer connection with colleagues. On the other side of the theoretical fence, an analyst who has a need for connection can advocate for the importance of authenticity or the need "to use ourselves most fully as analytic instruments so as to best advance the analytic process…" (Ehrenberg, 1995, p. 223). Such an analyst must, however, remain aware of her need for privacy so that she does not find herself revealing more than she is comfortable with or reacting against the felt intrusion with anger or withdrawal. Not surprisingly, an analyst's theoretical orientation cannot be separated from who she is as a person. Someone who defines herself as a classical analyst will have different needs, wishes, and conflicts than someone who defines herself as a relational analyst. This is not to say that there is a one-to-one correlation between an analyst's personality and her theoretical choice, for the theoretical position might well represent a compromise between various internal pulls, rather than an expression of the analyst's predominant personality style. We saw this earlier in Mendelsohn (1996) who embraced "a belief in the therapeutic value of candor and directness" while viewing himself as "quite formal and reserved" (p. 25). And just as it is important that an analyst knows, as best as possible, why she discloses or does not disclose, so too is it important that she understand why she has made her theoretical choice and how that choice affects both her life and the lives of her patients.

This conflicting need for connection on the one hand and protection on the other can be seen whenever an analyst is faced with an extraordinary life circumstance that necessitates some information be disclosed to her patients. This same conflict operates in more commonplace self-disclosures as well. Even if the analyst consciously thinks about the disclosure only in terms of how it advances the treatment, the analyst's need for connection with her patients versus her need for protection from them will unconsciously inform whatever she chooses to say and not to say. By extension, even an analyst's theoretical orientation can be seen as an attempt to feel neither too alone nor too exposed. It is not that this subjectivity can or should be removed from the consulting room, but rather that being as aware as possible of why we do what we do remains, as always, a most laudable goal.

6

FROM DISCONNECTION
TO RECONNECTION

I open the door to usher in the first patient I am seeing in my Boca Raton office. It is only my therapeutic training that allows me to not react when I see Andrea, the woman sitting there. I have never seen anyone who looks more like a Barbie doll: teased blond hair piled high on her head, incredibly long false eyelashes, gobs of blue and green and brown eye shadow, thinly shaped eyebrows, and red-red lipstick. As she stands I see that she has huge breasts and an extremely narrow waist. I note her appraising me as I gesture her into the chair across from me.

This office is on the second floor of a modern office-building complex, with large windows on two sides. I see only the tops of trees and watch the wispy clouds glide through the clear blue sky. I like my office. I like the light and the airiness. But these days the sense of limitless space leads me to feel untethered, as if I were going to float off into nothingness. I miss my tree-house office in Ann Arbor. I miss the feeling of being held and cradled in the boughs of the trees. I miss watching the squirrels on their busy daily routines. I miss the familiarity of the old and am uncomfortable with the new. Still, I feel fortunate to be sharing office space with two like-minded colleagues. As a whole, the culture of south Florida is not particularly friendly towards therapists with a psychoanalytic orientation. Generally this is an area focused on external appearances and a "quick fix."

Early on in my obsession about whether or not to move, I interviewed with several group practices to see if I might work somewhere part-time while building up my independent practice. It was a rude awakening. First, almost all the administrators — whether they were psychologists, social workers, or business people — looked and sounded like the stereotype of a used-car salesman. They were sure I had good credentials. No reason to see my vita as long as they took more than fifty percent of what I made. Their volume was terrific, spectacular; they were sure they'd be able to provide me with a full practice in no time. Sixty patients, no problem. But working for them while I built up my own practice, that was definitely not part of the arrangement. I'd be expected to sign a non-compete contract that would remain in effect for a year after I left their employ. The entire interview experience brought the ping-pong ball back to the "we're not moving" side of the table. Until that traumatic plane ride, until George's heart problems, until my increased anxiety about losing him, until we were, indeed, moving.

Fortunately, I also made contact with the psychoanalytic psychotherapy group in the Boca Raton area, attended several meetings and even gave a presentation. There I found my like-minded colleagues and office-mates. Now I believe I can be comfortable here professionally, as long as I can find patients, a not insignificant problem. In fact, it is a problem that frightens me a great deal. Leaving a well-established practice in Ann Arbor and starting anew feels like jumping off the proverbial cliff. I am the sole breadwinner and there is definitely no guaranteed income. George is not worried. He's sure I'll do well. As always, he has the greatest of confidence in me, convinced that I cannot possibly fail. I hold the anxiety for both of us. I have more than enough to go around.

The other not so insignificant problem is finding a house in which to live. We look at sixty-six houses before I accept that we are never going to replicate our Michigan home on the lake. Water remains a prerequisite. Since ocean-front property is way too expensive, we have to live on a canal or a man-made lake. And it has to have trees. I can't stand a barren, desert-looking landscape. I also don't want to be looking into my neighbor's kitchen across a tiny canal cluttered by too-big boats and jet-skis.

In the end, we buy a house on a pond. It's much larger than our Michigan home – four bedrooms, which we actually have no difficulty filling. There are large vaulted ceilings, a coral fireplace, and a wonderfully open, airy feeling about the space. One huge plus is that the roof of the house extends over part of a large screened patio and pool, making it possible for us to eat most of our meals outside. I like the house. I don't love it. I objectively understand that I should love it, but liking and appreciating is about as far as I can go. Out back there's enough lawn that our neighbors across the pond are sufficiently far away. But the outside space feels too open, too gaping. There's no large elm tree. In fact, there are no trees at all except scraggly looking pines that definitely don't count. We will change it, George assures me. As always, I recognize and appreciate George's attempt to take care of me, to provide a place where I can feel safe and comfortable. Yet my pain over all the Michigan losses separates me some from him. It is as though I feel the need to steel myself, to hold myself together in order to make this transition and do what I need to do in what is now my new home.

"I'm not sure if I really need to be here," Andrea begins, batting her eyelashes at me and giggling. "It's just that I'm worried about Katrina. Well not worried about her exactly, I just don't know what to do about her," she continues, gesturing expansively with her hands. Her exceptionally long fingernails painted in pink and red flash like flags in the wind. "I think she might be a lesbian," she continues. "I mean, I'm fine if she is. That's not the problem. And truthfully, just between us," she laughs, covering her mouth. "Silly me, I know it's just between us, that's what therapy is all about. I mean I know that you're not going to tell anyone. But anyway, she's always been my favorite. I have two other children – a boy and a girl – but Katrina, I don't know, I was just always closest to her. Maybe it's because her asshole Dad and I broke up when she was so small and she and I just had this special connection." She frowns when she mentions her ex-husband, but immediately reverts to her doll-like demeanor. "It would be fine with me if she's a lesbian although I suppose I would worry about her more. I mean I know the gay lifestyle isn't so easy. People don't accept it regardless of what they say. But I don't know if I should talk to her about it. What if I'm wrong? Would she be insulted? But I'm really sure she is. So what do you think? What should I do?"

I find it hard to listen to this woman. I am both mesmerized and put off by her appearance. Her waving hands and rapid, staccato-like speech is jarring.

"How old is Katrina?" I ask mostly to avoid addressing her question.

"She's twenty-nine," she says smiling. "I bet you didn't think I'm old enough to have a twenty-nine year old daughter. And a thirty-one year old son. And a thirty-three year old daughter." She laughs.

I smile but say nothing. I am stymied by Andrea, unable to take the session beyond the superficial level she is presenting.

"How old do you think I am?" she says, as though challenging me.

Here again, I find myself tongue-tied, unable to address the question of what age means to her or why she wants me to guess. "Why don't you just tell me," I suggest lamely.

"I'm fifty-two! Well, are you surprised?"

"You do look younger than your age," I reply, as though I were meeting Andrea in a social setting, rather than in my consulting room. What is making it so difficult for me to be an analyst in this room?

She beams. "Everyone says that! I work at a gym so I get to exercise every day for hours at a time. But that's not my real secret. It's plastic surgery! I love it! I love plastic surgery," she continues, drawing out the "love" for emphasis. "I've had everything done. I've done my face, my eyes, the whole thing. I had my neck tightened, my boobs enlarged, ribs removed, my ass pulled in. I used to work for a plastic surgeon so he'd give me a great deal. And he's wonderful. The best! I recommend him to everyone. I'll give you his name if you like."

"No, that's all right," I say quickly, leaving me to again wonder why I don't open up what might be an interesting discussion about what it means for her to want to give me the name of her plastic surgeon. Instead I ask, "Do you have any idea why plastic surgery is so appealing to you?"

Andrea looks at me as though I have just arrived from Mars. "What do you mean?" she asks placing her hands on her breasts. "Look at me! Why wouldn't I love plastic surgery?"

I am unable to engage with Andrea, to ask more in-depth questions, to place myself in the consulting room and reflect on the interaction between us. I am not sure why. At the time, I tell myself that Andrea is just so different from the patients I am used to, just so different from me. Not surprisingly, the therapy is short-lived.

"I'm so glad that you could see me at 4 p.m. on a Tuesday," says Shirley, a slim, elegantly dressed sixty-year-old woman who sits primly in the chair. "It's about the only time that I'm not busy. My husband doesn't understand what I do with my days," she says with an exasperated shake of her head. "I don't know what more he wants me to do. And I don't know why he should care. He's always busy working.

A lot he cares about me. But he complains about everything. That's my problem, my husband. I tell him I play tennis and golf and bridge. And I'm involved in all these charities – the Cancer Society, the Alzheimer Association – those are the two big ones – and then there are the smaller, local charities. But I'm always on some board, usually doing fund-raising of some sort or another. I love to put together these elaborate charity balls. They're such fun! Besides, I think it's important to give back. I wish my husband understood that. And my low-life son for sure doesn't get it," she continues, rolling her eyes. "He's always more interested in going off on some adventure – backpacking for goodness sakes – and never thinks that he shouldn't be all that high and mighty since he couldn't very well be doing any of that if he wasn't living off our money. I tell my husband he should be tougher on him, but of course he ignores me as usual."

I say nothing during this diatribe. As I will soon discover, Shirley wants to do little but complain. She is a woman who takes her wealth and privilege for granted and experiences herself as mistreated by everyone in her life – husband, son, friends, acquaintances, fellow board members or partners in any of her games. I know almost nothing about her background because she brushes off my attempts to discuss her history with a wave of her hand. "Oh, we don't need to go there. That Freudian stuff is all passé. Besides, I had a wonderful childhood. My parents gave me everything. It's my husband who's the problem." Or my son. Or my bridge partner. And so on.

She is another patient I have difficulty engaging with. Is she also too different from me, too different from most patients I have worked with in the past? I suggest to Shirley that we can't fix her husband, that we can only help her to see things differently or perhaps even react differently herself.

I sense that she is displeased. I am unable to address her displeasure, unable to point out that I have become another of the people with whom Shirley finds fault.

This therapy is also short-lived.

I join groups – professional, political, and civic. A long-time member of the National Organization for Women, I become more actively involved, looking for both like-minded friends and potential referrals. I join the board and become chair of the Committee for Gays and Lesbians. Having worked with many gays and lesbians in Ann Arbor I am sure that I will be comfortable in this role. I become close to many of the older women on the board. They're firebrands who in many ways remind me of my grandmother. I go to Gay Pride meetings, speak out against including homosexuality as a psychiatric disorder, become a consultant and supervisor for a gay and lesbian outreach center. I am on more familiar ground.

Barbara is a thirty-three year old lesbian who has been in a relationship for three years. She's getting bored. She and her partner Tanya almost never have sex. She's not sure what she ever found attractive in Tanya. Barbara finds herself looking at other women. She considers having an affair. She considers breaking off her relationship.

She's not sure what she wants to do.

"What did you love about Tanya when you first got involved?" I ask.

She shrugs. "I don't know. Like I said, I don't know what I ever saw in her. She's too fat. All she wants to do is sit around and watch movies," disgust oozing from her words. "I'd like to go out to the bars. Or how about the beach?" she says gesturing emphatically. "This is south Florida. There's so much to do out there. The weather's so great. Who wants to be in all the time?"

"What about previous relationships? What was your longest relationship?"

"This is my longest relationship. Maybe that's another reason I'm reluctant to break it off. But relationships never last anyway. And it's not just lesbian relationships. We won't even talk about gay guys. But look at my parents, they got divorced when I was three."

"It sounds like you expect all relationships to end badly."

"That's because they do."

Although Barbara is indeed a more familiar patient to me, I still do not feel actively engaged with her. There's a contemptuousness about her I find off-putting. But why don't I ask her more about her feelings that all relationships end badly? Why don't I ask her what she expects from our relationship?

The following session Barbara comes in and places her keys, sunglasses, and an envelope on the floor under her chair.

"I met this woman, Pamela, while I was riding my bike the other day. We were instantly attracted to one another," she says smiling, more animated than I'd seen her previously. "We exchanged phone numbers and agreed to get together. I've been to her house a couple of times. We haven't done much besides kiss. She knows I'm in a relationship. At least I guess I am. No, I am. I'm in a relationship until I break it off. But I still haven't decided to do that for sure. I don't know why."

"That's a very good question, why don't you want to break it off with Tanya?"

"I guess because I don't want to hurt her. And it's such a hassle to break up. The deciding who gets what chair, or what plate, or even who gets to stay in the apartment or move."

"How do you think you'd feel about breaking up with Tanya?"

"I just told you."

"I meant on a more feeling level. Would you miss her? Would you feel sad? Relieved? Unburdened?"

She shrugs. "I don't know, relieved I guess. But, as I said, it's such a hassle."

At the end of the session, Barbara is gone before I realize she has forgotten her letter under the chair. I pick it up with the intention of hurrying after her but notice that the envelope says Dr. Linda Sherby. She's written me a letter? I open it. Enclosed is a check for our sessions along with a note that says today will be her last session, thank you and good-bye. I'm stunned. I feel hurt, dismissed, discarded. In all the years I've been doing treatment no one has ever left me a note terminating. It's particularly extraordinary since she spent an entire session in my office during which she obviously could have discussed her intention, rather than just leaving the note. She had clearly made up her mind before coming to the session and yet spent the entire time as if nothing unusual was happening. She has certainly demonstrated her inability to talk about her desire to end a relationship. I, on the other hand, feel totally cut off, in need of closure, wanting at least to be able to say good-bye.

I call Barbara at her office. Not surprisingly she doesn't take my phone call. Our relationship is over.

That Barbara chose a bizarre way of terminating cannot be denied. But what about what I did or, more accurately, did not do? Why did I never ask her if she expected our relationship to end badly too? Why did I never ask if she assumed that our relationship would be short-lived, just like all her other relationships? And why do I seem unable to keep so many of my patients since I've moved? At the end of my first year in Boca I joke – only half-heartedly – that I've lost more patients in my first year in practice here than I did in all my eighteen years of practice in Ann Arbor. I do consider why this is the case. On the most superficial level I say that it takes awhile to get referrals that are more in line with who I am and what I do. I also know that I am very anxious to build up my practice, and that perhaps I communicate a kind of desperation to my new patients, a desperation they may feel the need to pull away from. Perhaps they sense my neediness and are put off by it, unconsciously fearing that I will expect too much of them, that I will become the patient rather than the therapist.

There is, however, one possibility that I do not consider until years later in the process of writing this book. It is then, when I am keenly aware of how the analyst's current experience of love and loss can so dramatically affect her way of being in the treatment room, that I realize what now seems obvious. I am not yet ready to connect to new patients. In order to connect to the new I have to be ready to give up the old, to move forward, to embrace new possibilities. I am not at that point. I like, but do not love my new home. I may have moved away in distance, but not in thought. In my mind, the Michigan house is still my home, still the place I long to be. It is indeed possible that I feel similarly about my new patients. They are not my Michigan patients; they don't have the same psychological awareness, the same intellectual acuteness; we don't have the same history and connection. Although I intellectually understand that I cannot possibly have the same relationship with a patient I've seen three times as opposed to one I've seen for seven years, I react against the new in an effort to stay connected to the old. That explains why I didn't insert myself into the new treatments, why I left the intertwining of the relationship between myself and my patients completely unaddressed. It's why I didn't deal with Andrea's attempt to give me the name of her plastic surgeon, why I didn't ask Shirley if she wanted to use me only as the recipient of her complaints, and why I didn't talk with Barbara about her feelings and expectations of our relationship. Despite my conscious desire to have new patients, despite the financial necessity that I have new patients, I undermined my success by being unwilling to intensely connect to new patients because I was not ready to truly separate from the old.

Snapshots from our first year in Florida: Thanksgiving with just me, George, and Mark, George's schizophrenic son. We had been invited by friends to their large family gathering,

93

but thought Mark would be too uncomfortable. I know it's the right decision, but I feel alone, cut-off, adrift. Even George cannot lessen my pain and my feeling of being disconnected from so many important, loving connections.

We go to a Christmas Eve party where I enjoy the camaraderie of my professional colleagues. Christmas Day it is just me and George. I try very hard not to cry. George knows how miserable I am; there's no reason to make him feel worse. Despite the chilly weather I ask if we can go for a walk on the beach, even though I know that walking on sand is difficult for George because of his old back injury and dropped foot. He agrees. I know he's trying to please me. It's raw at the beach. There is no sun. I feel desolate. Even the elements are conspiring to keep me from feeling warmed. We stay only a brief while.

George is busy arranging for renovations to our house, as well as adding some unique touches of his own. He is back into the mode he knows best, back to making beautiful structures that can both please and contain us, as well as keep us safe. The roof needs to be replaced. It will cost $16,000. George says that's more than his first house cost. He installs Pergo floors throughout the house except for the bedrooms, crawling on his hands and knees for hours. He suffers for it, but I am delighted to see the fruits of his labor, and he is delighted with my delight. Perhaps the floors will be more than floors to our new house, but a sturdy foundation for our new life as well. They do create a look that recalls our Michigan house, while still maintaining the Florida flavor. Perhaps they can be one bridge between the past and the present. George builds another bridge between spaces, these quite literal – pull-down ladders in both the garage and the bedroom closet so that the attic can be easily accessed. I am again both amazed and thrilled by his ability to alter spaces, to make them both utilitarian and beautiful.

We go on a brief vacation to Oregon. When people ask where we're from I say that we're living in Florida, but that Michigan is home. I am not ready to claim Florida as my state.

We give a Fourth of July party. These parties in Michigan were legendary. People vied with each other to bring the most creative dish and spent the day frolicking in the lake and on our pontoon boat. We are both disappointed with the results in Florida. It is too hot to spend much of any time outdoors, although a few guests do take a dip in our pool. There is no lake to swim in, no boat to take out. And people bring mostly store-bought food. George is very unhappy about the latter. We both experience a feeling of absence. We give one more such party and then discontinue the tradition.

I continue to try to build my practice. I am more involved with professional activities than I ever was in Ann Arbor. I join the board of the psychoanalytic psychology association. We decide to have a fund-raiser. I'm designated as the chair. Suddenly I'm asking restaurants for gift certificates, asking colleagues for ads, asking friends to donate possible places in which to hold the fund-raiser and, in the end, even serving as auctioneer. I'm busy, busy, busy. My schedule has me out several evenings during the week. I feel more distanced from George. I still get to crawl in bed with him at night, to hold him close, and turn to him to allay my anxiety. But there seems to be less time for us, less time to really be together. At the time I consider my busyness necessary fallout of my need to build a practice. Today I believe my motivation was more complex. I believe it provided a way for me to withdraw from George, either to convince myself that I needed him less or as a way of expressing my anger at him for "making me" move to Florida or, still worse, for what I envisioned as his inevitable abandonment of me.

Still in practice-building mode, I randomly select five women psychologists from the phone book. I say that I'm new in town, would like to have lunch and introduce myself. Four of them return my call. One is an inexperienced but genuine young woman. We have a pleasant lunch. We never see each other again. The second is a more experienced therapist who graciously says, "Welcome to the neighborhood," and picks up the lunch tab. We both know that we will never become friends or referral sources. We are just too different. The third becomes a lasting friend. And the fourth refers a friend of hers to me, my first psychoanalytic patient in south Florida. Well, not exactly a friend, she tells me, more like a casual acquaintance whom she calls every so often. She doesn't think this woman has a friend. And I shouldn't be deceived by appearances. There's a lot of money in the family, even if Kathryn doesn't look the part.

I am indeed surprised when I open the door and see Kathryn sitting there. By Ann Arbor standards she would have been considered shabby; in Boca Raton she looks like a street person. A shapeless, creased gray dress covers her extremely large frame. She has brown scraggly hair that looks oily and unwashed, and full, bushy eyebrows. She wears not a stitch of make-up on a face that clearly communicates a depressed, forlorn individual. I invite her into my office. She seats herself uncomfortably in my chair, pulls alternately at her fingers and her hair, and stares at me.

"You seem really anxious," I say after a lengthy silence. "Is there some way I could make you more comfortable?"

"I'm not quite sure why I'm here. Gail told me I should come. She said I need help."

"And do you feel you need help?" I ask.

"I guess so."

Silence.

"What sort of help do you feel you need?"

"I don't know. With life. I guess I don't have a life."

Silence.

The muscles in my shoulders tighten. Kathryn's anxiety feels as though it is catching, or perhaps it is just adding to the anxiety I carry around myself these days. "Can you say what you feel anxious about right now?" I ask.

"You're here. I'm not used to being with people." Long pause. "I'm not used to talking."

I refrain from my desire to clench and unclench my fingers. I don't know if I have ever sat with someone who so quickly communicated her anxiety to me. But it's not only anxiety. It's anxiety accompanied by an absence, a withdrawal, a feeling of her not being engaged with me. How will I deal with a patient who feels so absent? Will I feel as though she is here and not here? Will that feel like another person who is lost to me? But I'm getting ahead of myself. This is just the first session. Most patients are anxious during their first session. Many are not engaged. I should not be jumping to such rash conclusions.

95

"How do you spend your days?" I ask, hoping to find some neutral topic that might lessen the anxiety while giving her a chance to further interact.

"I read."

Silence.

"Do you have friends?"

"No. I have animals."

Silence.

"Can you tell me about your animals?"

"I have two ferrets and two guinea pigs."

Silence.

"Ferrets are very intelligent. Guinea pigs not as much, but I like watching them."

Silence.

"Can you tell me a little about you, about your background, your parents."

"I knew I'd have to do that. I knew I'd have to talk about them," she says, her hand wringing increasing. "I was in therapy a lot as a child. My mother was always dragging me to one therapist or another."

"Because?"

"She thought there was something wrong with me."

"Could you be more specific?"

"No." Long pause. "She thought everything was wrong with me."

"That sounds very painful."

Silence.

With much skepticism and trepidation, Kathryn agrees to begin a three times a week analysis. She is not alone in her concern. Although I try to reassure myself, I am afraid that I am embarking on a very difficult treatment with a patient who may increase my own feeling of alienation and separateness. Still, I have wanted an analytic patient and here she is.

Over the course of the first several weeks, with much hesitation and silence, I learn that Kathryn is thirty-two years old and an only child. Her parents divorced when she was seven. Both had money of their own, so money was the one thing they never fought over. No, they never fought over her either. There was no question that she would stay with her mother. Her father never had much to do with her anyway. He's presently married to his fourth wife. Her mother remarried after she bought Kathryn her own apartment. It's okay. She likes being on her own. She gets to do what she wants. And to have her animals. Her mother never liked her animals. She wanted Kathryn to get a cat or a dog, but Kathryn didn't want to. They demand too much attention and, besides, she likes being different, sort of.

After a couple of months Kathryn brings in a typed document, about twenty-five pages long. She hands it to me. She tells me it's from her mother, who wrote it years ago when she was taking Kathryn to therapists as a child. Her mother thought it would be helpful for me to read.

"Do you want me to read it?" I ask. "Have you read it yourself?"

"Yeah, I've read it. It tells all the things that are wrong with me."

"Do you want me to read it?" I ask again.

"I guess. It's easier than telling you all about it."

"Well, if you want me to, I will read it, but can you tell me what you feel about what's written in here?" I ask, still somewhat uncomfortable about reading a document written by the patient's mother without any of the patient's input.

"I don't want to talk about it."

"All right. What would you like to talk about?"

"Nothing," she says, fidgeting in the chair.

Silence.

"We don't have to talk about anything if you'd prefer. It's okay to sit in silence." I wonder if I believe this. Although I have usually been quite comfortable with silence, I sense that Kathryn's silence would feel oppressively empty and isolating.

"No, it's not. It only makes me more uncomfortable."

Is Kathryn responding entirely to her own feelings or has she intuited my discomfort as well? I put that concern aside and say, "I can see what a bind that puts you in, Kathryn. It doesn't feel comfortable to talk and it doesn't feel comfortable to sit in silence."

"Yeah. That's why I avoid people."

Silence. I shift uncomfortably in my chair. Am I being an incompetent analyst? Was it just a fluke that I had a successful practice in Ann Arbor? Will I never be able to succeed with Kathryn? Will I never be able to succeed with any of my Boca Raton patients? Here I am now, unsure whether to be silent or to push. Should I encourage Kathryn to talk? Should I ask questions? Will the questions seem encouraging or intrusive? If I'm silent will the silence be experienced as respectful or punishing? What's wrong with me?

As agreed, I take Kathryn's mother's manuscript home to read. I am appalled. It is indeed a document about what is wrong with Kathryn, beginning with her having too small a mouth for her to be able to breast feed properly, continuing through her failure to be toilet trained by two, her rejection of her mother's embraces, her odd facial features, her lumbering gait, her awkward social manners, her unwillingness to bathe regularly, etc., etc. I find myself enraged at this woman I have never met and cannot imagine that my patient does not feel likewise.

"How do you feel about this document?" I ask, handing it back to her at our next session.

She pulls at her hair and says nothing.

I try to maintain the silence. Minutes pass. Anxiety fills the room.

"I'm going to leave," Kathryn says heading for the door.

"Kathryn, please, sit down," I say, almost desperately.

"I'll be back tomorrow," she offers.

This is the first of many times that Kathryn is to leave in the middle of a session. It is the only time, however, that she tells me of her intention both to leave and to return. Usually she simply gets up and goes. She doesn't look in my direction. She doesn't say anything. I give up trying to stop her. This first time I feel abandoned and insecure. What did I do wrong? What could I have done or said to keep her in the session? In time, I accept the inevitable, becoming more inured to Kathryn's abrupt departures.

Despite it all, Kathryn continues to come faithfully. She never misses a session. She is rarely late. I struggle to figure out how I can be more helpful. I understand that Kathryn and I are enacting a projective identification, unconsciously willing me to feel what she felt in relation to her mother – inadequate, not good enough, never able to please, never able to do anything right. Sometimes I contain these interpretations; sometimes I discuss them. Nothing. I talk to colleagues. I hire a supervisor. Just as I can't help Kathryn, they can't help me. As far as I know there is no change in Kathryn. Not in the sessions. Not in her life outside the sessions. To the best of my recollection, I do not at this time consider what I am bringing to the sessions independent of Kathryn. I do not think about feeling uprooted and disconnected myself, firmly tethered to neither my old life nor my new. I do not think about my own anxiety, my busyness as a self-protective mechanism, my withdrawal as a way to avoid potential pain and loss. I focus on the feelings Kathryn is inducing in me, neglecting the other half of the equation, the feelings I may be inducing in Kathryn.

We are well into the second year of treatment. Every once in a while I feel a glimmer of hope, a glimmer of what might be possible. Maybe Kathryn can talk about her anger at her father, at me. Maybe she can come to believe that I am interested in her, interested in what she has to say. But my hope is soon snuffed out, replaced by the usual anxiety, despair, and feelings of impotence and incompetence.

I see Gail at a conference. She comes up to me immediately and tells me what a great job I'm doing with Kathryn. I look at her incredulously. She wants me to know how much better Kathryn is, how she's able to talk so much more, and how great it is that she's begun volunteering at an animal shelter. I'm stunned. I also don't know what to do with this information. Kathryn obviously doesn't want me to know about these changes in her life. It's important to her that she remains intransigent in my eyes and that I continue to feel the inadequacy she's always felt. Yet I now have a secret from my patient. That also feels uncomfortable.

Within the next several weeks I detect no change in Kathryn; I hear no difference in the material; her anxiety remains rampant; she still leaves midway through many sessions. I do ask more questions about her life, about what she does with her time. She finally tells me she's volunteering at the shelter.

"It's no big deal. It's just a way to spend a few hours a week."

I am afraid to applaud Kathryn's success for fear that she will need to disown it, undermine it. I inhibit myself. Again I am being like Kathryn.

"It's not a no-kill shelter. I would have rather worked at one of those. Here there are so many animals killed each week. Some do get adopted. But a lot of them die."

I feel deflated. Kathryn has found another reason not to attach. Why attach to a being who will most likely be dead, and who will definitely be gone? In retrospect I wonder if I am also asking myself this question about my relationship to George, but at the time I am unaware of any connection.

Approaching the third year, Kathryn comes in with an amazing announcement.

"I'm going to need to look towards ending analysis. I'm pregnant. I figure I'll stay for another five months or so and then end. It will be too difficult for me to come in my last trimester. And I certainly can't come with a newborn."

"You're pregnant!" I exclaim.

"Yes, why are you so surprised? Did you think that no man would want to sleep with me?"

"No," I practically scream, "I didn't think you were or wanted to sleep with any man!"

"It was no big deal. A one-night stand with some guy from the shelter. We went out drinking one night and ended up in bed. I quit the shelter last week, as soon as I knew I was pregnant. I don't want him to know. I don't want him involved with the baby or anything. But a baby, I don't know, I kind of like the idea."

I have rarely felt so adrift in a session. I can't take in that Kathryn is pregnant. I didn't know that she had ever slept with a man. And it seems frightening to me to imagine her raising a child. I feel guilty about that thought, but must own it. I can't imagine Kathryn as a mother, a woman who can't allow herself to connect to a cat or a dog. Yet, I don't know what to say. To cast doubt on her ability to care for a child would be to join in the chorus of people throughout her life who has told her she isn't capable. I find myself at a loss for words.

Sensing my discomfort, she smiles for one of the few times in the treatment. "Looks like I've dumbfounded you," she says, obviously pleased.

"I don't know what to say, Kathryn," I say truthfully. "I didn't know you were sleeping with anyone. I…"

"I'm not sleeping with anyone. I slept with this guy one time."

"I don't think it's a good time for you to be ending treatment. You're going to have to deal with so many changes …"

"I'm ending treatment in five months. I'm not going to be dragging myself here. I'm not exactly a lightweight and I'm not doing anything to endanger the baby or me."

"Kathryn," I say, struggling to regain my voice, "You've understandably had such a difficult time relating to people. Now you're going to have a baby, an infant who's going to be totally dependent on you. Don't you think that's the time that you'll especially need to be working here, to be helping yourself relate to the baby as best as you can?"

"I can do it," she says defiantly. "I can do this on my own. I don't want to leave the baby with anyone, not like my mother left me with one nanny after another, and I obviously can't bring a baby in here."

I don't let go. Over the remaining five months I continue to try to change Kathryn's mind. I present rational arguments – it's only three hours a week, five maximum if you consider travel time. I try to understand her motivations – why it's so important that she do this alone, why she can't accept my help. But there is no budging Kathryn. She is going to have this baby. And she is going to leave treatment.

And she does. In our last session I tell her if she ever wants to return, even for a few sessions, she should not hesitate to contact me. The only communication I ever again receive from Kathryn is a birth announcement. She's had a healthy, six pound, five ounce red-headed girl. I send her a congratulatory note and again welcome her to come and see me. I don't hear from her. It is the end. I worry about Kathryn and about her baby. But my responsibilities as an analyst are over. There is no way I can intrude in Kathryn's life.

There is no question that Kathryn was a difficult patient, a prime example of Fairbairn's (1952) schizoid personality. She could neither move beyond her unconscious hope of winning love from her early caretakers nor come to terms with her overwhelming sense of need.[1] As a result she was unable to allow herself to form an intense relationship with me. But what about my side of the equation? Was I a good-enough analyst for Kathryn at the time in our lives that our paths crossed? Now I think that the answer is no. I myself was in a period of both intense anxiety and, to some degree, defensive withdrawal. I was struggling with feelings of inadequacy about starting a new practice. I was struggling with the pain of all my Michigan losses – my patients, my friends, my home. I was anxious about being in a new and very different place with new people and new expectations. My fears about losing George were ever present. Now I was in foreign territory with George as my only anchor. What would I do if I lost him as well? Although I realize that Kathryn and I did not share the same degree of pathology, I think it is important to ask: what happened when anxious, withdrawn Kathryn met anxious, withdrawn Dr. Sherby? Did my anxiety remind Kathryn too much of her own? Did she sense my neediness underneath and pull back because of her fears of engulfment or because of the terror of her own underlying neediness? Did Kathryn sense my withdrawal and take it as permission for her to withdraw or did my withdrawal make it less likely that I could effectively interpret Kathryn's withdrawal? These are all questions I raise today, clearly too long after the fact to be of any help to Kathryn. But these questions again point to the importance of therapists remaining aware not only of their past histories, but also the space they are presently in, a space that clearly affects how they are in the consulting room, thereby inevitably affecting their patients.

I am waiting for a new patient who is already almost a half hour late. She has called twice, first to tell me she is running late, then to tell me she is lost. I anticipate another ambivalent, reluctant patient. In comes Rachael, a tall, thin, dark-haired woman who looks frightened and withdrawn. Not another Kathryn, I think to myself. I've been seeing Kathryn for about two years now and I am not inclined to add another such patient to my practice. But there's a different feel here. Rachael seems more blank, more terrified, like a frightened rabbit who wants to scurry away before she's ever seen.

"I'm sorry for being late," she stammers. "It's not like me. I guess I'm not sure I should be here. Robin, she's my friend, she said I should come. It's really not like me to be late. I'm a nurse, a pediatric oncology nurse. I'm always responsible. I'm always on time."

"Maybe you're scared about being here. You look pretty scared."

"I guess. I guess I am. I've never done this before. I don't know if I should."

I am reminded of Alyce, the young woman I saw in Ann Arbor many years ago. There's a fragility about Rachael that hooks me. I haven't yet seen her toughness, but a pediatric oncology nurse has to have grit.

"We have very little time left today, Rachael," I say gently, "so maybe it would be best if you tell me a little of what brings you here and then we can find another time to meet."

She mumbles something I can't hear.

"I'm sorry," I say, "I couldn't hear what you said."

"I'm in a bad relationship," she says, barely audibly.

"What makes it bad?" I ask.

Her eyes widen in fear. She says nothing.

"Okay," I say, "why don't you tell me whatever you feel comfortable telling me."

"I love my job," she says, smiling for the first time. "People can't believe I'd want to do this job, being around sick kids all the time. But I love it. I get to make a difference. And they don't all die. People think they all die, but they don't. Some of them live. Some of them even come back to visit me."

I am more and more taken with this patient. In less than fifteen minutes she has drawn me in. I am definitely connected. I know she will not be an easy patient. I know there will be all kinds of difficulties, all kinds of pathology. But I feel relieved. I anticipate that I will care deeply about this patient, I will care deeply about a patient in Boca Raton. My self as an analyst has returned.

Rachael's story unfolds very slowly. Soon I am seeing her three times a week, using both her insurance and a reduced fee to make this possible. She is indeed in a "bad relationship."

"I don't know how I can tell you this. I don't even know if I even should tell you. I've never told anyone. Not even Robin and I've known her for years. She knows that Daniel is a bastard; she knows that he doesn't treat me well. But she has no idea."

Silence. She stares at me, her face blank. I've formed a hypothesis about that blank look. I've seen it many times before, that blank, vacant stare. My experience is that patients with that look have often been abused. It's a look that signals an ability to dissociate, to go elsewhere, to turn off, to not feel. But I keep my hypothesis as just that, a guess and a guess that could definitely be incorrect.

"He uses a gun," Rachael says finally. She says no more.

My stomach constricts. "For?" I ask.

There is a long pause.

"He puts it inside me," she mumbles, her head down, her eyes barely looking upward towards me.

"You mean he puts a gun in your vagina during sex?" I ask, shuddering inside while I try to keep my voice calm and non-judgmental.

She nods.

Once again there is a long pause. I am beyond horrified. And terrified for Rachael. I fantasize taking her home with me. Questions go flying through my mind. Is the gun loaded? Why does he do it? Why do you permit it? Does he do it every time you have sex? Does he get off on it? Do you? I say nothing.

"Do you... do you think I'm terrible?" she asks beseechingly.

"No, of course not. You're the same Rachael you were before you told me about Daniel using a gun during sex. But I would like for us to understand it, to understand what it means to you, to..."

"I hate it!" she says vehemently, interrupting me.

"Then why do you allow it?" I ask gently, again feeling that I want and need to protect this damaged young woman.

She shakes her head. "I can't talk about this any more today."

In truth, I too feel as though I've had enough for today. I need a break, some time to think about all that Rachael has told me and to be less overwhelmed by my own feelings of horror. I know we'll be back here many, many times.

And, indeed, we are. The answer – or more accurately, answers – to my question of why Rachael allows Daniel to use a gun during sex is complex and takes a long time to begin to answer. She allows it because she thinks she deserves it. She allows it because she's afraid not to. And, eventually, after many, many months she can own that having a loaded gun up her vagina during sex is exciting, like living on the edge. I'm even more certain there's abuse in Rachael's history, but I say nothing.

What she tells me about her background is both skimpy and relatively benign. She grew up in Los Angeles, the only child of middle class parents. Her father was a mid-level executive at various companies, her mother was a secretary. She was told she had a sister who died before she was born of some kind of illness. No, she didn't keep in touch much with her parents. They didn't have much in common. She always wanted to be a nurse. When she was eighteen she moved to Sacramento to go to nursing school. She met Daniel and moved to Florida to be with him. She's had other relationships. Some of them were okay; most of them weren't. She loves her job. She can't imagine ever leaving it.

Rachael becomes more and more attached to me. She talks about missing me over the weekends, fantasizing about my life, wondering if I think about her between sessions. I become similarly attached to Rachael. Although I don't miss her during weekends, she is in my mind. I worry about her. I think about that loaded gun. I have fantasies of calling the police – even anonymously – and imagine them scornfully rejecting the idea of their legally being able to intervene in two adult's consenting sex. "Consenting?" I imagine myself countering, but realize this will get me nowhere. Barring the intervention from an outside authority, I wonder if I should be more adamant about their banning the use of a gun during sex. I wonder if I should insist that Rachael leave Daniel. And I wonder if I can hurry the therapeutic process along. Can we understand her need to remain in this sadomasochistic relationship? Can we understand the connection between her past and this tremendously self-destructive relationship? I do none of the above. I am uncomfortable with the slowness of the process, but willing to have it take its course.

The winter of 1996 presents a series of challenges. First, my father dies in January. I am mostly relieved by his death. Our relationship had remained chaotic throughout my married life – long periods of estrangement, followed by violent verbal outbursts on his part, followed by another period of estrangement. I am, however, worried about my mother. She is devastated by my father's death. Despite the fact that my father had congestive heart failure and took nitroglycerine pills like candy, my mother is to tell me that she never thought about his dying. She has been caught entirely unaware. And she is all alone in her apartment in Mt. Kisco, without the ability to drive and without real friends to rely on. She spends weeks with us, returning occasionally to her apartment. We encourage her to move near us. We'll help her. We'll find her a place, pack up her current apartment, find the movers, and drive down her beautifully crafted sculpture that she'll entrust only to us. Overwhelmed by her aloneness in New York, she eventually agrees. The plan is to move her in the summer.

In the meantime, however, George and I get another shock. He is diagnosed with prostate cancer. I feel as though I have been punched in the gut. Cancer! Weren't George's heart problems enough?! I wasn't prepared to add cancer to our list of concerns. And now there's my mother to deal with as well – moving her, adjusting to living fifteen minutes from her. It's all too much. But, of course, we adjust and begin the process of dealing with this new problem. We meet with George's urologist to weigh the options: surgery and removal of the prostate, external radiation, or radioactive seeds which can be implanted directly into the prostate. The latter is a relatively new procedure. The clinical trials look good, although they only have data for five years. Given George's age, the urologist seems to be suggesting the seeds. I like the idea because I am terrified of George going through surgery given the difficulty he had with his heart only three years earlier. George would also prefer to avoid surgery and the possible side effects that frequently accompany removal of the prostate – impotence and incontinence. The decision is made. The radioactive seeds it will be.

Although the procedure is supposedly simple and risk free, I am extremely anxious. I cling to George's hand as they come to wheel him away from me into the operating room. George's mortality has again been thrown in my face, and I am terrified of losing him. I continue seeing my patients and follow up on my professional responsibilities, but my psychic energy is all focused on George. As promised, the procedure goes smoothly. George feels fine. It will be fine, he assures me. He'll just continue to be monitored and all will be well. But this health scare changes me. I am once again focused on George's health, more acutely frightened, and more aware of the inevitability of George's final leave-taking. There is, however, a positive side to George's new health crisis. My defensive withdrawal is shattered. I am back with George one hundred percent. I am more than aware of my need for him, more than aware of my terror of losing him. I am back totally and completely and am very glad for it.

It is from this place of greater openness and vulnerability that I deal with moving my mother from her Mt. Kisco apartment. It is an apartment I never lived in and that I have no emotional attachment to. The movers have taken all the furniture and packed boxes. George and I have put her fragile possessions, including her sculpture, in the back of our car. We will put her on a plane and then drive from New York to Florida. We are leaving the apartment for the last time. I imagine how painful this leave-taking must be for my mother – the home she lived in for the past sixteen years, the last place she lived with my father. The elevator is waiting. My mother leaves the apartment and never looks back, dry-eyed and stoic. I stand in the elevator crying.

"I moved out," Rachael announces one day. "I'm staying with Robin until I find my own place."

I'm surprised and pleased. "What led you to make that decision, Rachael?"

She shrugs. "I don't know. Lots of things I guess. I didn't like needing to have a gun up me in order to get off. And I knew you thought the relationship was unhealthy. I mean everyone thought it was unhealthy, including me. But your opinion matters to me. I don't want you to think I'm all messed up." She pauses. "And there was something else. I don't know exactly how this fits in but I know it does. There was this little girl at work. She died. I didn't want her to die. I really cared about her. I thought she'd get better. Maybe I even thought I could make her better. But I couldn't. She had cancer and she died."

Although Rachael is dry-eyed, I feel close to tears. "I can tell how very, very sad that makes you, Rachael."

"Yes. It does. She didn't deserve to die. She was just a little kid."

A thought occurs to me. "This may seem like a huge leap, Rachael, but I find myself thinking about your sister. Do you think there's any connection..." My voice trails off.

Rachael goes blank, more blank than I have ever seen her, as if she is not with me at all. She says nothing. It seems as though minutes go by.

"I didn't hurt that child," she finally says. "She just died."

"Of course you didn't hurt the child, Rachael. Did you think I was implying that you did?"

Rachael shakes her head and blinks her eyes as if she is trying to wake herself up or bring herself back to the present.

"What just happened, Rachael?" I ask, clearly concerned.

"I don't know. Nothing. Nothing. I just don't like to think of that little girl dying."

I am torn. Should I push her further or allow her to retreat? Should I encourage her to look in that place she clearly wants to avoid, or should I accept that she's had enough for today? I glance at the clock. We don't have that much time left. I decide to allow her to close up.

Rachael's treatment continues for many years. Throughout the agonizingly slow process I remain concerned about and connected to her. Ever so slowly her history emerges. Not at all surprising to me, she had been both physically and sexually abused by her father. She was beaten, chained, left to lie in her feces, forced to go without food for several days. He would punish her for her transgressions – she didn't suck hard enough on his penis, she didn't come herself, she had her period, she didn't welcome him with sufficient enthusiasm when he woke her in the middle of the night. Pleasure and punishment were inextricably interwoven. The horrors seemed unending.

"You know, don't you?" she says one day. "You know he killed her."

"I've thought for some time that you think he killed your sister, but I don't know that you know for sure."

"No. I guess I don't. It just makes sense. After all our work together, I still don't know when he started abusing me, but I know it was pretty early. She was three when she died. Maybe he put his penis or a bottle or some other disgusting thing inside her and ripped her to shreds. He could do it. I know he could do it."

"Rachael, what was your sister's name? After all these years I still don't know her name."

"I can't say her name. I can't. I can't. I don't even think her name."

Ever so gently, filled with love and compassion, I say, "I think it's important for you to say her name, Rachael. I think it's important that you name her, important for you and for her. She deserves her name and you need to allow yourself to say it."

Although Rachael looks terrified, I persevere. I feel it is important for Rachael to speak it.

"Sophie," she says very quietly. "Sophie. Her name was Sophie." And, for the first time in years, Rachael bursts into tears, then gut-wrenching sobs, for Sophie and for herself. It is as though she is crying for all the dead or damaged children.

This is a breakthrough in the treatment. After this point Rachael is able to cry. She loses some of the blankness in her expression.

"I think she watched," she says one day.

"I wondered where your mother was in all of this, but I figured you'd get to it when you were ready."

"I think she got off on it. Or maybe he made her. Or maybe after he was through with me he'd get into bed with her and they'd both get off on how scared I was or how I cried or how I came myself… I'm disgusting. How could I get off on it? I know, I know what you're going to say. You've said it often enough. I was the child, he was the adult. It was his responsibility, his fault, and if someone rubs on you long enough you're going to come. I know. I know all that. It doesn't help. I'm still disgusting."

Building on all the work we've done, in the end it is not me but another woman who is able to help Rachael feel less disgusting. Although never having been in a lesbian relationship, Rachael is wooed by Beatrice, a nursing colleague, and allows herself to fall in love with this kind, somewhat older woman who is obviously enamored of Rachael. I wonder aloud with Rachael whether she is substituting Beatrice for me, taking Beatrice as a sexual partner when she cannot have me. She reacts with horror. She doesn't want me as a sexual partner! How could I even suggest that?! I withdraw my interpretation. Given the horrific sexual abuse in Rachael's background, it is too much for her to contemplate having sexual feelings for me. Perhaps my interpretation is correct, perhaps not. Regardless, Rachael is in a far better place than she was when she began treatment, both psychologically and in terms of a life partner. We continue to work together for some time. She continues to love her job. She and Beatrice are happy together. Eventually it is time for us to say good-bye.

"I'll miss you," she says tearfully.

"I'll miss you, too," I reply honestly. "This is the part of my work I like the least, saying good-bye. But you've done amazing work, Rachael. You deserve to be proud of yourself. You deserve the very best always."

"I love you," she says as we hug good-bye.

My eyes fill with tears. I close the door.

7

ILLNESS AND DEATH
Self-Disclosure Revisited

2004 was the year our lives became preoccupied with illness and death, starting with the death of George's eldest grandson and the hospitalization of my mother. Then, in April of that year, George was hospitalized with what turned out to be an undiagnosed infection in one of his prosthetic knees. By the end of that hospital stay George's PSA – the marker for prostate cancer – had gone from around four where it had been hovering for the past eight years to thirty-six. The cancer was back with a vengeance and had spread to George's bones. He began hormone injections. The injections proved to be effective and his cancer went into remission.

I was ecstatic. George was to turn eighty in October and I had great plans for his birthday – a surprise party in September, that luckily happened to fall on the only weekend that month that we didn't have a hurricane, a second party at my friend Ann's home in Ann Arbor, a third at Melodee's in Ohio, and then a trip to the wine country in California. I expected that George would tire more easily, was determined to set a more leisurely pace, and, by and large, I succeeded. It was indeed a never to be forgotten birthday and a welcome respite to all the pain we had been dealing with.

But, the respite was not to remain. Although George's cancer remained in remission through 2005, his physical deterioration continued. This man who used to walk on roofs was now in tremendous pain, walked with a walker, and fell too often for either of our comfort. I marveled at his ability to cope, particularly since no physician seemed able to explain his increasing pain or physical incapacity. Since the prostate cancer was in remission it should not have been giving him bone pain. His cardiac stress tests were negative. His carotid arteries were clear. His back was a mess, but that was nothing new. He saw a pain doctor who put him on narcotics. George hated it. He couldn't think straight. His body temperature was out of whack. He decided the pain was preferable. Eventually he used a motorized scooter in addition to the walker.

Now, early in 2006, George's PSA again begins to rise. The hormone injections have become ineffective. George's oncologist tries two oral medications. Neither work. More aggressive treatment is necessary. In June of 2006, several days after our twenty-fifth wedding anniversary, George is to begin chemotherapy and embark on a still more treacherous journey. First, there is no guarantee that the chemo will work. Second, there is no way of knowing how George will react to the treatment. He is, after all, an almost eighty-two-year-old man who is not in the best of health. As is typical of us, the day of the first treatment George is calm and confident while I am frightened beyond belief. We are told the treatment will take three to five hours as various medications are administered through the IV prior to beginning taxotere, the actual chemotherapy. George's treatment takes much longer. When they begin administering the taxotere George becomes extremely cold and starts to shake violently. The treatment is stopped. He's given another drug to further prepare his body and the chemotherapy is started again more slowly. This time George is able to tolerate it.

I don't remember going home, although obviously we do. I don't remember if George lies down. I don't remember when or what we eat for dinner. I don't remember going to bed. What I do remember is being awoken at 2 a.m. with George throwing up and complaining of a tightness in his chest. He takes a nitroglycerine and feels better. Is this the affects of the chemo or is it a heart attack? Should we call the emergency number for the oncology office? Both George and I hate to unnecessarily awaken a doctor in the middle of the night. He feels better sitting up. He still feels some constriction. He takes another nitro. Again he feels better. We finally decide to call, me falling over myself apologizing to the doctor for waking her. She is professional and kind. She asks about George's previous cardiac history. I tell her he had two angioplasties in 1993. She tells me to call 911. George's symptoms are not a usual reaction to taxotere and given his cardiac history she thinks it best to have him checked out. I call. We get dressed and wait for the ambulance. George sits calmly in the chair in the library. I too am relatively calm. Although I can easily imagine the worst-case scenario, I also have some of my mother's capacity for denial and at this point the denial has kicked in.

At the hospital George is started on a nitro drip. He's soon entirely comfortable and joking with the nurses and the emergency room physician. They take blood. We wait for the results. The doctor comes back into the room.

"The blood work indicates you had a minor heart attack. It doesn't look too severe, but we'll move you to Northridge Medical Center for an angiogram."

That's the end of my denial. I start shaking. It's not the procedure I'm concerned about, but I'm immediately apprehensive about what they might find. I keep asking what will happen if the damage to George's heart is too great to permit an angioplasty. The nurse and the physician's assistant independently assure me that George would be sent home until he recovered some of his strength and then undergo bypass surgery. The cardiologist has a different answer. George is not a candidate for a bypass. As we know, George's cancer has metastasized to his bones. In bypass surgery the sternum must be broken; for George that would mean the possibility of releasing cancer into his bloodstream.

I go home before driving to Northridge. I have to feed Pippin, our cat. I have to get my patients' phone numbers so that I can call and cancel my day. I don't remember making those calls, but I'm sure I tell all my patients that I have a family medical emergency. I'm not interested in sharing any more information and I don't.

Once at Northridge, I sit by George's bedside until they take him for the angiogram. "We've done this before," he says confidently.

I must look terrified. The nurse reassures me, "He'll do fine."

Sitting in the small waiting room, I ask if I can turn off the TV. I can't stand the noise. I'm barely holding myself together, anxiety seeping from every pore.

After what seems like hours, the cardiologist comes into the room. "Your question was prophetic," he says. "This was only a minor heart attack, but your husband has massive heart damage. We can't help him. Not with a stent and not, as we discussed, with bypass. The additional problem is that he's just had chemo. And when the full effects of the drip goes into his system it's going to lower his red blood cells which is going to pose additional difficulties for his heart. I'm sorry."

I ask if he'd told George. He said he had. I ask how he'd reacted. He told me he seemed quite all right.

"Should I call his children?" I ask.

"I would," he replies.

"How is it possible that George has massive heart damage when his stress tests have been normal for years?"

"There are ten percent false negatives in stress tests. If the damage is too massive, the color contrast doesn't show up."

I call George's daughter, Melodee, and ask her to call her brother, John. Melodee makes plans to fly down immediately. I call Luke, George's grandson, and gently break the news to him. I call my cousin, Danielle, now an attorney in Florida, who immediately leaves work and comes to the hospital.

When George is wheeled into his room he looks pale and shaken, but still smiling and literally welcomes me with open arms. I rush for those arms, wanting so much to be embraced, to feel this man who is still very much with me. He tells the story of what he remembers of the procedure. I don't know if it is an accurate description, but it is his reality and he is to repeat it many times. He says that when the probe went into his heart all he could see was this blackness, a hole, nothing there. It scared him. I put my head on his hand and kiss it. I love his hands, workman's hands. He thought they were coarse and ungainly. I thought they were beautiful. "We've had a great life," I say. "No one could ask for more."

I am convinced beyond a shadow of a doubt that George will not survive. But I am most definitely incorrect. Although I don't minimize the expertise of the physicians, I do believe that it is my husband's spirit that pulls him through. The doctors are amazed by how well he responds to the treatment – Lasix to drain the fluid from his heart; transfusions and aranesp injections to lift his red blood cells out of the danger zone. Melodee is with me throughout, sharing both my despair and my elation.

After a week in the hospital we are home. But not for long. Two days later, George starts to sweat profusely and says he's feeling some mild chest pain. We call 911. We are back in the emergency room. For hours. Until he is again admitted to the hospital. At first George's cardiologist is not optimistic, saying that George's heart is unstable and that keeping George's blood pressure low enough without making it too low and complicating the problem of congestive heart failure is problematic. He leaves. George and I hold each other. We are both scared. In less than half an hour the cardiologist returns. He has good news. He has seen the films of George's heart. There is no evidence of congestive heart failure. It's just a question of tweaking the blood pressure medication and in a few days George can go home. We breathe a tremendous sigh of relief.

While in the hospital, George's oncologist comes to see him. He says that George's PSA dropped a few points, but is still way beyond normal. We'll have to think about when to do another chemotherapy treatment. I knew we would have to walk down this path again, but I'm less than eager to begin the journey. The oncologist says that we can wait an extra week, but that we can't afford to go beyond what by then would be a five-week break in the chemotherapy treatments. I feel sick at the thought. I understand that there is no alternative.

George comes home. Melodee returns to Ohio. Luke and his girlfriend, Emily, come for dinner. I like Emily a lot. She seems warm and caring and upbeat. I formulate a tentative plan. Perhaps Emily can move to Florida, live with Luke and stay with George while I'm seeing patients. It seems like a good idea all around but, in the meantime, I make plans to take off from work after George's next chemotherapy. I tell patients I have a family medical matter to attend to.

Don is a young, African-American internist I have been seeing in analysis for three years. He is an anxious, obsessive man who is driven to be successful and fulfill his family's expectations that he surmount all hurdles placed in front of African-Americans and produce great achievements. Our work has been slow, with me trying to provide a kinder, gentler voice to combat the harsh messages in his head and his critical judgment of both himself and others.

"I hope you don't mind my asking," he says tentatively, "But you seem to be having a lot of family medical issues. Is everything all right?"

Don is the first patient to directly ask me this question. I have generally given patients perfunctory explanations for my absences – I have a family medical emergency – and most of them have accepted it without question. Although I wrote an article on self-disclosure in 2005 – a revision of which appears in Chapter 5 of this book – I have given little thought to what I will or will not tell patients. I have been far too preoccupied with the stresses of my own life to consider how much and what information would be best for either specific patients or for my patients overall. And I certainly have not considered what would be best for me. Am I seeking connection or protection? The fact that I have offered so little information would seem to imply the latter, that I want to retreat into the safety of my office and my patients' lives and escape, however briefly, the trauma of my own.

Now that Don has asked me directly I regret not giving this inevitable question more forethought. I know I have a responsibility here, a responsibility to answer in a way that would be most helpful to my patient. But what would be most helpful? Possible responses flit through my head – What have my absences meant to you? What are your fantasies? How do you feel asking the question? But I need to respond to Don in this moment and in this moment I do not know what would be most therapeutic. So I say none of those things. I answer the question.

"My husband has metastatic prostate cancer, has been undergoing chemo, and also had a mild heart attack."

"Oh my God. I'm so sorry. I'm so sorry I didn't ask sooner. I'd been wondering about it, worrying about you, but I didn't know if it was my place to ask you. If I can help you or your husband in any way, please do let me know."

Oh my, I think to myself. This is exactly the problem with telling patients about my own difficulties. Now Don feels he has to take care of me and he certainly doesn't need anything else to feel guilty about. Still, would it have been better if I hadn't answered his question? Perhaps then he would have felt rejected or even guilty for intruding into my life.

"Thank you," I say. "I appreciate your concern. My husband and I are managing as best as we can. But here the focus needs to stay on you."

"But that seems so selfish! I don't see how I can just go on blithering about my mundane issues while you're dealing with such major problems."

"Again, I do appreciate your concern, but truthfully it's helpful for me to focus on you, to get outside myself, to put my own problems aside and become engrossed in you and your life."

Although Don was not totally convinced, he was able to return to himself and his problems. There were times he would ask me how things were going and I would respond truthfully. There were times – especially when he became blocked in a session – I would sense that he was thinking about me, but saying nothing. At those times I would ask what he was thinking about and he would often return to his guilt about focusing on himself when he knew that I was dealing with so much pain in my life. In retrospect, I think my disclosing my life circumstance to Don was both helpful and unhelpful to him, sometimes increasing his harsh judgment of himself, but also giving us an opportunity to work directly on his guilt while fostering his capacity for empathy towards others.

For my part, I found Don's knowledge about my life neither comforting nor intrusive. I felt neither a greater connection to Don nor a sense of having violated my own need for safety and protection. But I had set a precedent. Without much conscious thought I had decided that, if asked, I would answer patients' questions truthfully, regardless of who the patient was or how I felt about the patient. This "decision" was not always to serve me well.

Bill is a fifty-two year old orthopedist who has been in treatment with me for two years, coming because his wife said she would divorce him if he did not change. Although he has made some progress, he remains an opinionated, angry, rather arrogant man who always believes that he is right. His ability to empathize with others is limited, although he does have a good relationship with his two sons. He loves the surgical part of his work, but finds seeing patients in his office more difficult and loathes what he calls the hypocrisy of getting along with his partners.

"You're having too many family medical emergencies," he says abruptly one day. "What's going on?"

I feel immediately intruded upon, put off by the demandingness of his question. "I will answer that question," I reply, "but I wonder if you'd first be willing to look at how you've just asked it?"

"Why? What's wrong with it? It's just a simple question? Are you going to give me that shrink nonsense about my having to look at what my questions mean? And, no, I haven't felt abandoned by your having to cancel sometimes."

"The way you ask, 'What's going on?' – it feels very much like a demand, it's off-putting, and it makes me not want to answer the question."

"Yeah, I get what you're saying. But I have been thinking about your family medical emergencies and I just wanted to know if there was something serious going on with you or your husband or kid or mother or whoever."

"That's definitely a more caring way to ask the same question."

"Yeah, yeah. I said I get it. But I still want to know."

And so, I tell Bill the same thing that I told Don. But Bill is a different person and his response, both initially and throughout my husband's illness is likewise very different. Although an orthopedist and not a specialist in any of my husband's conditions, Bill is all too willing to tell me how my husband's treatment should be managed, as well as freely offering his own opinions and comments.

"Radiation is a preferable treatment to chemotherapy." "They're waiting too long between chemo treatments." "Oncologists never know what they're doing – it's just a shot in the dark." "He's how old? Well, you should be able to have him for a couple more years." "You're still a young woman. You'll find yourself another man."

I find it very difficult to deal with these comments in a therapeutic manner, experiencing Bill as insensitive, opinionated, and dogmatic. Sometimes I feel as though I have been punched in the stomach and all I can do is go into a defensive crouch, hoping that the comment will go by, that I can ignore its existence, and that we can return to Bill's life rather than my own. I know, even then, that these instances could be good therapeutic tools to help Bill see how his manner affects me, just as it does others in his life. But often I am too raw to respond therapeutically. I am hurting too much to feel sufficiently protected from Bill's bombastic voice. I regret telling him anything about my husband's illness. And I am more than a little relieved when he abruptly terminates, saying that he has changed as much as possible and that his wife will just have to accept him or "take him on."

Whether Bill's sudden departure is a result of his experiencing me as being overly confrontational or, on the contrary, his conscious or unconscious awareness of my withdrawing from him rather than "taking him on," I have no idea. But his leave-taking is a relief to me and a most blatant example of how my current life circumstances left me incapable of effectively treating a patient.

In contrast, there is Stella, a seventy-nine-year-old Russian woman I had been seeing for four years. She initially entered therapy because of problems with her husband and issues with her adult children. Soon, however, we were dealing with her persistent feelings of guilt stemming from her having eloped, leaving Russia, and never seeing her parents or siblings again. I always liked Stella. She was a strong, feisty woman whose accent and way of being in the world reminded me of my beloved grandmother.

Shortly after my return to work following George's second chemotherapy – a procedure he did tolerate, but one that left him feeling weak and debilitated – Stella comes in with a clear-cut agenda.

"The last time I saw you," she says, "I was worried about you. I started to ask you if everything was all right, but then I didn't and then I was mad at myself for not asking right then. You just didn't look right. You didn't seem like yourself. Is everything all right?"

The sincerity of Stella's warmth and concern brings tears to my eyes although I do manage to perfunctorily address Stella's guilt. "I'm sorry my distress was so evident to you for we certainly know it doesn't take much for you to get mad at yourself."

"What's wrong?" Stella persists. "You're so sad."

"My husband has prostate cancer that's spread to his bones and he's having chemotherapy which might or might not work."

"Oh! I'm so sorry," she exclaims, tearing up herself. "You're so special to me. I'm sorry this has to be happening to you. I wish the best for your husband. I wish the best for you."

Three months later in November of 2006, Stella herself is diagnosed with multiple myeloma, cancer of the bone marrow.

"I'm so scared," she says. "I know you're going through the same thing. Everything seems to be going wrong these last few months. First my back starts hurting and I can hardly walk, then my best friend dies, and now this."

I find myself almost unable to speak. "I'm so sorry," I say, feeling overwhelmed by yet another illness, yet another tragedy.

"They say it's not terminal. And I'll be able to be treated with medication, not chemotherapy. But the medication can have all kinds of side effects and I'm not good with medication, so I hope I'll be able to take it. I hope it will work."

"I hope it will work, too. I hope you'll be well. I know you feel as though your body has been letting you down. You've been well your whole life and now there's this, this betrayal of your body," I say overwhelmed by sadness for Stella, for George and for myself.

One month earlier, a day before George's eighty-second birthday, the oncology office calls. George's PSA is fifty-four. It's definitely not good news. But they will continue the chemo and still hope it may work. Uncharacteristically, I decide not to tell George until after the celebration. I tell Melodee and some friends, but spare George the news. When I do tell him, despite his pain and his fatigue, he remains optimistic. "Don't bury me yet," he tells me. And so we go on.

By the end of November George's pain is so severe that his oncologist puts him on morphine. It is Thursday, the 30th of November. I'm at work. Emily is with George. Around five o'clock she leaves me a message. George has fallen, hitting his head right above his left eye. There is blood everywhere. She has called 911. They are on their way to the hospital. My anxiety soars. I cancel my remaining patients and rush to the hospital. On my way I call my mother to tell her we won't be picking her up for dinner tonight. There's no answer. I call repeatedly, with no results. I finally call my cousin Danielle, explain the situation and ask her to go to my mother's. As it turns out, in a scenario I wouldn't believe if I saw it in a movie, my mother fell at almost the same time as George. Although she is unable to get herself up, she is not hurt in any other way.

Such is not the case with George. When I get to the emergency room, George is being stitched up by a doctor, but otherwise seems fine, except for being mad at himself for falling. Unfortunately, an MRI of George's head reveals that he has a subdural hematoma. He is transferred to the trauma unit at another hospital where visiting hours are strictly limited to three separate hours a day. For the first day and a half, George seems his usual warm, outgoing, intelligent self. Then I begin to notice a change. His memory isn't as sharp. He's more unsure of himself. I ask him who's the Secretary of State. He can't tell me. I tell him she's a woman. He gets mad at me for pressuring him. I tell the charge nurse. They take him for another MRI. Yes, the bleed in his brain has spread, although has so far spared the frontal lobe. In the next few days George has difficulty writing or making even the simplest decisions. I'm despairing. It doesn't seem possible that we will add cognitive loss to all of George's other losses. After a week, George's medical condition stabilizes. Neither the bleed nor his cognitive processes are worsening. He enters the rehab center at the hospital.

It's hard for me to recall the specifics of my life during this time, except to say that I am in a state of constant, sometimes unbearable anxiety. I work, although I rearrange my schedule so as to see George as often as possible. In addition to dealing with the terror of losing George, I am terrified about not knowing: not knowing how I'll find George, not knowing what will come next, not knowing how I'll cope with what comes next.

It is incredibly painful to see George struggling – with his mind, with his pain, with his walking, and, most of all, with his dignity. The worst picture I have of George in all the horrible images of all his terrible illnesses is when I arrive at the rehab center to find him sitting in a wheelchair by the nurse's station hooked to an alarm bell designed to go off if he attempts to get out of the chair. George is furious and mortified, as am I. George isn't suffering from dementia! Fortunately, George's neurologist is on the floor that day and I entreat him to unhook George from that contraption. Within minutes, the alarm is undone. Somewhat calmer, I ask the neurologist if George's mental condition will improve as the bleed recedes. "Perhaps," he says. "It will probably improve some, although I can't guarantee it."

At the same time Stella discovers that she cannot tolerate the medication prescribed for her cancer. Additionally, she too falls, and her back pain returns with a vengeance.

"I can't stand this," she cries. "I'm in such pain. Perhaps this is my punishment for abandoning my family."

"You know that's not the case, Stella," I counter. "You know that life isn't fair, that it isn't reasonable. You know there was no reason six million Jews were killed in the Holocaust. You know there's no reason that you have cancer, that my husband has cancer. It just is. It's part of life and something we must bear."

Crying, she says, "I don't know how you got to be so wise. I'm old enough to be your mother. I should be saying things like that to you, not the other way around. But I'm so glad I have you, that you're in my life. You're such a special person."

"Thank you," I say smiling, "You're a pretty special person yourself; a gutsy person. We'll struggle through this together. I'm here to hold your hand through whatever the future may bring."

Stella and I developed a unique bond. Although George's illness was rarely actively discussed, that she and I were struggling with similar difficulties in our lives made us particularly attuned to each other. Just as was my experience when leaving Ann Arbor, Stella's and my shared pain brought us closer together, made us feel more connected in our mutual sadness, made us each feel as though we were less alone. Although they were often painful, I looked forward to my sessions with Stella and was glad that I had told her about George's illness.

Still in the rehab center, George's PSA continues to climb. It's now 120. George becomes increasingly disgusted and increasingly determined to be home by Christmas. Christmas is on a Monday that year, so he is insistent about being home the preceding Friday. Christmas had always been a festive time of year for us, and George wants to celebrate it as we always had. He also wants to sleep in his own bed with me at his side. Because he wants it so desperately, I want it for him although, at the same time, I fear what it will be like to care for George at home. He's so much weaker than he was prior to this hospitalization. Will he be able to get in and out of his wheelchair? Will he be able to get in and out of the shower? Will his cognitive deficiencies make it more difficult for him to do what he needs to do? I know for sure that he can't be left alone. Not even for an hour. The logistics are daunting.

With great persistence and determination, George is indeed home the Friday before Christmas. It's wonderful sleeping with him again, cuddled up in his arms. It's the one place that life almost feels like it once had, where I can feel safe and protected in his arms and deny his sickness and frailty. We do a family Christmas, smaller than usual and perhaps not as festive, but Christmas nonetheless.

Later that week I take George for his long delayed hormone injection. They make his next appointment for the end of June 2007. "I'm glad you think I'll live that long," George says. I say nothing. In my heart I know he won't.

Starting the New Year, George's days are filled with visits from nurses, aides, physical therapists, and cognitive therapists. George finds his cognitive difficulties totally demoralizing. All his life he prided himself on his beautiful handwriting. Now he struggles to make it legible. He calls it "chicken scratch." Numbers and drawing, both of which had been so easy for him, become painstaking endeavors. He finds it humiliating. I suffer along with him. It's yet another loss, his mind now diminished along with all his physical incapacities. But slowly George does seem to show some cognitive improvement. We welcome the small changes and feel a degree of hope.

And then it seems as though George's improvement is not confined only to the cognitive arena. By the second week of January he seems perkier, less fatigued, perhaps even in less pain. Shortly thereafter we go for George's blood work. Two days later the physician's assistant from the oncologist's office calls and tells me that George's PSA is twelve. "What!?" I practically scream into the phone. "How is that possible? It was over 120 last time."

"Oh," she says, checking the past records. "You're right. There must be some mistake. We'll run it again."

And again the results come back as twelve. They send the blood to a different lab. Same results. They have him come in and give a new blood sample. This time the PSA is eleven. Although still clearly an abnormal reading, it's a far cry from 120. George's oncologist is mystified. There's no explanation. "I've never seen prostate cancer go from being hormone resistant to hormone responsive," he says. Explanation or not, George is definitely feeling better. We accept our good fortune, determined to enjoy whatever respite we have.

In the meantime Stella is not doing well. They try her on one medication after another, each bringing intolerable side effects – muscle cramps, rashes, restlessness, and inability to sleep.

"I don't know if it's worth it," she says. "I'm an old lady. Maybe I should just forget it all. Give up. Let whatever happens, happen. They tell me if I don't do anything I'll start being in tremendous pain. This cancer is so impossible. There's so much of it around. I go to the oncology office and see all these people sitting there – young people, old people, people without any hair, people who don't even look as though they can communicate any more. Why bother? Why should I bother?"

I have been battling inside myself while Stella is speaking. Would it be helpful to tell her about George? Would it be helpful to tell her how much he's struggled and how, at least for the moment, he's doing so much better? Would it give her hope? Or would it diminish her, making her feel she doesn't have his strength? I make my decision.

"Stella," I say tentatively, "I don't know if this will be helpful to you, if you'll find some hope, some encouragement in this, but let me tell you a little about my husband's journey with his illnesses, about some of his ups and downs. There have been lots of them. He was a man who once had enormous physical strength and stamina and now he needs a walker and gets short of breath when he walks twice around our living room. He's in constant pain both from his chronic back problems and the spread of the cancer to his bones. He fell and has some brain damage. And yet he's shown a tremendous will to live. He keeps fighting and fighting. And right now, although no doctor can explain it, he's actually better. His cancer markers have decreased and he's feeling better. No one knows how long it will last, but for now, with all his limitations, he's trying to enjoy his life as much as possible."

Stella is silent for a moment. "Thank you for telling me all that. He sounds like an amazing man."

"And you're an equally amazing woman," I add.

The following week, Stella is smiling, eager to begin her session. "I thought a lot about what you told me last week about your husband. I could tell you weren't sure whether or not you should tell me. But I'm glad you did. It was helpful. I could see what a fighter he was. And it made me more determined to fight, too. So thank you. I'm going to stop whining like a baby and do what I need to do."

"You weren't whining like a baby. You're scared and tired and in pain. And it's okay to feel all those things. But if you can take some strength from my husband's story, I'm glad. I'd like to keep you around as long as possible."

Stella is another patient I have come to love. Her survival is important to me. More important because I'm struggling with George's survival as well? That is most likely the case, another example of how my current life situation coincides with and affects my relationship with a patient.

June of 2007. The month for George's next hormone injection. He has indeed survived to receive that injection, something I never anticipated. I'm anxious. The results of the last injection were miraculous. I want another miracle. For a while it looks as though all might be well. George's PSA remains fairly stable. We get Hadley, our piebald miniature dachshund, a new bundle of life and joy added to our lives. All seems well. But it isn't. By the end of July, George's PSA again begins to climb and he begins to crash. George is philosophical. "We knew it couldn't last," he says. I'm devastated. And weary. George becomes more and more fatigued. He feels weaker. Showering becomes exhausting. Even going to the bathroom saps his energy. But still he perseveres. His birthday is less than two months away. He wants his party. I make the plans.

George lives to have his party. Jaundiced, he enters the hospital two days later. He has cancer in his bile ducts. He decides he does not want to be resuscitated if his heart stops. He enters hospice one week after his birthday and dies thirty-six hours later.

George is no more. His absence surrounds me; I am enveloped in emptiness. I go through the necessary motions – people to notify, a memorial service to prepare, an obituary to write. I take some comfort in the presence of family and friends. But it is George I long for. I will never again experience his love, his embrace, his smile. Forever after these things will exist only in my memory. He is gone from me. I must continue my journey without him.

When George went into hospice I did not know when I would be returning to work, knowing neither how long his dying process would take nor how long I would need to take off after he died. I called all my patients, talked to some, left messages for others. Depending upon what they already knew, I gave them different amounts of information, ranging from my having a family medical emergency to a death in the family to the fact that my husband was dying. When I did return, most, but not all of my patients asked me who had died. Here again I was at a choice point. I knew that telling patients my husband had died could place an unnecessary burden on them. I was their therapist. My problems were just that, mine. But we also had a human connection, often a close, intimate connection. Could I expect them not to want to know who died? Could I expect them not to sense the degree of my sadness? I vacillated. In the end, I hedged. I told them they should consider whether or not they wanted to know. I would tell them if they did want to know, but could certainly understand if they preferred not to. It was as though I gave patients a second chance to say they didn't want to know, although I did understand that the complex relationship between patients and analyst, a relationship that combines elements from both the past and the present, makes it impossible for them to make a real choice. Again, most, but not all of my patients said that they did want to know.

Not surprisingly, what patients did or did not want to know was usually consistent with who they were as people. An older woman who had been widowed many years earlier made the implicit assumption that it was one of my parents who had died. She could not imagine that anyone, and most certainly not her therapist, could possibly be suffering as she suffered. A depressed woman who felt that she too easily experienced other's pain as her own, asked me nothing, and went on to talk immediately about what had transpired in her life in my absence. Yet a third person expressed her condolences, but said she didn't need to know who had died. I saw her as someone who thought of herself as empathetic and sensitive, but whom I experienced as quite distanced from her own feelings and those of others.

Some patients brought in cards. Many expressed their most genuine and heartfelt condolences.

Stella gives me a hug and a box of sweets. "You're my hero," she says. And then, "Did he suffer?"

She herself has not been doing all that well. "He went quickly at the end," I say. "He was ready." I am telling her the truth and perhaps preparing her for her future.

Some patients cry briefly, both for me and for themselves in identification with me, not convinced they could survive a similar trauma. Some patients express guilt over not having known; others marvel at my capacity to keep working through all my pain and grief. I respond to patients' comments and questions as honestly as I can, but do attempt to focus the session back on them. Some patients never ask me again how I am doing; others ask every so often, wanting to know both that I am all right and that I can continue to function as their analyst. Some patients' treatments seem completely unaltered by what were momentous events in my life. For other patients, my life circumstance seems to intensify underlying issues.

"I feel so bad for you," says Charles, a thirty-year-old librarian who came into treatment because of his difficulty in forming intimate relationships. "I don't know how you can stand it. But I know that I feel bad for me too. I've been preoccupied with dying again. I keep thinking I'm having a heart attack. I knew it was anxiety, but I went to the doctor anyway, just to check it out. I guess with your husband dying, it just made me feel more vulnerable. Although I'm sure he was much older than me. And I do feel sad for you, really sad."

"Thank you. And do you feel anything else?"

"What do you mean?"

"I'm not sure. I just wondered if there was something more going on."

"Well," he says rather sheepishly, "I did have this dream. I dreamt that I came into the session and you were like flirting with me, not exactly coming on to me, but being kind of coy and cute. And I felt like I was the one who had to keep the boundary, like make sure that nothing got out of hand."

"What are your thoughts?"

"I don't know. I suppose it's like with my mother. I couldn't trust what she'd do. She could be so inappropriate, not sexual exactly, but just too touchy-feely, too close. And I guess that's how I saw you in the dream. Classic transference, right?"

"So you're saying that now that my husband's dead you're afraid that I'll become more like your mother, more sexually inappropriate."

"Yeah, I guess, although I know that you won't. Not really."

"I wonder if there's something else in that dream though, after all it was your dream, you created the scenario. I wonder if there's a wish in there, if you wish that I'd come on to you, if there's a wish for some sexual contact between us and that wish makes you feel guilty and afraid you'll be punished and die."

"Wow! That's interesting! I never thought of that."

The following session Charles' fears of dying have intensified. We return to the theme of the previous session.

"I just keep thinking over and over that I'm going to die of a heart attack. I imagine that your husband had the chance to say good-bye, but that I won't, that I'll simply be gone. And I'm worried about losing you too. I'm worried that you'll want to get away from here, that you'll move and leave your practice. And then I'll die all alone."

"Have you thought, Charles, that you've won?" I ask. "My husband is dead and I'm here and you have me all to yourself?"

"I get anxious just hearing you say that! … I had another dream. I dreamt that we were in a session and that some man stormed into the office. He looked kind of scary, like a crazy, homeless person. I felt I had to protect you. But I was scared, real scared."

"Is that the frightening father? The father who returns to punish you for your victory?"

"I suppose. It does seem to follow."

Over the next several weeks Charles' fear of dying recedes. My sense, however, is that this issue has not been resolved, but rather put aside to appear again at another time. Perhaps its reappearance requires a time when my husband's death is less fresh and the fear/wish of Oedipal victory has less immediacy.

Some treatments were greatly affected by George's death, often in vastly different ways, for vastly different reasons. One of these I will chronicle in-depth in the following two chapters on the power of love and loss in an analytic treatment. At the moment, however, I turn to Christine, a forty-five-year-old vice-president of a large company, whose treatment was affected by George's death in that it allowed me to experience her in a different light and, by so doing, enabled me to facilitate her growth into a more feeling person.

At the time of George's death I had been seeing Christine for two years. Twice divorced, she has spent the last three years in and out of a relationship with Rick, a married man who has separated from his wife and gone back to her innumerable times. Christine complains bitterly about the back and forth, but is unable to definitively end the relationship. And when Rick is with her, she's not even sure that she wants him in her life. She thinks she loves him. But he can be very self-absorbed, short-tempered, and, at times, sharply critical.

She grew up as the oldest of two daughters, in a family that prided itself on success and achievement. Both her parents were attorneys. She describes herself as never getting along with her mother, who was always too busy with either her younger sibling or her career and who seemed to always have an antipathy towards Christine. Her father could be more loving, especially when pleased with Christine's accomplishments, but could also be harsh and angry and critical. We had come to talk about Christine's early childhood as lacking in any sense of being cherished.

In Christine's first session after George's death she asks how I'm doing and expresses her condolences. I feel, however, that we are not really connected, that there is a blandness or superficiality to the words. In the second session, I ask directly if and how my husband's death has affected her feelings about Rick.

"I don't know. I'm not sure I made much of a connection. I mean it's not the same circumstances. He was your husband and Rick isn't dying. My relationship with Rick is what it always is, in and out, in and out. I want to accept that it's never going anywhere and just get out."

I find myself very sad during this session. But given that sadness is a fairly prevalent feeling for me these days, I don't know whether I am feeling my own sadness or Christine's. Is it I who longs for connection and feels sad without it or is Christine unconsciously communicating her own unmet longing to me? At the moment, I do not know.

Before the next session I receive a card in the mail. Christine has made a donation in George's name. I'm initially surprised and then realize the donation is an easier, more impersonal way for Christine to express her feelings. I start the session by thanking her for her donation.

"Sure, no problem," she says, almost dismissively.

"What led you to make the donation?"

She looks startled. "I don't know. That's what people do. You lost your husband, I made a donation."

"But was the donation expressing any feelings you might be having?"

"Well, yeah, I felt bad for you."

"I don't mean to be hurtful, but you don't sound as though you feel bad for me. You sound as though you don't feel much of anything. In fact, I find myself wondering whether you feel afraid of my sadness and are running from it."

There is a long pause. Christine looks both thoughtful and sad. Finally she says, "I don't think it's that I'm afraid of your sadness. I don't think I feel your sadness at all. In fact, I don't think I feel my own sadness. I don't feel much of anything. I act. I do. I do what I'm supposed to do, like making a donation when someone dies. But feel it? I don't think so."

"I believe you. I hear you and I believe you. It's as though you turned off your feelings a long, long time ago and can't bear to feel all the loss of not being loved and cherished."

"Now I feel sad," she says. "I don't know why."

"Perhaps because you feel understood. Perhaps because you feel just an inkling of what you didn't get as a child."

This session proved to be a turning point in Christine's treatment. She increased the frequency of her sessions and set herself the task – still the task-setter – of feeling her feelings, however painful they might be. We learned that the relationship with Rick was both a way to focus on external problems as opposed to her own thoughts and feelings, as well as a safe relationship where she never had to risk being truly close and intimate. Our relationship deepened. I felt more genuine connection when she was in the room.

But then Christine had the opportunity for a further advancement in her career. She would have to move. I knew that Christine was far from ready to end treatment, but this was a decision only she could make. In the end, she decided to make the move. She saw it as a way to finally, finally be done with Rick.

"Do you also see it as a way to be done with me?" I ask.

"Oh! I don't think so!" she replies. "Leaving you feels like the hardest part of this decision. With maybe the weather being a distant second."

I talk about referring her to another analyst. She resists. She doesn't want to start over. She isn't ready to begin again. We try telephone sessions, a medium I've discovered works quite well with some patients. Not surprisingly, with Christine it works less well. She can too easily fall back into her distanced, non-feeling stance. I ask her to return to Florida for a week so that we can terminate in person. She does.

"It's good to see you," she says, smiling broadly. "I didn't know how I'd feel seeing you again. Whether it would feel strained, awkward. Except that seeing you reminds me that I won't be seeing you. I don't know, I don't think I'd really thought of that. It's as though I'd anticipated the meeting, but not the… I don't know."

"Not the what, Christine?" I ask gently.

"Not the loss. Not the good-bye. I've been so busy with my new life I really haven't thought much about myself. I've just been doing my thing – getting settled in my apartment, figuring out how to get around the city, learning what's expected of me in my new position. It was different on the phone. I never could get beyond all these mundane things."

"It's hard for you to remind yourself to stay in touch with your feelings."

"Yes, it is. And yet just seeing you, it all came back. I'm going to…" She smiles. "I almost didn't say what I thought of next. But I will. I'm going to say it. I'm going to miss you!"

"Thank you. I'm going to miss you too. And I do hope that you'll be able to figure out a way to hold onto your feelings, to remind yourself to feel, when you're not with me in my office."

"Yeah, that's definitely going to be my challenge."

Although clearly far from ready to end treatment, Christine has come a long way since George's death, becoming both more aware of her feelings and more able to express them. My experience of Christine in the sessions immediately following George's death allowed me to feel on a very personal level how removed Christine was from her feelings and to intervene in a way that allowed her to recognize her own difficulty in feeling either her own feelings or those of others. For Christine, working with both my disclosure and my feelings about George's death was helpful in advancing her treatment.

So what did I learn about self-disclosure in dealing with patients regarding George's illness and death? First I would say I learned that it is difficult to learn much of anything during periods of extreme stress and, in fact, that what I had learned earlier in my life was often totally absent from my mind. I say that not to excuse any lack of thoughtfulness on my part, but rather to illustrate, yet again, that analysts are only human beings who must try to stay mindful of their life difficulties and the impact such difficulties invariably have on their patients.

That having been said, I do believe that my previous thoughts about self-disclosure remain applicable, that analysts do want varying degrees of connection with and protection from patients. How much of each any therapist desires will depend upon her own dynamics, the current situation she finds herself in, and the particular patient–analyst dyad. For myself, when George was ill, my first response was to crave protection, to look to my time with patients as a way to escape from the unrelenting anxiety and worry of my daily life. However, once asked directly about my family medical emergencies I responded truthfully and then automatically assumed that I would answer similarly whenever asked, regardless of my relationship with any particular patient. This led to my difficulties with Bill whose intrusiveness and bombastic manner was difficult for me to tolerate. If I had considered more carefully who I might tell what, I might have had the forethought to conclude that I could comfortably share more with Don than with Bill. On the other hand, perhaps no amount of forethought would have accurately allowed me to predict the interaction that would have followed whatever disclosure I offered and that it is only hindsight that leads me to understand why some patients responded as they did. I do think, however, that just as when I was leaving Ann Arbor, my desire to be "fair" to all of my patients and to not treat one differently from another, ignored obvious patient differences and did not serve either me or my patients well.

Although I sought more protection during this most difficult time in my life, my desire for connection was also evident. My relationship with Stella, although itself laden with pain, brought both of us warmth, solace, and love. Stella herself died five months after George. I remained with her through the end, visiting her at home when she could no longer make the trip to my office. I held her hand as she lay in bed shriveled to half her already small size. Although angry about both her pain and her impending death, she took comfort from both my presence and her awareness of the pain I too bore.

With Stella my need for connection took precedence over my need for protection and proved to be helpful to both of us, nurturing us through the process of living, dying, and grieving. In this instance, I have no doubt that my self-disclosure was helpful to Stella. With some other patients the outcome was similarly positive, while with others the results were either not as clear or not positive at all. Might

Bill have remained in treatment if I had not disclosed George's illness and not felt as intruded upon by his unwanted comments? Was Don helped or harmed, opened up or inhibited by his awareness of George's medical condition and eventual death? Did Charles' knowledge of George's death and subsequent intensification of his Oedipal conflict facilitate or stymie the treatment? These are all questions that are difficult if not impossible to answer. And if they cannot be answered in hindsight, how much more difficult to attempt to anticipate beforehand what the results might be. Still, I do regret that I did not give more thought to both what I did or did not want to tell some or all of my patients and how I thought my disclosure might affect them. Interestingly, I did struggle with this question with Stella when I debated in my mind whether telling her of my husband's physical battles would have a helpful or deleterious effect on her. In her case, I feel I definitely made the correct decision. But with most patients I responded more spontaneously, more in line with how I was feeling at that particular moment, with that particular patient. As a whole, I feel that I dealt with my patients as thoughtfully and conscientiously as I could given my life circumstances. And, although there were some exceptions, I do believe that most of my patients who knew about George's illness and death grew through the experience of taking that journey with me.

With no one is that more true than with Caroline, whose story is told in the following two chapters.

8

THE POWER OF LOVE AND LOSS IN A PSYCHOANALYTIC TREATMENT

Looking Back

It is a month since George died. Caroline Feldman walks into my office. Since half her analysis is conducted by phone, this in the first time we have actually seen each other since his death. She gives me a big hug and, for the first time since we began treatment almost five years ago, she sits across from me in the chair.

"We can talk about it if you like," she says, "but I wanted to take you in. I woke up in the middle of the night last night and sat up in bed and thought, "I can't turn my back on Linda.""

We both fight back tears.

Caroline is a different person from the one who initially entered my office in December of 2002. How she evolved into the person she is today and how she continues to evolve is very much the story of the developing closeness and love in our relationship, a story that is itself much influenced and affected by George's illness and death.

I clearly remember the woman who first came to see me, a woman perched at the edge of the brown club chair, hands folded primly in her lap, with perfectly coifed white hair, a beige, long-sleeved blouse, and tailored tan slacks. Although I am generally not attuned to designer fashion, even before Caroline uttered her first word, I suspected that she was a woman of means, her clothes tastefully expensive, not flashy, but expensive.

In what I will come to know as Caroline's style, she speaks clearly and distinctly, providing much clarifying detail. "I'm sixty-one and I've been depressed most of my life. I've been in all sorts of therapy from cognitive behavioral to past life regression. I've done meditation, hypnotism, acupuncture. But the depression always comes back. Or maybe I should say it never goes away. I've been on medication – Prozac, Paxil – and it does help, but I'd like not to go back on it. It ruins my sex drive and I'd like to have more of a sex life with my husband.

"And I always seem to get more depressed when I'm in Florida. I'm from North Carolina, you see, from Charlotte. We split our time between the two, though we're probably in Charlotte a bit more. Anyway, my husband and I – my husband more than me – we're pretty well known in Charlotte. Milton – that's my husband – made a lot of money in real estate and we're very philanthropic, particularly in the Jewish community – but not exclusively, we give to education and the arts as well. Anyway, here in Florida, no one knows us, no one knows me, so I suppose that I feel less appreciated, less important."

"Are you saying that you feel less nurtured, less fed?" I ask, trying to get beyond Caroline's words to what she might be feeling underneath.

"Yes, I suppose you could say that," she answers. Cocking her head slightly to one side, she looks at me more intently and settles back into the chair. She continues.

"I'm sure the depression is chemical. It runs in my family. Both my mother and sister are bipolar. One of my sisters, the other is just depressed. I have two older sisters and one younger brother. So I'm obviously the third girl, which I'm sure tells you how important I was in that family."

"So being in Florida reminds you of being back in your family, unimportant," I say. There is something distancing about Caroline's recitation, almost as though she is telling a story about people other than herself and her family, people in whom she is vaguely disinterested or perhaps even contemptuous. Still, so far I find myself liking her well enough. I feel no antipathy, no regret that she has crossed my threshold. But I also do not feel immediately and powerfully drawn to her. Perhaps like the patient, I am not fully engaged and have taken a wait and see attitude. I want more of a sense of who she is, more of a sense of her humanity.

"Yes, that's true. I hadn't thought of it like that, but, yes, that's right." After a pause she continues.

"You certainly couldn't say I had a happy childhood. First of all my parents were Jews from Brooklyn who moved to Charlotte wanting to become Southern gentry. And they became Christian Scientists. It wasn't good. We continued to live in the Jewish community, but we weren't Jewish. And the Jewish community never forgave us. They saw us as traitors. So we didn't fit in anywhere. Daddy wasn't around much. He traveled a lot. When he was there he always deferred to Mother anyway. As for her, she vacillated between being grandiose, having wonderful, stupendous ideas, to being utterly depressed, locking herself in her bedroom. She also had a violent temper. It wasn't much directed my way. I learned from Betty, she's the sister just older than me – actually we're all five years apart – it was Mother's five year plan – Betty always took Mother on and always got beaten for it. I was the good girl. I wanted to be Mother's favorite. Mother would always talk about my being 'God's perfect child,' and that's what I wanted to be, 'God's perfect child.' Mother's still alive by the way. She's ninety-two and as impossible as always. She lives in a retirement community – that I pay for, of course – and I still do her bidding."

"You sound angry." I am relieved at the expression of a more intense, genuine feeling.

"You could say that," she says, nodding her head vigorously. "I'm angry at her for being her usual demanding, impossible-to-please self, and at me for still caring! You'd think by sixty-one I would have learned!"

"So it's hard for you to feel compassion for yourself."

"Compassion?" she says, scornfully. "Yes, it's very difficult for me to feel any compassion for myself. Truthfully, I'm as critical as my mother. I focus on little things,

things that don't matter at all, like what someone is wearing or how their house is decorated, and pick at them and pick at them. In my mind, of course. I don't mean I tell them. That would be far too unladylike, definitely not a genteel Southern lady."

"But what I'm suggesting is that you turn that criticalness on yourself as well. That you're critical of yourself, just as she was critical of you."

"I do find it difficult to be kind to myself. But then again there are so many reasons I have not to be kind to myself."

"Such as?"

"Well, I haven't done anything with my life. I do have a Master's and I did teach English for a number of years, but basically I've done nothing with my life but live off Milton's money and flit from one thing to another. I'm a total dilettante. And," she continues, taking a big sigh, "There's Alexa. Alexa is my daughter from my first marriage, my only child. I had her when I was twenty-one. Her father was twenty. Obviously I was pregnant when I got married. Milton and I couldn't have children, although he adopted Alexa and was the father who raised her. She's a delight – a lawyer, a successful businesswoman – she's in the business with Milton now – a wonderful mother of three and a respected woman in the community. I had been involved in the business earlier myself, but I stepped aside to make room for Alexa. Anyway, I was married to Greg for five terrible years and I was a horrible mother. When they put me in the stirrups to deliver, I said, no, there must be some mistake and started to get down. I just couldn't love her, not when she was little. Now I adore her. But it's too late. I know she doesn't forgive me. And she shouldn't. But she won't talk about it. She says everything turned out fine. Except it didn't. Somehow we can't be close."

"It sounds sad for you."

"Not as sad as for Alexa."

"There's not much forgiveness in your life. The Jewish community didn't forgive you for becoming Christian Scientists, Alexa can't forgive you, you can't forgive your mother, and you certainly can't forgive yourself."

"Yes, I suppose that's true. I know I keep myself apart. I don't trust anyone, not really. Except for Milton. Milton is always in my corner, he always worries about me, he's always there for me," Caroline says, brightening considerably.

"Sounds like you have a good marriage."

"It's a great marriage, a far better marriage than I deserve. I was destitute when Milton came calling. And that's what he did, he came calling. He was the true Southern gentleman. He's fifteen years older than me and he'd never been married. He was too busy building his business and now he wanted a wife and family. I was beautiful back then, and although I certainly didn't have the pedigree, I did have the looks and the manners. And I was a quick study. I learned everything I needed to know to be a good wife to him. He adopted Alexa – that was a messy business – and although it wasn't all easy – Milton can have quite a temper – we became a family. And I got to reclaim my Jewishness."

Talking rapidly, Caroline continues. "Milton was never the best lover I had and it's certainly slowed down since he's gotten older. As I said, I wanted to stay off antidepressants so that I'd have more of a drive to approach him. That's what we do. I go into his bedroom and cozy up to him."

"You go into his bedroom? Do the two of you not sleep together?" I ask, trying, somewhat unsuccessfully, to keep the surprise from my voice.

"No. We haven't slept together for years. Milton snores and I have difficulty sleeping under the best of circumstances, so we've found it works best to just have two separate bedrooms."

"So you feel close to Milton, but keep yourself apart from others. Does your criticalness serve to keep you apart?"

"Most definitely." Caroline concurs.

"And that increases your sense of aloneness, isolation, and then depression."

"Yes, that's it."

"Well, sounds as though we know what we need to work on – your criticalness – towards both yourself and others – your desire to be close to people and your fear of being close and learning to be more forgiving – again, both to yourself and others."

"And I don't want to be at the end of my life, to be on my deathbed and think, 'Is this all?'"

In the second session I experience Caroline's criticalness first hand.

"This is hard for me to talk about – my Southern upbringing says one should always be polite – but I know that here I'm supposed to talk about whatever comes to mind and I have to tell you your office is very off-putting. At least to me that is. It's not at all how I expected an analyst's office to be. I thought it would be elegant: a mahogany desk, built-in bookshelves, wood floors, antique Oriental rugs, a black leather couch, and African sculptures artistically arranged throughout."

Well, I think to myself, that's certainly not a description of my office: beige carpeted floors, one free-standing formica maroon bookshelf that matches my desk, a brown and white fabric couch and no African sculptures. Mexican and Haitian prints line the walls, but I suspect these are not to her liking.

She continues.

"And your waiting room is even worse, very uninviting. It's so barren. Why would you only have one picture? And those chairs look like they came out of somebody's basement."

They came from Bloomingdale's, I think to myself. Her criticisms are beginning to rankle.

"What does it mean to you to not like my office, to criticize it?" I ask.

"Part of me feels liberated, like I don't have to be the good girl here, I get to say whatever. But part of me feels great shame. Like why do I care? Why do these superficial things matter to me? Isn't your skill, your professional training far more important?"

"So in being critical you get to break out of your role of having to be the good girl?" I ask.

"Yes. But there's a problem with that. Because I hate myself. I hate myself for picking apart this nonsense. And I sound just like my mother, who now puts on all these airs, as if she didn't come from nothing, as if all her little luxuries aren't the result of my largess."

"You sound very angry."

"I am. I hate her! But the problem is I hate myself too!"

"So you hate your mother and you hate the mother who walks around in your head, the mother you've become like."

"Yes, that's it exactly. And why do I care about all these superficial things?"

"Well," I ask gently, "why do you, why do you think these things matter to you?"

Silence

"I feel a tremendous amount of shame about my early upbringing," Caroline says. "About never having enough, about always being on the outside, never being accepted, so when I'm the fancy lady, I get to feel, aha! I'm now the one who has the power, I have the power to reject you."

"So it's an expression of your anger and a way of retaliating for all your past hurts."

"Exactly! But it doesn't work. Because I'm not really this fancy lady, that's not who I feel like inside, so I'm just presenting this phony person and I don't ever really feel known or accepted."

"And inside?" I ask.

"I'm empty. I'm a shell."

"Sounds pretty sad," I say.

Silence.

"I know that all we've said is important. And true. But it doesn't change my feelings about your office. It's tacky. It doesn't give a good first impression. I would have thought you could do better."

I am aware of feeling somewhat deflated, not devastated, but deflated. I hoped for a more positive response to my intervention, but Caroline does not deliver.

Despite Caroline's reaction to my office – or perhaps because of her freedom to give voice to both her criticalness and shame – she soon asked to move to twice a week and then to a three times a week analysis. I was initially reluctant to begin an analysis with Caroline ostensibly because more than half the analysis would have to be conducted by phone. My reluctance, however, may also have mirrored Caroline's own conflict between closeness and distancing with, in this instance, my playing the role of the rejecting – or at least reluctant – parent, rather than the rejected child. It was a role that could switch in an instant, with Caroline as the rejecting parent criticizing some facet of my furnishings or, as the needy child, requiring that I live "a monastic life in the office" so that she could feel "safe." In the end I agreed to an analysis, with the caveat that we would have to see how the phone sessions worked out.

So the treatment begins:

"I had a dream about toilets last night. In real life, when we were children Mother would put each of us on the toilet and we'd have to sit there until we took a shit. Then she'd come inspect it before we could flush the toilet. If you didn't have to go you'd just sit there. I used to turn around and play with the knick-knacks behind the toilet.

I'd make up stories, just to keep myself entertained. In the dream, I was in a house with a man friend and his father. I went to a huge bathroom and I poured menstrual blood and shit. My friend wanted to help, but his father was disgusted. It reminds me of how betrayed I felt when I got my period and Mother told Daddy. I didn't want her to tell him. It was embarrassing, embarrassing like when I was in my ballet outfit. I wanted to dance for Daddy. I wanted him to see how pretty I was. I came prancing and pirouetting down our staircase. Everyone was at the table at dinner and started laughing at me. It was awful. I felt so deflated. But it wasn't always that way," Caroline adds with a smile in her voice. "There was the time – I was older though I don't remember exactly how old – I was with Mother and Daddy at a theater or something and we were waiting to pick up our coats. I was standing behind them and I overheard Daddy whisper to Mother, 'She doesn't look Jewish.' I knew they were talking about me. And I knew that somehow this was a good thing, that Daddy was pleased with me, pleased that I didn't look Jewish."

"So it sounds as though your father was both figures in the dream, the Daddy who is disgusted by you, who laughs at you and the Daddy who accepts, who wants to help."

"Yes, that definitely makes sense."

"But I wonder if I'm also both figures in the dream. Here you are, spewing out all your blood and shit and you're wondering if I'm going to applaud or laugh at you."

"I think you're right. I have so little to offer. I'm not smart enough. I haven't done anything with my life. All I do is shop. And I hate myself for it. I shop and shop and shop, just to fill myself up. And then after I do it it's just like if you've been on an eating binge. It makes me totally sick. Seriously, I actually get physically nauseous. So I take the stuff and stick it in the back of the closet and try to pretend it isn't there. What's there to love?"

"So shopping becomes a replacement for love, a way to try and fill yourself up."

"Yes, and of course it doesn't work. But I can't go back either, I can't have a do over. And even if that were possible, it's not like mother would be any different. She's not any different now. She sits in her room, holding court, waiting for us or for one of the aides to come calling, to do her bidding. Her bedspread has to be perfectly made so that the medallion sits perfectly in the middle, an inch off one way or the other is definitely not permissible. Each of her shoes – shoes she never wears any more – are in separate plastic bags, placed just so in her closet. She rules her compact domain just as she ruled our household. And I'm the same too. I'm the pleaser, the fetcher. I get to bring her just the toothpaste she wants, only a certain kind of mouthwash, only a certain size. She could buy all these things at the commissary of her retirement home, but no, she wants me to bring them. And I do, the supplicant, still trying to please. I never learn. I see some little trinket or a sweet and think, I'll bring this to mother. And she never wants it, she always rejects it, always in her sweet, phony voice. 'Oh, I don't need it, I have no place for it.' Or, 'We get plenty of sweets with our meals. I wouldn't want to lose my girlish figure.' I get so mad just talking about it. I don't know why I keep trying."

"You keep trying to win your mother's love."

"But it's so futile," she says plaintively. "The only one of us that got mother's love was Robert, the anointed boy, mother's pride and joy. It's a miracle he's not a horribly obnoxious man. But he's not. He's very sweet. I hate her. And I hate myself."

"So you feel angry with your mother for not loving you and you feel angry with yourself for wanting that love, angry rather than having compassion for the deprived, needy child."

"I hate her. I have no compassion for her. I want her to grow up already and accept the realities of life."

"So you treat that needy, child part of yourself just like your mother did, rejecting her rather than embracing her."

She sighs. "Yes, I suppose you're right. I do want mother to love me. And I hear you, I need to be more accepting of that part of myself as well – I almost said sniveling part."

"Do you feel that anyone loves you?"

"I do know that Milton loves me. He doesn't believe in saying it; he thinks words are too easy, that he shows me by how he provides for me and how he cares for me. And it's true. He does love me. I know he can get really angry sometimes, although not usually at me. And he's totally and completely rejecting of my family. He won't have anything to do with them. I don't like it, but I've grown to live with it. He's definitely the only person who's ever loved me. No one else in my life ever cared for me; no one else ever loved me. I don't know what I'll do when he's gone. I mean, he's very healthy, but I still worry about his dying. I worry about how alone and bereft I'll feel when he's gone. I worry I'll be all alone in the world."

My reverie leads me to compare myself with Caroline. With all my mother's shortcomings, I never questioned her love for me. As unable as she was to protect me from my father, she gave me a strong foundation, one that let me know that I was loved and valued and that my being in the world mattered. Although I spent many years chasing after my father's love and approval both directly and through a long line of narcissistic men, I had finally been able to feel the impossibility of ever achieving that goal. I had been able to give up hope and to find and choose George, a man who easily expressed his deep feelings of love and devotion. I did, of course, strongly identify with Caroline's fear of losing Milton, reverberating to her words about feeling alone and bereft once he died. In retrospect, I believe that, in time, Caroline's ability to capture in words both her feelings and mine were to form the bedrock of our ever increasing connection to each other. But that was unknown to me at the time, far away from where we were at this early point of the treatment.

Bringing myself back to the session, I say, "You're wondering whether I'll care for you, whether I'll love you."

"Well, not love me, I wouldn't expect that, I wouldn't even think that's appropriate. But I do want to be your best patient, your best student. I do want to be worth your time."

I've scared her. Love is too big a word. It's way too early to be talking about love.

So, at the beginning of treatment, we see a Caroline who felt depressed, angry, unfulfilled, isolated, unloved and unlovable. Her ambivalence about getting close to me was clear. Caroline wanted me to be her neutral and unknown analyst, a role I felt completely comfortable in fulfilling. Since George more than fulfilled my need for closeness, I felt no press to push for greater connectedness with Caroline. I also experienced Caroline and myself as very different. We came from different backgrounds, had different experiences with our respective parents and lived extremely different lives in the present. We were both married to older men, but the similarity seemed to end there. I did resonate with Caroline's thoughts about Milton's death and her fears of feeling bereft and forlorn, but at the time that Caroline began treatment with me George was well and my concerns about loss and death were not center stage.

As detailed in the previous chapter, however, that was soon to change, a change that was foreshadowed by George and my vacation in the fall of 2003.

Twenty-four years earlier, two years before we were married, George and I took our first European trip, visiting Spain and Morocco. We had, however, never seen Barcelona or northern Spain and planned this current trip to correct that omission. Barcelona brought all that we had hoped – the cosmopolitan atmosphere of a major city, fabulous food, the massive and fanciful architecture of Gaudi, and incredible museums filled with Picasso and Joan Miró. But the years had worn on George. Although steadfast and determined as always, it was soon apparent that he did not have the stamina he brought to earlier trips. On the first day, after a long walk both to and through the Picasso Museum, George was tired. "I'm not tired," he assured me. "My legs are tired." This was typical of our days in Barcelona. George's legs or back began hurting after one museum, or one walk, or one church. And the effect was cumulative. We accommodated. We took more taxis. We took shorter walks, had longer lunches, and more rest time before dinner. One day I left George in our hotel room and took a walk through the downtown area on my own. I was painfully aware of my singleness. Everyone seemed to be in groups or in couples. I wondered what the future held. When would George be unable to make these trips? When would he no longer be here to make any trips at all? I hurried back to the room, into his welcoming arms and, for the moment, tried to put my fears at bay.

Much of Caroline's treatment focused on her need to both protect and hide the deprived, needy, greedy child inside of her. On the one hand she feared that this part of her could be mortally hurt, while on the other hand she was terrified that it could and would devour anyone and anything in her path. Feeling unloved and insufficient from birth, Caroline had closed off her needy childhood self, becoming "an empty shell," while her underlying desire for love festered, feeling increasingly dangerous and destructive (Fairbairn, 1941; Guntrip, 1968). As a result, much, although certainly not all, of our work involved her swinging like a pendulum between allowing herself to be closer to me and then reacting against that closeness by pulling away to a place that felt as though it offered greater safety.

Caroline welcomes me back from vacation. "I felt you were with me the whole time, although I needed to keep myself quiet. I wanted to make sure that nothing bad happened. It was safer to disappear. I don't want to expose the vulnerable me, the me that wanted to dance for Daddy and have him take me on his knee and say 'you're my precious baby' and have everyone look on. Instead I danced and got laughed at. I feel sad and sorry for that little girl."

"It's really good that you can feel sorry for that part of you, rather than hating yourself."

"Yes, that is good. I can feel how it feels different."

Reading a book by Bonnie Friedman, Caroline resonates with the author's description of having some key part of herself be kidnapped, of having her voice imprisoned. Caroline says that her own voice is starting to talk now that she knows she has someone to listen. "It makes me feel less empty, less hollow," she says.

But still she resists: "It's not pleasant to need anyone."

Back and forth she swings. She is more aware of her attachment to me, more aware of the needy little child inside her, and more aware of her underlying sadness. On the other hand, she still hates to need, feels humiliated by that need, and continues to reject the "baby" in her.

At the same time, her feelings about her relationship with Milton also fluctuate. "I felt sad when I came back from a quick trip to New York with Milton. I decided to feel it rather than just getting busy. I lay down in the window seat where I talk to you and gave myself permission to feel sad. Milton feels more aged to me. I felt tender toward him. I was pleased to feel tender, rather than impatient."

During another session, however, she says, "I miss the aliveness. There's a quality of youth and juiciness that seems gone. It's like a harbinger of old age and death. I don't want to have to go into Milton's bedroom at night. I don't want to because I will come to rely on him. And then he'll be gone."

How differently Caroline and I respond to our husbands' increasing frailty, I think. She withdraws in an effort to protect herself, while I cling all the more tightly, as if my presence alone could magically thwart George's death.

Caroline's progress continues. She talks about being nurtured by me and feels less humiliated by her need for that nurturing. She also recognizes that she can be kinder to others and, sometimes, even to herself.

The issue of love comes up once again. "I want more," Caroline says. "I want what I didn't get. What I really want is love."

"From me?" I ask.

"It's not appropriate to look for love from you. I definitely feel cared about by you. And that matters. It most definitely matters."

Although Caroline's response is not so different than it was when she first started treatment, there is a softer quality to it, more inviting, less distancing. And soon after she reports the following dream:

"I am a grown-up, but a young adult, twenty-five to thirty-five. I'm in a dorm setting or a hotel, not my own home. I'm given a room. In the small hallway there's a little girl who's crazy. I don't want to be near her, but I am. The little girl is screaming, running up and down the walls like a bug, trying to get out. We have an adjoining room and I'm trying to lock the door and the door won't shut. Then the scene shifts. The same dorm setting with college age girls, like a sorority setting. This same little girl is sitting in the bed across from me and she's calm. The little girl is content, she's quiet. She's loved. She just needed to be loved. I wake up and think I need to tell Linda. That child was wild with anger, trying to get out and I was scared to death of her. Locking her up seemed the thing to do. But with you I'm learning to be less afraid of that little girl, more able to let her out, more able to care for her so that she's not so desperately crazed."

Later, Caroline reports having a tender moment with Milton when listening to a song with the lyrics, "Don't go changing just for me, I love you just the way you are." Then she finds herself crying.

"Crying for whom?" I ask.

"For that little girl. It's a terrible loss to be that little girl and not know that you're loved just for who you are."

But in the next session, Caroline again talks about her fear of needing. "It's like wanting to eat everything in the refrigerator. The want is huge and could engulf me. I can do that with you too. If you were gone six months, I'd say it's fine, but then I'd shut the door completely. I know you say, 'Tis better to have loved and lost than never to have loved at all,' but I don't do that. It's better to have not loved and not lost."

Oh no! I think to myself, feeling incredibly sad, both for myself and Caroline. It is definitely better to have loved and lost. I could not imagine what my life would have been like had George not been a part of it, how devoid of love and pleasure and richness. My heart breaks knowing that I will lose George, but I would not trade places with Caroline. I would not want to have steeled myself against connection for fear of eventual loss and I do hope that this is a place where Caroline will one day arrive.

When Caroline makes plans to return to Charlotte at the end of April 2005, she acknowledges feeling anxious about being apart from me, knows that her feelings are different from last year, and realizes that this signifies a change for her. Once home, Caroline feels glad to have returned, but wishes she had me with her. I suggest she feels less given to by me on the phone. "I feel more embraced by you in the office." Fears and defenses notwithstanding, Caroline is definitely moving closer and I am pleased and welcoming.

A year goes by. For me it is a year of watching George decline further physically, being more preoccupied with his health, and somewhat curtailing the scope of our lives. For Caroline, the reverse is true. She is becoming more alive, more able to feel, and more engaged with both organizations and people in her life, including me.

She and I have a greater sense of connectedness. Despite the external differences in our lives, I am struck these days more by our similarities. One month before she is to leave Milton to go on an overseas trip with Alexa and her family, a time that coincidentally coincides with the first of George's chemo treatments, she reports the following dream:

"It was a sweet dream. I was in a shop. Milton was with me. We're about to leave. I notice that the back of Milton's jacket is threadbare or ripped at the seams. I think, 'Maybe the jacket is important to Milton. Doesn't he want a new one or does he really like it and should I have it rewoven?' I was pleased with my response. I was more understanding. I connected to my own sense of value."

"The plaid jacket? The woven jacket?" I ask.

"The jacket was beautiful quality. It was old. It was loved. … Perhaps it's a metaphor for Milton."

My eyes fill with tears. I'm grateful to be on the phone, unseen. I marvel at how Caroline can capture in a brief metaphor not only her feelings, but my own. Beautiful quality. Old. Loved. My George.

Caroline continues, "I so like my kindness towards him. I help him downstairs. He seems not steady, like he could tumble. I'm protective of him. It's a relief to feel that way towards him, the loving concern and to know that even unconsciously I have that capacity."

By the time Caroline returns from her trip, George has had his first chemo, his heart attack and his near-brush with death. As she describes missing Milton, it is all I can do to keep myself from weeping. "I missed Milton so much. I missed being cared about. I missed having a peer. I missed having a buddy. I missed someone who missed me in the same way. I missed someone who truly loved me. And I knew I was going home to Milton. What will it be like when there is no Milton to go home to?"

And, several weeks later: "I went to an old friend's funeral this morning, an old dear friend. I had a sudden wish that I still had God as I had God as a child, God as a palpable caregiver. God was my biggest protector as a child. That's sad. I wondered if after I married Milton, Milton became God – paternal, always there, loving. And then I thought about Milton's death, about whether that will be like losing God all over again. I also had a memory of my childhood home hovering over me. No, that's not right. The memory was more solid and the house was behind me, not over me. It was behind me like you sit behind me. And I was looking forward to a homecoming. When I pictured myself walking inside, nobody's home. I'm alone in the house, but there's still the security of a place to go."

Caroline's story and mine were coming ever closer together. We both yearned for the safety of home and the protection of the kind, loving father. At this point Caroline consciously knew nothing of what was going on in my personal life. What she intuited on an unconscious level is of course impossible to know. I do believe that Caroline's ability to express both of our deepest feelings – the dread, the longing, and the love – was, in the end, what led to our blossoming connection. It was as though her language was poetry, providing a direct access to the unconscious, facilitating a depth of feeling of both self and other not consciously available (Akhtar, 2000). This depth of connection led her to feel known and understood by me and eventually made me want to be known and understood by her. My growing concerns about George's illness and possible imminent death made me all the more raw and especially attuned to longings for safety and protection, as well as to the fragility of life and the need to find meaning and fulfillment and connection. As I faced the ever increasing reality of George's death, my need for connection with Caroline may have increased as well. If this need was unconsciously communicated and if my need did not feel overwhelming, Caroline may have taken solace in the unconscious awareness that she was not the only frightened, needy person in the room. Perhaps some of her shame about needing could dissipate. Perhaps she could come to see the need for connection not as a weakness, but as a strength and a testament to what it means to be truly human. And perhaps as I struggled with my overwhelming sadness anticipating George's death, she could move closer to feeling that the joy of love did outweigh the pain of loss.

On the other side of the equation, two concerns can be raised. First, did my feelings overshadow the sessions, determining the direction the treatment took and making it difficult to know whether the feelings in the room were mine or Caroline's? Second, did my current life experience present an extra burden to Caroline, forcing her to deal with my feelings and my problems, rather than her own? My response, at least for this portion of the treatment is, I don't think so. For the most part, until George's death, my work with patients still seemed like a welcome respite to the intense anxiety and pain of my personal life. I had no wish for my problems to be the focus of the treatment. I wanted my patients to talk about themselves, to take me away from myself. The one significant exception was that, at times, when I felt particularly moved by Caroline's expression of sadness or longing or anticipated loss, such as the session reported above, I knew that there would come a time when I would want to tell Caroline about my journey through George's illness and death. Was this an anticipation of my need for greater connectedness? Quite possibly. Whether it benefited or harmed the treatment is something I will return to in the next chapter when I explore Caroline and my relationship after George's death. And that death, although I of course could not know that at the time, was a year away.

In October of 2006, Caroline had one of the most significant dreams of her treatment, a dream we came to call "the closet dream" and one that we returned to again and again.

"I enter my childhood bedroom. There's nothing in there except a single bed. The room is spartan. There are wooden floors. Where's my stuff? I'm alarmed. Where's my computer? Where's my chest of drawers? In real life we had weekly inspections of our drawers to make sure everything was folded just so. I run into my parent's room. Mother is puzzled at my dismay. She doesn't know where my stuff is, it's not important to her. Perhaps she says that they needed the chest of drawers. Or that they took it apart to be refinished. But where's my stuff? I must find my computer. My computer holds everything about me. It seems we do find my laptop. I'm relieved and take it to my room. As I'm leaving, Daddy says, 'You don't need anything anyway. You still have your closet. Go back to your room.' I open the closet. I gasp. It's completely bare. There's nothing there. The paint has faded. The wood is distressed. It's old. I feel a sadness and a gentle tenderness. When I get my things, I think, I'll just lay them on the floor. I'll keep them with me. I'll have them even if I have only the floor. I sit in the closet and sob. Daddy appears in the doorway. He's angry. 'Stop your sobbing,' he says. I feel threatened. I wake up." She pauses, the room laden with a heavy sadness. "There are no words," she continues. "This is why I shop. I will never have enough stuff. It seems like such an important dream – such an impoverished childhood. How silly that I would think I could fill that closet, that I could fill the void."

"There's so much sadness in that dream. That there's no place for you but the closet, no place for your things but the floor," I say trying, however unsuccessfully, to put the despair of Caroline's dream into words.

"I wish I could cry like that child in the dream. My father was also Milton who can't allow tears. And the computer was my insides, everything I know. It was such a relief to find it. But I wasn't cradling the computer. The computer was all I had, all that was left to me. And I took it and went into the closet and made the closet my house, my special place."

"The emotional void in that dream is so overwhelming."

"After that dream I thought, 'You'll never, ever fill up the emptiness. It doesn't matter how much you talk to Linda, you'll never fill that loss.' And the future looks as bleak as the past. The world without Milton is the world without love. I wondered if I could be in your office and sit in a corner and just sob and sob. If you came over to comfort me, I'd push you away. I cannot be stroked. When I'm that vulnerable, it would just be pity."

Although it is obvious that Caroline and I still have much work to do, that she remains terrified of her needy self banished to the closet, I do take some hope from this despairing dream. At least Caroline now knows the sad, deprived, yearning child inside her. She still may not be able to cradle her, she still may not be able to give to her, but she knows of her existence and does feel some compassion for that part of herself.

And that little girl continues to make her appearance. Some three months later, Caroline reports the following dream: "I've come to look for a little girl, three or four, who was angry or upset or something. She's hiding under the bed. I lift up the duster and see her lying on her back. She has her dress up and diapers on. I ask if she wants me to change her diaper and she says, no, but I check them anyway, very gently and discreetly. I'm maternal. I'm both mother and child in the dream. She makes a move to come out, but in order to do so she has to pick up something like a chicken wire and crawl out from under it. Either I'm helping or I'm not helping because she has to do it herself. Something about the fencing feels both dangerous and protective. I'm happy or relieved that she's willing to come out. It's important that she not hurt herself."

Although Caroline is indeed both mother and child in this dream, a dream in which protection is still required, although that protection is far more porous, I am also the mother. I am the person who must be careful and patient as Caroline makes her way out from under the bed. I am also the person who can help to make the world she enters into as safe as possible. It is a role I may have fulfilled without realizing it when I inadvertently "stepped aside" to make room for Caroline in the psychoanalytic writing program from which I had graduated and frequently returned as an alumnus. Definitely going outside the analytic frame, I had told Caroline about this program, knowing that she was very interested in writing and increasingly interested in psychoanalysis. I thought that it was a program where she could shine and alleviate some of her doubts about her intellect. What I didn't know when I initially told her about the program was that George would become increasingly ill and that I would become a non-participant for a number of years.

Early on in the treatment, Caroline had told me that she had "stepped aside" to make room for Alexa in Milton's business. What I would later realize was that Caroline had great conflict around competition, Oedipal strivings, and either winning or losing. She always wanted to appease her mother, a woman she experienced as beautiful, dangerous, and prone to violent outbursts. She also desperately wanted to be Daddy's little girl, the girl who "didn't look Jewish," but she couldn't reliably count on him and she couldn't afford to antagonize her mother. She had a small part in a high school play and when she stole the show from the leading lady, she never tried out for a part again. She was a self-described "dilettante," someone who would immerse herself in an activity, become good at it, and then withdraw. When I "stepped aside" to make room for Caroline, we were able to see her competitive strivings, her wish to be best and her sense of fulfillment and satisfaction upon completing the three-year program with the appreciation and respect of many. Unlike her mother, I could cheer her on and applaud her success.

In May of 2007 Caroline comes down to see me for the first visit of that year's summer break.

"I'm feeling Milton's loss as the powerful man he was," she says. "And I so fear his absence after he dies. Sometimes I think about what I'd do if he died before my mother. That seems intolerable. Not only unfair, but intolerable. I couldn't stand that. Not having Milton and having to deal with my mother!"

I'm struck by how astonishingly similar we've become and how even our life issues have come to coincide. Although I certainly don't share the very negative feelings Caroline does for her mother, I do feel certain that George will die before my presently ninety-seven-year-old mother. And although I can usually accept the randomness of the cards that life deals, I find myself piqued by this seeming unfairness.

When Caroline returns to North Carolina the theme continues:

"I felt I had a good week in Boca. But it did feel lonely, more like a stopover. It felt empty. I'm not going to stay in Boca after Milton is gone. Life there doesn't feel as though it has any texture. It feels dead. But, who knows, maybe I will stay there. Maybe it will be comforting. Maybe a smaller place in the same community. Or maybe I'll have three places – North Carolina, New York, and Boca. I'll need to go from place to place to stave off the loneliness. But there would still be the emptiness of walking into the house. I keep thinking about the song, 'I'll be seeing you in all the old familiar places.' I live the moment again and again. I wallow in it."

"No, I don't think so," I say tearing up. "You're rehearsing." I'm all too familiar with such a rehearsal. "You're imagining and preparing yourself. Although you can't, of course, not really," I say, talking to myself as well as Caroline.

"I've gotten morose. I don't want to do that with you. And I also don't want to be constantly rehearsing our ending either, the one you and I will eventually have. I always told myself I'd work with you for seven years. It pleases me how far I've come since I began. How much more understanding I have. How much more encouraged I am and you should be too."

As I type this session today, I wonder about Caroline's sudden shift in focus and her strikingly more upbeat tone. I wonder if at some level she sensed my own despair, felt that it was I who had become too morose. Perhaps she feared inflicting additional pain on me, both because it felt aggressive and because she unconsciously feared rendering me an ineffective analyst/caretaker. So instead she declared herself too morose and sought to save us both by turning to her progress and towards greater optimism.

In line with this optimism, Caroline's life involvements, including the psychoanalytic writing program, continued to expand. In addition to the literary prize she endowed, the political candidates she supported and the philanthropic organizations whose boards she sat on, Caroline underwrites a building for international studies at a prominent university. She is excited and proud. And I am her most ardent champion.

At the end of July 2007, George crashes for what will be the last time. His cancer has returned to being hormone resistant, his PSA numbers are increasing, along with his pain and his fatigue. Although I have incorrectly anticipated his death in the past, I watch him growing more and more weary and doubt that he will persevere for much longer.

Caroline reports the following dream: "I was in my early forties. I was with my husband, perhaps my first husband, Greg. We weren't married in the dream but we were definitely together. There was a doctor there. I say, 'I'm going to have a baby by that method where there's an injection of a fetus. Time is running out. I don't have a womb anymore, but it's okay because this new procedure will allow you to grow my egg somehow.'"

Struggling to stay focused on Caroline's associations to this dream, rather than my own, I ask, "Time is running out?"

"Alexa's children are growing up. I don't have time to form a close relationship with them and time is getting short with Milton. I think how it will feel to live without him. Not having him to call before coming home at night. Not having him to kiss before going to bed."

I am once again grateful for the telephone, as tears run down my face.

She continues. "I feel so appreciative of the relationship with Milton. It's matured. What was lost or even what never was, I've mourned it, I've moved through it. There's an acceptance of him as an aging man. I feel protective of him. I feel both given to and giving."

I am unable to speak. I am too raw. She has come too close to voicing my own feelings. Once again, Caroline obligingly – although unconsciously – comes to my rescue and shifts the focus to talking about calling two of her friends, a big breakthrough for her. She ends, however, in an interesting way: "I'm discomforted on the phone. It's harder to read your audience."

Although Caroline is ostensibly addressing her discomfort talking with friends on the telephone, I now wonder if she unconsciously sensed my great distress and sadness and felt both uncomfortable and perplexed.

A month later Caroline is talking about feeling uncomfortable around needy people. "When someone gets needy I withdraw."

"Because?" I ask.

"It makes me anxious, feels heavy, perhaps like Mother or my sister Betty."

"I wonder if it also reminds you of the needy, vulnerable part of yourself."

"I'm sure it must. But I really do want to connect. I want people in my life. What I like in a relationship is parity, give and take, equality."

"What about me, about us?"

"I'm evolving. Like when you laugh at something I say that's funny. I like that. I think now I'd be more comfortable with your being revealing. And I like when we bandy around ideas."

"But what if I were needy?"

"That would be hard. But you don't seem needy."

"What if I had some personal tragedy?" I persist.

"I'd be concerned for you, the way you are concerned about people you love. I've gotten past needing you on a pedestal."

"What if we shared similar vulnerabilities?"

"That would feel possible, good."

It is clear that I had an agenda in this session. As Caroline became more open, as her needy, vulnerable child became more available to her and as I was more vulnerable and needy myself, I felt more and more connected to her. As mentioned previously, her ability to poetically express her feelings, particularly those related to longing and loss, often captured not only her feelings, but mine as well. We were becoming closer, the bond between us growing, the love more palpable. As I struggled with George's tortuous decline and his now imminent death, I knew that I wanted to tell Caroline about it. I wanted to feel known and understood by her, just as she felt known and understood by me. Yet it was I who was the analyst, not her. It was I who was there to counsel her, tend to her needs, do that which was best for her. This session was obviously my clumsy effort to ascertain what Caroline might want or not want to know. As of this time, Caroline consciously knew nothing. I had revealed nothing of my struggle. But as George's death drew closer, I had less of an idea of what that experience would be like for both him and me, and less of an idea of what I would need or want to tell Caroline or my other patients.

Caroline follows up on the previous session. "I'm wanting more out of my relationships or at least moving in that direction. I've also thought more about us. Sometime this past winter I began to think of us more as partners in this. You present an idea to me as a possibility, not as a voice from on high. Perhaps it was always like that, but now I hear it the way you probably always meant it. I remember the first time I saw you driving into the parking lot and found out what kind of car you drove. It felt dangerous to me. Like I shouldn't know it. Now I have a warm feeling about your car. It's like a little talisman. If you changed your car I'd be curious."

Perhaps here Caroline is again reassuring me, letting me know that she has grown enough to handle what life has in store for us. Then again, it is a long way from knowing about my car, to knowing about the death of my husband to cancer.

A month later, Caroline and I are both preoccupied with loss. First, she is planning a trip with Milton to Israel, bringing up concerns both about being away from me and dealing with an aging, more fragile Milton in a foreign country. There is also the sudden death and funeral of a woman only two years older than herself from a massive stroke. And there is Yom Kippur.

"We were in synagogue on Saturday. It pulled on my heartstrings. They list all those who have died. You can pay more to have it read in perpetuity. My sister paid to have my father's name put in. Milton thinks it's just hypocrisy. This time I was really touched. I was thinking about the fragility of life, here and gone, so brief. I thought of Milton's death. He won't be here to touch. But when they read out my father's name and I went to touch Milton he gave me one of his snide laughs. I was devastated. I felt cut off from everyone. I felt lost. I tried to hold back the tears, but they fell down my face. I felt angry with him. I talked with him about it yesterday, crying and sobbing. He can't bear when I cry. I explained he was the only person who loved me and what a loss it would be when he was gone. He said he didn't feel he'd survive if something happened to me. I don't know if I have the strength. I've been feeling so emotional lately. Am I depressed? I thought of something you said – be with the sadness, try to understand it. It gave me some peace of mind. I'm yearning for something less transient, something that gives meaning. Life is so fleeting. There's loss and more loss."

Once again, barely able to hold myself together, I say, talking to both Caroline and myself, "You fear your aloneness. You yearn for something that will take away that aloneness."

On October 4, 2007, Caroline and I have our last session before she leaves for Israel. Prophetically, she talks about her father's death.

"He ceased being Daddy except in fragments or glimpses for a long, long time."

"So did his death feel painful, like a loss, or did your distance from him make his passing easier?" I ask.

"Hard to say. He left Mother and moved to Mexico and had a pretty good life for five years. When he got so sick and had to return to the United States, he made a suicide attempt. Then he came back to Charlotte and wanted to make amends with Mother. She'd have none of it. She didn't want to take care of him. At the time I felt she was entirely justified. Yet there were those few moments when I found out he'd died. I knew he was going to die and yet when he did I was suffused with sadness and started crying. I didn't want any consolation. I fled the building. I ran into my oldest sister and we embraced each other and cried. I could take it from her. When I brought his little bit of clothing home I felt this huge loss of him." She pauses, thoughtfully. "This afternoon I drove into the driveway of the first house Milton and I lived in. We lived there for thirty years. I couldn't figure out what was happening, what I was doing there."

"Maybe there's some longing for the past," I suggest, again understanding that all too well.

"I think maybe. My first sense of myself was my nanny holding me and my looking up into her face and her allowing me to suck my thumb and my knowing I was me. There was a moment of recognition."

"Sounds like you're talking about both connection and separation – being safely connected to your nanny, but also knowing yourself as a separate person. I also wonder if you're talking about us, about knowing I'm here, while also knowing that my seeing and knowing you helps you to know yourself."

"I know I can reach you if I need to, but I have you with me."

Caroline leaves on her trip.

We celebrate George's eighty-third birthday.
He enters the hospital.
He goes into hospice.

Knowing that Caroline will be returning from Israel and expecting to resume our telephone sessions on Monday, I leave a message on her voice mail, as I have done with all my patients who I could not reach directly. I tell her that I am really sorry to be unavailable to her, especially after an already long break, but that a family member is dying and that I am not sure exactly when I will be returning to work. I assure her that I will indeed return, but that I cannot give her a specific date and that I will call as soon as I know the time of my return.

9

ENDINGS

The Power of Love and Loss in a Psychoanalytic Treatment

George dies early on Monday morning, thirty-six hours after entering hospice. He is to be cremated. His memorial service takes place on Friday at a Unitarian church. The minister reads the piece I wrote and read to George at his birthday celebration. Family and friends, some present, others contributing via e-mail, give tribute to George's life. They speak about his generosity, his love, his humor, his intelligence, his engagement in life. Luke's song, "Son and Rain," about himself, his father, and his grandfather fills the room. I've read the tributes previously. I've heard Luke's song many times. But my tears are unstoppable. And then there is this poem, a poem written by Jane Dobija, a writer friend we knew from Ann Arbor. She read a poem at our wedding. Now her words, which echo that poem from long ago, ring out through the chapel.

Sky Light
For George Brandeberry

I haven't any words for this death.
My mind insists upon a skylight
Cut into a friend's roof,
The installment of stones, a sapling, a stream
In the living room.

I recall the walls pushing out,
To make room for him, for family,
For a dog as devoted as Jane Eyre.
With these shifts,
My friend becomes his wife.
They climb together
Like moonflowers
Blossoming even in the dark.

I remember how he watched her
Stretch out the window,

His smile underscored
By an impeccable goatee.
"This is what the hammering was all about,"
his grin said,
"and if you'd like to partake, sit here.
The fish is grilling.
The wine has been poured.
The sky's light waits."

This is the only image that works for me:
George climbing out a window
Of his own making;
Showing us the distant point to which it leads.
Waiting, as always, for us
To follow.

Everyone comes back to our house, except it's my house now, right? My house, not ours. Friends have brought food and food and more food. I am grateful. I feel the outpouring of love. Earlier today, before the service, I was uncharacteristically short, irritable. I even threw my set of keys when repeated trips to the grocery store by Melodee and Emily – what would I ever do without them? – didn't bring the type of paper plates I so irrationally demanded. I go, steeling myself against the store's too bright lights and nonchalant people. How could life be progressing so normally? How could life be continuing at all? But now, back home, after the service, I feel more held by the love around me and by the house itself. I have returned to our home, OUR home, and feel more embraced by George's love as well.

George's ashes have not yet arrived. I'm glad. Melodee won't leave until we receive them and scatter them in the pond by our home. I want to keep her with me as long as possible. She brings me comfort, both because of the person she is and because she's George's daughter. I am, however, ready to return to work, at least part-time. I am eager to resume my professional role, eager to escape my unrelenting feelings of loss and grief, eager to immerse myself in someone else's pain rather than my own.

The Saturday after George's memorial I called several patients, including Caroline, to say I would resume work on Monday. Caroline was tremendously relieved to hear from me. Unbeknownst to me at the time, after hearing the voice mail I left before George went into hospice, she wrote me a letter, part of which is reproduced here:

> I listened to your voicemail twice last night when I finally remembered to check messages at past 11PM. I couldn't quite make out how long you said you'd be away, was it 2-3 days, weeks, months – it wasn't clear, and you only promised that you would, eventually, come back and that you would be in touch at some time. I wanted to call immediately to leave a message for you to let you know that I was concerned for you and that you sounded so despairing, your voice

seemed heavy with sadness and whatever you said gave me the impression that when/if you returned, it would not be the same you I left behind two weeks ago when we went to Israel.

My very first thought after absorbing your message was: Can I go it alone, am I ready? I thought I might survive, but that my work with you was not complete, that I am unfinished like a dress basted along the seams, but not yet securely stitched. Then, I took my pills and drifted into sleep.

The letter goes on to describe a terrifying dream about a woman group leader and an ominous man. The woman believes the man has committed multiple murders before burying his victims in the ground. She encourages her group, including Caroline, to dig for the skeletal remains, which Caroline, believing in the leader, eagerly does. After finding the evidence Caroline feels she might throw up and jumps out of the grave, saying she can't do this anymore. The letter continues:

I wonder why I had this awful dream. My first thought is that it might be the lingering effect of being in Israel and of our day at Yad Vashem… Then it occurred to me that the dream might be related to your phone call. Who is dying? Is it the death of our relationship? And I believe it is a combination of all these things and I wish we could talk about it.

So, for the first time in perhaps years, I find myself writing it down to make myself feel better, or at least empty my apprehension onto the paper hoping it will make me feel better.

From this letter it is clear that Caroline felt very much abandoned and threatened by my unexpected cancellation and ambiguous return date. She was literally unsure if she could survive if she was left on her own. Her fear was so intense that even though she heard my reassurance – that I would return – she could no longer count on my previously unquestioned reliability and trustworthiness.

Interestingly, Caroline was the only patient who so clearly heard and understood the depth of my sadness and despair in the message I left. Was it her years of learning to stay attuned to her mother's moods that made her particularly astute in reading others' moods as well? Or was it that on an unconscious level Caroline had known for some time that I was struggling with my terror of the death of someone especially close to my heart? Or, is it possible that the message I left Caroline was somehow different than those I left other patients? Did I impart more of my sadness, more of my despair?

When I called that Saturday, Caroline immediately wanted to know how I was and who had died. When I told her it was my husband, she was not surprised.

"I knew it. You sounded so sad, so bereft. I knew it could only be your husband. Was it sudden? What did he die of?"

"I'll answer your questions, but are you sure you want to know?"

"Definitely! I care about you. We've come a long way from when I didn't want to know what car you drove."

"Yes, we have, we've come a long way. And I've known for a long time that we'd be at this place; that my husband would die, that you'd want to know, and that I'd want you to know."

So I told Caroline that my husband had died of metastatic prostate cancer, that he had been very sick for a year and a half, and that he had put up a valiant fight. I told her I would speak with her at our regular time on Monday, reassuring her that I did indeed want to return to seeing her and other patients and that I looked forward to focusing on someone beside myself.

Over the next several sessions I told Caroline that George was twenty-one years my senior; that, as she was concerned about Milton, I always worried about George's dying, and that he and I had a very close, loving relationship. She felt guilty that she had talked about her fears of Milton's death, worrying that I would have found those sessions particularly painful. I told her that on the contrary, I found comfort in the similarity of our feelings and believed that it fostered the connection between us.

My self-revelations were fueled both by Caroline's desire to know and, most definitely, by my desire to reveal myself to her. When I ask myself why it was with Caroline that I wanted to be most candid, the closest explanation I have is the one that I have offered previously, namely that I felt a kinship with Caroline both because of the similarity of our present life experiences and because her capacity to express herself so poetically captured, on an unconscious as well as conscious level, both her feelings and mine. These similarities and shared understanding increased my sense of closeness to Caroline at a time in my life when I had lost the person I was closest to in the world, thereby heightening my desire for connectedness. From this place of greater neediness, I forgot that Caroline's desire for and comfort with closeness was not a constant. I forgot that the woman who moved toward greater connection, who said, "I can't turn my back on Linda," often followed such movement by a defensive need to move away. She sought to protect the needy, vulnerable part of herself both from further hurt, as well as from the danger of devouring any loved person by the intensity of her need (Fairbairn, 1940, 1941; Guntrip, 1968). As we will see, my increased vulnerability and self-revelation would lead Caroline to even greater swings between closeness and distancing for much of the remainder of our work together. A related problem was that Caroline now experienced me as a damaged, fragile caretaker whom she needed to protect, leading to greater fears of her own anger, as well as concern that certain topics would need to be off-limits to avoid hurting me.

And then there is the issue of competition, of who's winning and who's losing and the ramifications of both the contest and the outcome.

Shortly after his death, I am surprised when Caroline says, "I was most touched by George saying that he didn't want to leave you." Tears come to my eyes as I recognize the truth of those words, but realize I have no recollection of saying them to Caroline. Whenever I talk about George and my relationship I talk about the great love and closeness we shared. It comes naturally to me. I want to proclaim our love to the world which is, no doubt, one of the motivations for this book. But I must be careful, I silently admonish myself at the time. How unfair to my patient to paint an idyllic picture of George and my relationship, only to stimulate her feelings of competition, jealousy, and envy.

But there is an alternative side to this competition created by the now different circumstances inherent in our lives, namely that Caroline has a husband and I do not.

Caroline's discomfort with this discrepancy becomes evident when, turning her head to stare at the rain streaming down my window, she says, "I've come to a place where I feel that magically Milton only has two more years to live. Then he'll be eighty-three. Just like George."

Knowing that I am only mouthing words, I reply, "You know, it is all right for you to have more than me, to do better than me. You don't have to be limited, not by George's age or anything else about me."

"No, it's not like that," she protests. "It's entered my mind as a way to treasure Milton. These times to be with Milton and the family are not to be squandered. Eighty-three means something. Just seeing him sitting on the bench – he looked old. I see who he was and who he's not any longer. It touched me. He's fading. It made me very sad. I talked to Milton about my fear of his dying. He said that he knew I was strong and that I could go on. It was a disappointment to me that he didn't feel he had to stay to take care of me. I wanted it to be harder for him to give me up."

Here we see both sides of the competition and Caroline's discomfort with either winning or losing. She's uncomfortable if Milton lives longer than George, that is, if she has more than me. But she's equally uncomfortable when she feels she's lost, that George didn't want to leave me while Milton focuses more on Caroline's ability to care for herself.

Although I have thus far in this chapter addressed some of the difficulties created by my being so revealing to Caroline, I do also believe that Caroline's growth as an open, related, loving person was fostered by my increased vulnerability and openness. In addition to seeing my strength and capacity for love, she saw my ability to persevere despite overwhelming feelings of loss, grief, and neediness. Even in the preceding example of the competition between Caroline and myself, there is evidence of Caroline's increasing ability to open herself to Milton. Although this did not begin with George's death, I believe that Caroline's knowledge of my capacity to both love and withstand loss helped her to believe she could follow a similar path.

Thanksgiving. One month to the day since George has died. I go out to walk and meet a neighbor I know casually. I end up crying in her arms. How will I get through these holidays? First Thanksgiving and then Christmas. Yesterday I ran into Target to buy Christmas toys for my cousin Danielle's little girl. I was in and out and laden with toys in less than thirty minutes. Going into stores feels oppressive. I have fortuitously solved the problem of Christmas presents. Wandering by a gift shop I happened to see the 2007 Swarovski Christmas ornament, a crystal snowflake, hanging in the window. I buy ten of them and eventually write the following note: "For all of us who loved George, I thought

I would send this eternally shiny, sparkling snowflake as a symbol of his essence so that we can keep him with us for this Christmas and for always."

But that's Christmas. Now there's still Thanksgiving to get through, Thanksgiving at the home of a good friend. Luke and Emily are there. I find myself following Emily around like a puppy dog. I tell her she's the person who makes me feel most safe, most comfortable. Is that because she's naturally maternal? Is it because she took such good care of George? I don't know. I'm just glad she's here.

Thanksgiving has not been good for Caroline either. The first day back after the holiday we are both morose. I struggle to keep myself focused and present.

No longer captivated by the magical eighty-three, she says despondently, "I feel that I might have ten more years with Milton. But he'll be just a shell of his former self."

I am immediately swamped by images of George's last months, last weeks, last days. I don't ask how the magical eighty-three has come to vanish.

She continues. "And I will disappear just as he does. Once he's dead, I'll be gone. I envision myself at the dinner table with Alexa and her family. When Milton isn't there, I won't be there either"

Is that what I felt at Thanksgiving dinner? That I was there, but not there, inconsequential, reduced.

More acutely aware of the finality of life, it is not surprising that Caroline's relationship with Milton takes center stage. She struggles to feel closer to him, to be more tolerant of him, while she simultaneously registers his limitations, notes his increasing fragility, and fears his ultimate decline and death. Although issues concerning Milton were prominent prior to George's death, they now have an added intensity, an increased sense of time running out. As before, though, she tends to vacillate. In one session she is angry that Milton is self-centered and unable to respond lovingly to her. In another session she realizes that like herself, Milton's background limits his capacity to reach out. The latter, "takes away the feeling of desperation and makes me feel closer to him." Simultaneously, she begins to recognize how much she longs for connection herself, how she wants to be closer, to me, to Milton, to Alexa.

It is the last session in my office before Caroline returns to North Carolina.

"This is our last session. I worry about you. You seem so fragile, so easily hurt. I could never imagine getting angry with you."

"Are you angry with me?"

"Oh no, not at all. If anything I'm angry with myself. I feel badly that I made all those negative comments about your décor. It was so irrelevant. What does it matter what you have in your waiting room, on your walls? You just seem so tender. I wouldn't want to hurt you."

I wonder if Caroline, anticipating the loss of our in-person contact, is projecting onto me her own feelings of vulnerability and loss. On the other hand, she could be intuiting my pain. The past several weeks have definitely been wrenching.

My patient Stella dies. I attend her funeral, the first funeral since George's memorial. I listen to the eulogy given by both her daughters and granddaughters. It's unbearably sad. Who am I crying for? Stella, myself, my long-dead grandmother, George? Perhaps all of us. When they proceed to the cemetery I leave. I just can't make myself go.

And then there's my birthday, my first birthday without George. Melodee comes. That helps. A dozen of my family and closest friends meet at a restaurant. I try to be pleased, upbeat, but previous birthdays flash through my head. My fiftieth when George baked me an L shaped chocolate cake, L for Linda and L for fifty! My sixtieth, the last very large gathering we had at our house. It was pre-chemo and although George was having difficulty walking, he was still very much his warm, affable, outgoing self. And then there was last year, when George was hurting but in his apparently miraculous improvement period. We went out to our favorite restaurant. It was a hard evening for George, but he smiled and we enjoyed both the food and each other. And then, the next day, George couldn't walk. He couldn't even stand up. I panicked, wondering how we would manage if George lost total control of his legs. Then, three days later, as quickly as it came, the paralysis reversed itself and George was back to walking as before. All this swirls through my mind as I sit smiling at the table, trying to enjoy, but feeling mostly a lack, an absence, a void.

So, is it that Caroline feels my "tenderness," or is she reacting more to our upcoming physical separation?

Regardless, the theme of being afraid to hurt me continues.

"How would I feel if Milton wasn't here?" Caroline asks herself quizzically. "I tried to think about that again this morning. Would I be sad all the time? Would I be imagining my life with Milton? [Pause.] I don't think I can do this work anymore. There are too many things I don't want to talk about. I don't want to talk about my sadness for fear of making you sadder. I don't like to think of you hurting. And I certainly don't like to think of my being the one to cause you pain."

"And if you hurt me, then what?" I ask.

"Then you won't love me. Or you'll be dead and then I won't have you anymore. [Pause.] Do you still believe it, do you still believe, 'Tis better to have loved and lost than never to have loved at all?'"

"Yes, I most definitely still believe it," I say, nodding my head unseen behind the couch.

"Well, that's helpful. Somehow that makes me believe you might be stronger than I think."

"It isn't weak to feel pain, to feel sadness."

"I know. But I always feel as though I'm under a cloud, that I'm always coming from a place of scarcity, always fearful of the future, always feeling 'woe is me.' On the other hand, I'm concerned that I'll hurt you by my good fortune, that I have Milton and you don't have anyone."

Here again we see Caroline's difficulty in both winning and losing. If she has more than me she damages me or incites my envy, so that one of us is harmed and our relationship is threatened. If she has less than me she feels diminished, deprived, and humiliated. Although it could definitely be argued that these conflicts intensified for Caroline because she knew so much about my life and my relationship with George, it is also true that being able to deal with these issues directly between us in the present may well have facilitated her ability to work on and come to terms with these same issues.

Look, for example, at a session that occurs while she is away from Milton in New York, considering whether to buy a New York apartment and have a third home there.

"Loneliness surged over me. I missed Milton. I can't imagine a deeper sense of loss even when he's really dead. How will I manage without him? The feelings just wash over me. It's especially true when I'm away from home. Is this New York apartment what I want? It feels like me. It also feels scary. The anxiety rises at night, in the darkness. Being alone feels more alone here because I'm a stranger in this city. My sense of being lost here is that I'm lost and won't be found. In Charlotte someone would find me and get me home."

She continues, "I saw 'Gypsy' last night and I experienced the envious, rivalrous part of myself, the part of me I see as ugly. Before I had identified with the girl who wasn't loved. This time I was the stage mother who pushes her girls, but who competes with them. The mother was portrayed with such envy. I know I feel that too. I don't want to feel envy toward Alexa."

"You want to continue to step aside for Alexa."

"Right," she says.

"But when you stole the show in high school, when you surpass me, when you have a husband and I don't, you're not comfortable either."

"That's true. I had too envious a mother. She couldn't handle my success and still can't. It's what she wanted for herself. I have more compassion for her, but I'm ashamed of my feelings of rivalry with Alexa. Alexa will surpass me financially. I don't know how I feel about that."

"And how do you feel about your having a husband and my not having one?"

"I'm really glad to have Milton." Softly she adds, "And I'm sad for you."

"And can both those feelings exist at the same time?"

"Yes. At least today they can."

But "today" doesn't last very long as Caroline's needy, deprived child reappears and she responds by becoming more distanced and defensive. Now she no longer trusts me and cannot imagine that I or anyone else could ever love her. Obviously she isn't worthy of love. Her mother certainly didn't love her and look how she has behaved towards her own daughter. And now Alexa rejects her and treats her just as she treated her own mother.

This conflict comes to a head when Caroline flies down for one of her summer trips to see me in my office. She announces that she wants to cut back to twice a week. I strongly oppose the idea, saying that she is clearly struggling with wanting more and wanting less and that we need to battle through this conflict. She says that

I feel like "a stranglehold" and that she needs to get rid of me before she can move forward. She does capitulate to my "professional opinion" and agrees to continue at her present frequency. At this point she has become less afraid of hurting my feelings and more assured of my ability to survive. Not surprisingly, though, now that I am no longer the "weak" child who needs to be protected, I become the "dangerous" mother who is to be feared.

Caroline dreams. "Someone is out to harm me and puts a plastic Ziploc bag over my head and asphyxiates me. I know it's you. You've become a demand on my time."

"I've gone from a homecoming to a suffocating obligation."

"There's a danger in having my back to you. You could leap out of your chair and smother me, put a plastic bag over my head."

"I'm more and more the dangerous mother."

"To this day when I leave my mother's room I back out of the room rather than turning my back on her. Last time I saw her I was completely lost to her, an interruption. But I don't care," Caroline says angrily. "She's old and she has no life and she's going to die. I wish she'd die sooner than later, but she will die and then I'll be rid of her."

"You know, Caroline, what just happened was really interesting. You started with me or your mother as the dangerous one. Then she became the rejecting, abandoning mother who hurt your feelings. Then you became the needy child, except that's a very uncomfortable place for you, so you became the angry, dangerous mother. It's a flip you often make. You have difficulty tolerating yourself as the needy child so you become the angry mother. I think you also assume that others make a similar shift, which is why I too can go from 'weak' to 'dangerous' in your mind."

"It's so hard to put my vulnerable self out there. I'm afraid to expose myself."

I tell Caroline that I will be gone for two weeks in October. She knows immediately that the time corresponds to the anniversary of George's death.

I carefully orchestrate this October anniversary. It looms before me like an abyss. Nothing feels right. Working and pretending it is like any other day is completely out of the question. Being alone does not even enter my mind. Perhaps I should just have Melodee come to the house. But I wouldn't mind getting away. Of course, getting away presents practical problems, as well as psychological ones. My mother, now ninety-eight, is seriously deteriorating. Her red blood count is extremely low, she is having seizures, and she is increasingly confused and uncommunicative. Hospice has been called in, although her primary caretaker remains, Cossette, the incredible woman who has been with my mother for four and a half years. Cossette assures me that she will take care of everything. I need to do what is best for me. But deciding what is best is far from easy. Going to Ann Arbor enters my mind, but is soon dismissed. I would see George everywhere. No, that's the problem. I would see him nowhere. In the end, I decide to spend time with friends in both Oregon and California, to spend George's birthday with John and Melodee and to go to a small spa for the anniversary of George's death, something George would never have been interested in doing. It's a plan.

In the session that I tell Caroline about my upcoming vacation she reports the following dream: "The dream was about a deer, a suffering deer. The deer had stepped on the quill from a porcupine. The thorn had to be extracted perfectly. It was a delicate operation. If it wasn't done properly the leg would have to be amputated or the deer would die. I woke up concerned. My immediate thought was Betty. [Shortly before this session, Caroline's sister Betty was diagnosed with liver cancer.] But then I thought it was about analysis too. If the painful thing is not carefully withdrawn the patient will die. There's some danger to the patient. I don't think it was until later that I connected it to grieving. It's like you need to carefully extract my pain or grief or I'll die."

"What's going on right now that makes it feel that we're at this delicate point?" I ask, wondering again if Caroline has been intuiting my pain, my grief. Am I the deer with the potentially deadly thorn of grief?

"Good question. Maybe a couple of things. I've been angry with you lately and that feels dangerous. And I have difficulty grieving. I don't permit it and that means I'm disconnected. I can appear to be compassionate or understanding, but I don't feel it. I want it to be there. Until I deal with my anger I won't be able to get to my grief. If I can allow that to happen with you it will move us forward, although it feels dangerous. It could poison the relationship. And then I'd die without ever having really lived."

I take a picture of George and myself with me and put it on the different nightstands overlooking whatever bed I'm sleeping in, wearing, as usual, one of his long T-shirts. He is with me constantly. I am reliving those October days last year. George's jaundice. My almost insisting he go into the hospital and cancel his party. The party itself. His actual birthday when we sat together for the last time on our porch.

This October 14, one year later, John, Melodee, and I go walking in a woodsy forest in Oregon. I suddenly realize that George and I had been here before with John and his family. It was one of the times George and I had that unique confluence of experience, walking along and simultaneously speaking of how the arrangement of path and foliage reminded us of scuba diving through the underwater reefs. I like remembering. I have no choice but to remember.

I continue tracing my days of remembrance. When George went into the hospital for the last time. When we learned he had another cancer. When he had the first failed procedure; the second more successful one. When he said, "It's enough already." When he went into hospice. When he died. It's a very hard time for Melodee as well, the daughter who loved and idealized her Daddy. And then it's October 23. The first anniversary of George's death is over. Not surprisingly, not much feels different.

But much is different when I return to Caroline.

"I didn't miss you. But that was because I have you in me. That feeling was stronger than I thought. I didn't feel needy of you even in the difficult times through Betty's surgery and the family dramas. But I did feel a deeper loss about the time we don't have together. I feel the need to be closer to you. I may want to sit face to face rather than be on the couch. I have a yearning to be closer, to see your face, your body, to really take you in. It wasn't that I needed you. I was glad to have the time, to not have the structure."

"So you simultaneously felt yourself not needing me, but wanting to be closer to me."

"I definitely want you in my life. And I feel good about that. And I have been able to build new friendships. I've learned with you that I can trust myself revealed. Friendships are where the future lies. I don't feel I'll ever lose you unless you pass away and then I'll feel terrible grief. I can imagine turning to you when Milton dies, or Betty, or even Mother. I feel kindly rather than critical. It's enlivening. I'm ready to risk being more emotional. I'm still afraid that if I start crying I'll never stop. That's why I need to be in your office and feel held by you. If I allow the grief I'll melt like the wicked witch. Being hard and angry protects me from the terrible grief. I asked Milton if he really loved me. He took me by the shoulders and said, 'Do you not know how I feel about you?' I wanted to burst out crying but I didn't. I buried my head in his shoulders, as if I'd hurt him. Then I felt loved by him. Then I felt a shudder of sorrow and joy. The little girl who had never been loved, getting it now and feeling ... I don't know what."

"Perhaps feeling loved now makes you all the more aware of what you didn't have in the past."

"Yes. That makes me sad."

"And if you are loved now, that means you are and were lovable."

"And that brings me close to tears. I do know how much I'll miss him when he's gone. As if I could never fill that hole up enough. Maybe I can. Maybe we can repair that hole together."

And, not surprisingly, within a week Caroline again experiences me as the smothering one, as the one who wants to hold on to her.

"I feel as though we've trod all this. I want less time. I want a different approach."

"I thought we were just talking about your trying to take in my positive voice?"

"Not to hurt Linda. If I leave Linda, if I reduce my time, do I hurt Linda? Why am I in this caretaker role? I'll stay longer than I want not to hurt you. Am I taking care of you rather than vice versa?"

This is indeed a good question. When I look back from a period of several years, I find myself not much clearer about the answer than I was at the time. I do know that I was at a very sad and vulnerable period in my life and that Caroline knew more about me than any of my other patients. I also know that I would have been very sad to have her leave treatment, both for herself and for me. I still deeply felt our connection and relished the richness of her words. So, yes, her leaving would definitely have pained me. But the fact that Caroline could shift so quickly from closeness to distance and back again, led me then, and still leads me today, to believe that most of what was being enacted here came from Caroline's internal dynamics, including her fear of her needy, greedy child and her tendency to protect that child by becoming rejecting herself. Additionally, as elucidated by Fairbairn (1958), Caroline needed to reject the new good object, in this instance me, for fear that it would replace the internalized bad object which would set off a period of intense mourning for the parents who never were and never could be.

And soon, despite her fears, Caroline again talks about wanting to be closer, to take in, and even to risk the threat of pain and loss. Coming from this place, she decides to get a dog, a standard poodle, the dog she always wanted. In making this decision, Caroline is simultaneously deciding not to get an apartment in New York. She is choosing home and attachment, rather than excitement and distraction. When she returns to my office in the beginning of December, Caroline chooses to sit in the chair. We understand that there are pros and cons to this arrangement and that we may or may not continue with it. Although Caroline is allowing herself to be closer, we both know that she can pull back in an instant if she feels too close, too suffocated.

Two weeks later Caroline tells me she loves me. I tell her I love her too.

Had I ever before directly told a patient I loved her? Not to my memory. I have most definitely felt love for a patient, but I do not think I ever stated it so clearly. My response was no doubt motivated by more factors than I will ever know – who Caroline is as a person, her ability to so beautifully capture in words both her feelings and mine, my loss of George, my awareness that my mother was soon going to die, my own need for attachment and connection, plus all the unconscious reasons I shall never know. I don't regret the words. I still believe in their truthfulness.

My mother dies on January 19, 2009, exactly one month shy of her ninety-ninth birthday. I cancel patients. I am sad, but not overcome by grief. Her life was definitely a full one; her death was long overdue. There was no unfinished business between myself and my mother. She had been more than a good-enough mother and I had been more than a good-enough daughter. We were both ready to say good-bye.

During the next several months Caroline continues to open up – to Milton, to Alexa, to her new puppy Gretchen, and to me. On her birthday she feels so loved by Milton that she cries, both for her present good fortune and for all the losses and deprivations of her past. She is determined to forge a closer relationship with Alexa. She reports a dream:

"I was given a child – I don't know by whom. And then I lost her and felt frantic. I had to go back to get her. I felt as though the child was me, but also Alexa. [Pause.] I still have to bring my child with me. It's not safe to leave her. I'm afraid of being too porous. I called Alexa to tell her about the dream. I want her to know how important she is to me. She has to know! [Caroline starts to cry.] It feels like such a terrible loss not to have had this mother/child connection, not with Alexa and certainly not with my mother. I know I saw myself in Alexa when she was an infant. I saw my own neediness, my own vulnerability and I was terrified of that little baby, terrified of her and terrified of me."

The next day Caroline continues, "I felt that crying was a breakthrough. Yet I still had a little background voice that said, 'Well, you win, I cried,' but I realized that was a defense and I was able to put it away. I actually felt very held by you while I cried – neither intruded upon nor abandoned."

Not long thereafter, Caroline raises the issue of termination, suggesting that she end in a year, in April of 2010 when she returns to Charlotte. By then it will be seven years that Caroline has been in analysis, the time she always imagined herself stopping. This time I do not hear her request as defensive, but rather as a desire to spread her wings and move on in her journey. Are there still issues Caroline needs to work on? Most definitely. But we still have a year. And, besides, there is no one amongst us who could not continue to parse and struggle with our issues forever and ever. If Caroline feels that she is ready to stop, I will not stand in her way. Will I grieve her loss? I know I will. But my loss is certainly not a reason to keep her in treatment.

Another loss looms before me. First George. Then my mother. Now my fifteen-year-old cat, Pippin, may have cancer. Pippin, named by George, meaning one of a kind. Pippin, our Florida cat, rescued from a humane society when our Michigan cat, Kali, died suddenly almost immediately after our move, leaving both George and I bereft. Pippin, a black and white tuxedo cat with her regal bearing and prim, ladylike manners. I can't bear it. I can't tolerate another loss.

As it turns out, Pippin does not have cancer, but rather a blocked nasal passage that inhibits her sense of smell and therefore her desire to eat. But she has kidney disease as well, an often fatal disease that affects older cats. Pippin will require twice weekly visits to the vet. She will need me to watch her while she eats and sometimes to feed her by hand. But she is not dying, at least not yet. I am again caring for an aging being. I am again anxiously returning home, wondering how she is faring. The déjà vu is excruciatingly painful, but it is better than the alternative.

A few sessions after setting a termination date, Caroline asks me for a picture of myself. I suggest that she is dealing with feelings of loss. She agrees. "I'm getting more and more in touch with my sad feelings, as well as with my open and loving feelings. I saw a movie in which a father clearly showed his five-year-old son how much he loved him. I cried and cried. I've never, ever been loved like that."

I think immediately of both George and my mother and know that I have been fortunate enough to be loved in that way. But I vibrate so intensely to Caroline's pain. I feel the loss as she feels the loss. And of course there is now that loss for me as well. The two people who loved me so unconditionally no longer exist. Except in my heart. Except in my thoughts.

But Caroline was certainly loving her puppy, Gretchen, as she herself had never been loved. Gretchen became the needy child in the closet who Caroline had to protect and whom she couldn't bear to be separated from. Gretchen was also the infant Alexa, the opportunity for a do-over, although accompanied with the guilt that she was being a better mother to Gretchen than she had been to Alexa.

154

It was in April of 2010 that Caroline was to graduate from the psychoanalytic writing program. She had tremendous ambivalence about attending graduation, both because she didn't want to "abandon" Gretchen and because she didn't feel she deserved to graduate.

"I feel like I'm not being a good-enough mother. I can't bear the thought of leaving her. But if I don't go I'll feel regret. I don't want to just peter out, to not be prepared. It's all a no-win," Caroline says shaking her head.

"I think this is about you as the helpless, dependent child. You don't want to graduate without taking care of that helpless, dependent child."

"I also don't feel I deserve to graduate. I feel like an impostor," she adds, more emphatically.

I persist. "Maybe you need to feel like an impostor so that you don't have to leave home. And maybe you feel this fear of leaving home particularly acutely because we've set a termination date. You're going to lose me and then what happens to the needy, dependent child?"

"I hadn't thought of that and I wouldn't have said that's my experience. But maybe now that we're getting close, maybe I am scared. Maybe I'm not ready. Maybe I'm not grown-up enough yet. But that would be on an unconscious level. Consciously I'm ready for us to reach closure. I expect to grit my teeth and get through it."

"It's important for you not to forget either the helpless, dependent child or the competent, capable adult," I say, hoping that Caroline may yet learn that she doesn't always have to grit her teeth.

"That helps – to not deny either." She pauses thoughtfully. "I feel we're on to something. I wonder if I'm practicing leaving – Milton, you, Florida, my own death. What was the original loss? It's too huge to remember. You're the only person I ever asked to understand me. [Pause.] I wonder what people love about me?"

"Are you asking what I love about you?"

"Perhaps."

"Well, what I'd say is probably very different from how you see yourself," I say smiling at her. "I'd say it's your warmth and your sensitivity and your lovingness."

She looks down. "I started to choke up when you said that, but I pushed it away. I'm sure you described the sweet little girl who existed underneath. But I unlearned all that. It surfaces sometimes, but mostly I'm the ironic, sarcastic person looking in on the world."

Prior to the graduation weekend, as Caroline and I continue to discuss her feeling of being an impostor, I suggest to her that she write about our work together. She says that she will think about it and soon becomes very excited about the prospect of writing a memoir and giving it to me as a gift when we end. It is only in retrospect that I wonder about my offering such a specific suggestion to Caroline and one that involved her writing about us. Consciously, my motive was to encourage Caroline in her writing by giving her a discrete topic that she might be more likely to complete. Perhaps unconsciously, however, I wished Caroline to memorialize us, to put down on paper our work, our relationship, so that the bond between us would forever exist in concrete form.

Caroline does attend graduation, a milestone for her. I am in the audience to support and applaud her success.

Several months later, I tell Caroline I will be going on vacation for three weeks in August. In the next session she reports the following dream:

"I am dying. I'm in my fifties or maybe forties and diagnosed with a rare disease. I'm with three other people, one of whom is my brother. We've been given a protocol to see if it will cure the disease. Things are breaking down in our bodies. I find out the protocol has worked for them but not for me. They've been told they're getting better, but not me. They leave. I'm devastated. I'm all alone. I feel like I want to sob. My brother left without even hugging me or saying good-bye! I yell out, 'How could you leave me?' But no one hears me. I can't see the point of crying with no one to hear me. When I woke up I started to cry. I'd be all by myself at the end. Yesterday when you told me about your vacation I thought, 'She's going to have fun and not with me. You don't like it when she leaves you.' That must have been what it felt like when mother went away on a fun trip – Linda/mother/Alexa. Alexa gone off and leading her exciting life. The sorrow of being left alone. I'm beginning to grieve for the end of our year, an end cut short by three weeks. I'm pleased that grief is coming up. All alone in life. All alone to die. Everyone drifts away. There is no comfort. How could you not even hug me or feel my pain? You have a life apart from mine that doesn't include me. I'm not the central character in your life. I'm okay if your time away is sorrowful, but not if it's a fun time. Termination is definitely a death word. It's not a leave-taking. If I have sorrow, if I have grief, I'm glad for it. I'm glad not to be alien to my feelings. I remember how outside myself I was when I first began with you. How I felt untethered, remote, a distant observer and how different I am from that now. I'm so inside myself now. I like feeling all the emotions. I like owning all the feelings. What made it happen? What made it possible for me to change in this way? [Pause.] I don't know how to answer that. What do you think?"

"I think that for us, it was our relationship that made it happen. As you came to trust that I accepted and understood the vulnerable child in you, you could begin to lower your wall and as you lowered that wall we became closer, enabling you to feel still further embraced, leading to a further lowering of your wall, making you more open and genuine, leading us to become closer still."

"That's sweet," she replies, smiling. "I always struggled to win intellectually, but that's not where the prize is. I don't think I knew that until this very conversation. I needed a real connection to that little girl who was me. The sweet little kid."

As Caroline packs to leave for what will be our last winter together in Florida she muses, "You won't be coming back with me. That will be a big loss. But I have you in me. I take walks with you. I think about you when I read. You've given me a great deal. I'll always have you inside me. It will be very different when Milton isn't here. I don't have him inside me in the same way. Maybe I will after he's dead. I have his presence. But I'll always be able to talk to you in my head."

156

Another similarity. I don't much talk to George in my head. I don't wish him good morning, tell him about my day, or ask his advice although I know friends and patients who do have such conversations with their deceased spouses. My memories of George are far more of the experience of him, of his warmth, his openness, his presence, as Caroline put it. I can hear his laugh, remember his welcoming embrace, see the love in his eyes, and hear the melodic tone of his voice as he said, "My love." He surrounds me. But it is not through words that we communicate any longer.

"What if I were dying?" Caroline asks herself. "Would I call Linda? I wouldn't want her to find out from someone else. But what could she offer me? Soothing, solace? Could I take it in? The thought is frightening, as if I might melt away. All my defenses would be gone. Then I'd have to feel not having love for all those years. That's what would destroy me. Yet I want it."

"I really do hope, Caroline, that you're able to take in my positive feelings for you before we terminate."

"I know you'll be sad about my leaving, just like you'd be sad about any of the people you've seen for a long time."

"Yes, I do feel sad when most people I've seen for a long time end, but we have had an especially close bond and I will feel your leaving – not that you shouldn't do it – as a profound loss."

"I believe you, but I don't take it in. I'm afraid I'd melt if I really took it in."

Several points need addressing in this session. The first is my insistence that Caroline take in the extent of my caring and accept the uniqueness of our relationship. It could be argued that I am encouraging Caroline to experience herself as "special," thereby increasing her narcissism or feeling of entitlement. It might also be argued that this is my agenda, that I need Caroline to take me in for me, rather than for her. The second, but definitely related, issue is why Caroline feels as though taking me in is so dangerous. As always, I am more than willing to concede that I cannot know my own unconscious and therefore cannot be absolutely sure that my motive did not include an element of self-interest. Consciously, however, I did and do believe it was my concern for Caroline that led me to strongly encourage her to take me in as someone who was different from the people in her past, as someone who truly loved and cared about her. If she could accomplish that taking in, she could accept herself as loveable and allow herself to separate from her internalized others, mourning their loss, while allowing both her needy, vulnerable child, as well as her competent, capable adult to be genuinely accepted and loved. It was a difficult task for Caroline, but one I hoped we could come close to accomplishing by the time of our termination.

Luke calls to tell me he plans to break up with Emily. My anxiety soars. More uncertainty in my life. The prospect of another loss, the loss of a young woman who has, in many ways, come to fulfill the maternal function in my life. I'm also concerned for Luke. Given his background I always thought that Emily was an amazingly healthy choice for him. Now what? Emily is devastated. She moves in with me, at least temporarily. I tell her she can live with me and go to graduate school in the fall, but I suspect that she will return to her home in Oregon. I try to be present to support both Luke and Emily. I yearn for George to be present to support me.

Caroline reports the following dream: "I'm leaving in a convertible with a young, sexy man. I realize that I've left Gretchen behind. I insist we return immediately and we do. It's not Gretchen, but this little lap dog. She's scared, in a complete panic. I say, 'I'm back.' The dog relaxes immediately. I think the dog is you. You don't want me to leave. You don't want me to go off on my exciting new sexual adventure. You need me to return to you, to calm you down, to keep you safe."

I counter. "I wonder, Caroline, if the little dog is the vulnerable, child part of yourself, if as you get ready to end and go off on your adventure, whether that part of you is frightened and wants to stay home, is afraid to embark on your new life."

She shakes her head. "Maybe, but I still think it's you. I have so much more in my life right now. I have Milton. I have Alexa in a way that's closer than I ever imagined. We've just bought this new summer home on the beach, the home that will be right next to Alexa and her family. It's so different from anything I ever imagined! That I'd actually to able to be embraced by her and her family, perhaps even when Milton is gone. He was so sweet the other day. He said that he was glad that he had me settled. I'm going to have it remodeled and then I'll even have a room where I can write and look out over the ocean. It's all so perfect. It's like I'm leaving you and going to my own family, my real family. I have so much. You have so much less than me."

As I prepare to again lose part of my "family," I know that much of what Caroline is saying is true, that there are many ways she does have more than me, including being embraced by a ready-made family. Has Caroline somehow intuited this? Perhaps such intuitiveness would strain credulity, but Caroline certainly does know that there have been many losses in my life. On the other hand, I remain concerned that she is ignoring her own vulnerability, as well as still struggling with issues about being victorious. "Is it all right for you to have more than me?" I ask.

"There's always that, isn't there? I guess not. I can't imagine allowing myself to soar and to leave you behind. Just as I could never imagine publishing if you don't."

"Why? Why can't you be a successful author even if I'm not?"

"Because then I'd kill you. [Pause.] Because then you wouldn't love me."

"So there are the two sides of you. There's the part of you that has murderous fantasies and both fears and wishes to kill me off, just as you wanted to do away with your mother. And there's the part of you who's the vulnerable child, the panicked little dog, who wants both my love and your mother's."

"I still think you're the dog," she insists.

"Perhaps we're both that dog, Caroline. After all, we all have a scared little child inside. And perhaps by making me that little dog you diminish me without killing me."

"You have a point. I think of my mother. She's so diminished these days, so fragile. She even looks like a porcelain doll. And I find myself feeling more kindly towards her, like she can't hurt me anymore."

Shortly thereafter Caroline talks more about the new beach house. "I'm doing a renovation again, rather than building a house from the ground up. I've always wanted my doll's house, but I never quite get it. Maybe it's only in fiction that I can have my doll's house."

Images of my Michigan house flash through my mind.

Caroline continues, "Maybe I'm being childish, always wanting more. Or maybe I don't deserve it."

"So now you're blaming yourself, rather than feeling powerless to find what you're really looking for, a refuge, a safe haven."

"Yes, that's true. I want the perfect place where time stands still, where there's no aging, no death."

"You're looking at a lot of losses – your mother, us, Betty, Milton."

"Yes, that's it. There's loss all around me. And I carry George's loss with me too."

"What do you mean?" I ask, perplexed.

"You're living proof that you do lose people, that death is inevitable."

"That's true. There's aging, loss, and death and not even a doll's house can keep that away," I reply softly.

When Caroline leaves, I allow the tears I have managed to contain during the session. I recognize that I am crying for myself, as well as releasing the sadness that remains difficult for Caroline to express. This is a dynamic that will remain with us through the end, as Caroline begins to subtly distance herself from me emotionally and I feel more and more of both of our sadness about our upcoming termination.

The following are excerpts from the last six sessions of Caroline's analysis.

In the first of these sessions, talking about her ever-diminishing mother, Caroline says, "I wonder what people's last thoughts are just before they slip away. Are they regretting that they're leaving? Have they gone to a comfortable place?"

"You're also talking about the end of analysis."

"I don't know what I would say. The gift of the memoir – the treasure between us that keeps it from feeling like I'm just walking out the door and not leaving a piece of me behind. I don't know what else I'd say beyond, 'I love you.'"

In the second, she says, "I never asked you certain things, like what other commonalities we might have in our background? Is there a reason we worked so well together? Is there an underlying similar experience that made it easy for me to say anything? I know you appreciated my language skills. If you didn't that would have been a great loss. I needed you to listen to all my words."

In the next session, despite Caroline's words, I sense a certain aloofness, an emotional disconnect. After listening to her talk about her mother, I say, "You're moving away, both from your mother and from me."

"I am. I'm looking for a sweet exit."

"Can you not move away and still have a sweet exit?"

"But it will be a literal away."

"Not until next Thursday."

"That's true. But it seems normal for me to distance myself before the end. I'm practicing loss."

"You can practice or try to prepare yourself for loss and still stay emotionally present."

"Are you concerned that I'll be devastated?"

"No."

"That I won't feel enough?"

"Yes."

"I'm losing the person who knows me better than anyone. I bring myself to you, the person who knows me and loves me and enjoys my little pleasures. That will be the biggest loss. That will be leaving home. On Hallmark cards there's always homecoming, the idealized version of coming home. You've been that for me. That's what I'll miss."

Yet, as Caroline says these words, I sense that it is me rather than her who is close to tears.

With three sessions remaining, Caroline reports that she has been up until 1 a.m. finishing her memoir. "I'm proud of it and proud that I could allow myself to feel proud. I realized writing it how much I've grown and changed during our time together. And I'll never again say that I never completed anything and that I'm only a dilettante. And besides, I realize that I'm intelligent!"

"That's terrific!! And it's true. You're very different from the person who began treatment seven years ago."

"I think you're correct that it is words that bound us. But I'm not sure I know exactly how that worked."

"I just had a thought. I think I was emotionally affected by your words before you were affected by them yourself. So it's as though you gave them to me and I held them until you were ready and then I gave them back to you."

"That's so sweet! And true."

Although Caroline had continually said she would give me the memoir in our last session, she brought it to me in the next to last session. "You asked me three times whether I wanted you to respond to the memoir, so I thought I would bring it to you before the ending. Besides, I was so moved by what you said about holding my words I ran and changed the acknowledgement page. It says, 'For Linda B. Sherby, Ph.D. who held my words until I found the courage to write them down.'"

"Thank you," I say, hoping that those two words can capture my profound sense of connection.

"How are you feeling?" she asks me.

"Sad."

"I'm glad you're sad. It means it mattered."

"You matter."

We sit in silence.

"There's no need for any more words," Caroline says.

The last session starts with my telling her how much I loved her manuscript and what a great tribute it is to her, to me, and to our work together. I again encourage her to continue writing, perhaps even doing more with her beautiful memoir. She tells me the memoir is my gift. That is all she wished to do with it.

She then goes on to talk about saying good-bye to various of her friends in Florida and how surprised she is to see how sad they are to have her leave, often crying, while she remains dry-eyed and detached.

"Yes," I say, "That's what you do, it's what I've tried to point out that happens between us and obviously it happens with your friends as well. It's just like I affectively held your words. Well I hold your feelings as well. When your sad feelings get to be too much to bear, you split them off and deposit them in me or in Wilma or Patty or any of your friends. And then we carry not only our own sadness, but yours as well."

"I know you've said that a dozen times before, but this time I got it. It's like my dream of the child in the closet. You always remember that dream with so much more sadness, while I remember the withdrawal, the attempt to keep myself safe. Although I have come out of that closet in so many ways – reaching out to others, exposing myself, being more genuine – I still haven't exposed myself entirely to myself. I guess I'm not cured," she says with a sparkle in her eyes.

"There are always issues still to be dealt with."

"If I start crying and crying and crying in a week or a month, should I send you a postcard?" she asks smiling. "I know, you want me to do it now."

I smile in return.

"I also wanted to tell you that Milton started to read my manuscript and that he wanted me to tell you how much he appreciated all that you did for me."

I tear up.

"That touched you," Caroline says, seeing my reaction. "It touched me too."

We give each other a big hug.

"I love you," she says.

"I love you too," I reply.

Caroline leaves.

I cry.

MOURNING

Letting Go and Holding On

The Five Stages of Grief

The night I lost you
Someone pointed me towards
The Five Stages of Grief.
Go that way, they said,
it's easy, like learning to climb
stairs after the amputation.
And so I climbed.
Denial was first.
I sat down at breakfast
carefully setting the table
for two. I passed you the toast –
you sat there. I passed
you the paper – you hid
behind it.
Anger seemed more familiar.
I burned the toast, snatched
the paper and read the headlines myself.
But they mentioned your departure,
and so I moved on to
Bargaining. What could I exchange
for you? The silence
after storms? My typing fingers?
Before I could decide, *Depression*
came puffing up, a poor relation
its suitcase tied together
with string. In the suitcase
were bandages for the eyes
and bottles of sleep. I slid
all the way down the stairs
feeling nothing.

And all the time Hope
flashed on and off
in defective neon.
Hope was my uncle's middle name,
he died of it.
After a year I am still climbing,
though my feet slip
on your stone face.
The treeline
has long since disappeared;
green is a color
I have forgotten.
But now I see what I am climbing
towards; *Acceptance,*
written in capital letters,
a special headline:
Acceptance,
its name is in lights.
I struggle on,
Waving and shouting.
Below, my whole life spreads its surf,
all the landscapes I've ever known
or dreamed of. Below
a fish jumps: the pulse
in your neck.
Acceptance. I finally
reach it.
But something is wrong.
Grief is a circular staircase.
I have lost you.

(Pastan, 1998, pp. 114–115)

In "Mourning and Melancholia" (1917), Freud had not yet understood the concept of grief as a "circular staircase," instead seeing the goal of mourning to be detachment from the deceased person, so that the individual could again be free to reinvest in new people and in the world. His later work, "The Ego and the Id" (1923) was to foreshadow the work of more contemporary theorists who see mourning not only as a relinquishment of that which has been lost, but also an internalization, a taking in, of the deceased person in the mind of the bereaved (Aragno, 2003; Baker, 2001; Clewell, 2004; Gaines, 1997; Hagman, 1995; Horowitz, 1990; Kaplan, 1995; Kernberg, 2010; Klass, 1988; Pollock, 1961; Shapiro, 1994). Bereaved spouses do not detach from their loved ones, but rather find ways to keep a connection, whether that be through concrete personal possessions, dreams, imagined conversations, or a sense of feeling their presence, all of which contribute to the building of an internal connection with the person who is no longer present (Schuchter, 1986).

In order to build this internal connection the mourner must first accept the reality that the loved one is indeed forever absent. Then, the bereaved can take inside the mind an image of the other and an image of the self in relation to the other (Kernberg, 2010). This internalization of the deceased, along with the internalization of the self in relation to the deceased, is what is called internal structure and enables the mourner to stay connected to the person who has been lost. This connection provides comfort and relief from the unmitigating sorrow of loss. If the loss is still very new and the strength of the internal tie between the loved one and the mourner has not yet been formed, this relief remains elusive and the mourner remains trapped in pain. Even after this internal connection has been established, however, when absence looms especially large in current reality – an anniversary date, a family celebration, the aroma of Mexican food – the comfort of the internal connection can be broken, so that the mourner again feels engulfed by grief, and the journey around the circular staircase continues.

In August of 2008, ten months after George's death, I hear the following message on my answering machine: "I'm Molly Callahan. I can't remember who referred me to you, but I need to see someone. I lost my husband, Mitch, six months ago and I'm having a hard time." Her soft but determined voice wavers towards the end. She leaves her number. I sit staring out my window at the darkening sky, shades from light gray to black, trees whipping wildly in the wind, all warnings of the storm headed our way. I think about this woman I have not met. The timbre of her voice suggests that she's young, certainly younger than me. I've worked with widows before, some young, some older. There was the woman whose husband died suddenly while they lay in bed, she nursing their first, newborn child. And the widow who couldn't stop herself from screaming, unable to contain the despair she felt at her husband's sudden death. And the woman who aged dramatically after her husband died and when, several years later, she was diagnosed with ovarian cancer, chose the route of no treatment, more than ready to give up her life. I had envisioned myself in each of these women's shoes; their pain resonated with me. But that was before. That was before George died. The question now is: Am I ready? Am I ready to hear another widow's pain? Will I be able to put aside my own grief to work effectively with hers? Or perhaps I should ask if I could use my own grief to hear hers more deeply, communicating on an unconscious, as well as conscious level.

I decide that I'm up to the task and that is how Molly becomes my patient. As it turns out, two other widows call me within the following sixteen months and I agree to work with each of them. What I don't know at the time is that they will present very different styles of grieving. Molly, closest to my own experience, makes repeated trips around the circular staircase internalizing memories of her husband and herself and building internal structure. Paula, unable to build this structure, goes round and round on the circular staircase but never places more than a toe on the step of

Acceptance, before scurrying hurriedly away, while Flora flies towards Acceptance trying valiantly to avoid any steps at all.

I begin treating each of these women believing that my own experience will bring added understanding to the treatment and that I am capable of withstanding both their pain and mine. My conscious awareness is that these treatments will bring added comfort to all of us, as we bask in our unspoken, but nonetheless unconscious connection. Since I had told none of my new patients that I was a widow, I never consider telling these women either. My conscious concern, especially with these women, is that we might become overly enmeshed and that the boundaries between us too fluid. And, in fact, there are times that the boundary between myself and each of these women is less clear, when my responses come more from my own needs and experiences rather than theirs.

But what I unfortunately forgot was my own earlier work on self-disclosure, on seeking not only connection, but protection. I didn't consider that my not telling any of these patients that I was a widow was my attempt to protect not them, but me. While I consciously told myself that I looked forward to the added connection our similarity would provide, on an unconscious level I was afraid, afraid that I would feel too much pain, too much vulnerability. It was as though I feared the melding of our grief, a melding that might fill the room and destroy my capacity to function as an analyst. Did my failing in this regard damage these treatments? It's difficult for me to say. I do think I provided more support for these women than I usually do in treatment, sometimes sounding like a cheerleader, encouraging them along. It was as though I had in my mind, both for them and for me, the belief that grief involves great sadness, but not sadness that becomes an endless morass of despair, not sadness burdened by guilt or regret, not sadness that offers no hope of an enlivened future. I wanted them – and me – to feel better. I will leave to my readers the question of how much my stance in this regard affected each of these treatments.

Molly is a striking, curvaceous, dark-haired, forty-two-year-old woman, with big, sad eyes. She immediately plunges into her story.

"I lost Mitch, my husband, in February. I can't believe it's been six months," she says, shaking her head. "I miss him so much. We had such a great relationship. He was my best friend. He would have been forty-seven on October 14." Her voice is strong, determined, as if she is willing herself to tell her story without breaking down.

Goose bumps appear on my arms, as I keep my face impassive. How is this possible? What are the chances that the deceased husband of the first widow I see after George's death would share his birth date?

"He died of a heart attack. He wasn't feeling well that day. In fact he hadn't been feeling well for several days, but he continued working. He was a construction supervisor."

Is this some sort of cosmic joke? I wonder. How many other similarities will there be?

Molly continues. "He didn't take good care of himself. There was a lot of heart disease in his family and the last time he saw his doctor – maybe two years before –

he was supposed to get all these follow-up tests, but of course he never did. But that Saturday he seemed to be feeling especially lousy. I offered to take him to the hospital, but he wouldn't hear of it. I was supposed to go shopping with my best friend and he told me to go. I said I'd stay, but he said, no, I should go, that he'd be fine. I tried calling him during the day, but he didn't answer. I figured maybe he was sleeping. When I got home he was slumped over on the floor in the living room. I don't even know if he was still alive then. I called 911 and they came over and started working on him and then they took him to the hospital and they wouldn't let me go back there and then they came out and told me he was gone," she says in a rush to get her words out. And then, much more slowly, more quietly, she adds, "Then they let me go back. He was cold, so cold."

I am back in the hospice room staring down at George's body. He isn't cold. I'm glad. I wouldn't want him to be cold; I wouldn't want my last experience of him to be cold. Not cold. Warm. Warm, like always.

"I keep asking myself why I left him that day. To go shopping of all stupid things! What if I had insisted that he go to the hospital? What if I hadn't left? Would he still be alive today?" she asks plaintively.

"Those questions are of course unanswerable, but I certainly understand your asking them. Beating up on yourself doesn't help though. It won't bring Mitch back."

"I know. Nothing will bring him back," she says angrily. "I'm angry at God. How could he do this? Mitch was such a great guy. There are so many other shits out there, why couldn't he take one of them? And I'm angry when people say dumb things – 'He's in a better place.' Oh yeah! If it's such a better place why don't you go there?" She takes a breath. "But my anger doesn't get me anywhere either."

"Do you ever feel angry at Mitch? For not taking care of himself? For leaving you?"

"Yeah, I do. And I'm also scared. I hope I'll be able to manage financially. I have a thirteen year old at home, Patrick, from a previous, terrible marriage. I'm a dog groomer. I have my own business. And then I work a couple of nights a week as a hostess at a neighborhood restaurant. But we really relied primarily on Mitch's salary and now it's going to be all on me. I'm going to have to make the mortgage. I did get some money from Mitch's retirement, but not a whole lot. It's scary. I hope I can make it. And it reminds me way too much of my past. My father died when I was fifteen, also of a heart attack, and left my mother to raise us seven kids in rural West Virginia. It was tough. But she did it. And I'll just have to do it too."

I like this woman who radiates pain and suffering, as well as tenacity and determination. Despite the obvious differences in our lives, my liking for Molly grows throughout the treatment into an intense feeling of connection, a connection born not of words, but of feelings. Molly and I mourn similarly, not identically, but similarly, both taking in our respective husbands and holding them close.

"I miss Mitch so much. I feel this hole all the time. It hurts. There's like a physical pain," she says pulling at the top of her sweater over her heart. "Sometimes I wonder if I'm having a heart attack, but I know I'm not. I just miss him. Every moment of every day I miss him. It helps when I'm busy. I don't know what I'd do without my business, but I still miss him. I talk to him all the time. I say 'good morning.' I tell him about my day. Sometimes I ask his advice. And sometimes I tell him that he can stop joking now, that he's taught me that I can take care of myself and he can just come home. I sleep with his picture. And his ashes are on my headboard. I wish you could have met him. I'm sure you would have liked him."

I miss George all the time, too, constantly aware of the void, the emptiness, the hole. I, too, am grateful for my work which brings some distraction from the pain, except at times like these when I feel the pain even more acutely. I don't talk to George, but his presence is always with me. I don't sleep with his picture, but there are pictures of us on both nightstands and the headboard, pictures of us smiling, dancing, looking lovingly at each other. His ashes are mostly in the pond by our home, but some remain in the wood box placed discreetly on my bureau.

In September, one month after Molly has begun treatment, I tell her that I will be out of town for two weeks in October. I don't tell her that I am leaving to both immerse myself in and escape from George's birthday and the first anniversary of his death. Molly will thus be left to deal with Mitch's birthday without me. I feel guilty about leaving her. The last session before the break is difficult for us both.

"I've been having a terrible time. I feel as though my heart is being ripped out of my chest. And sometimes it's as though I can hardly breathe."

"I'm sorry. You must have a lot of feelings about my not being here for you these two weeks."

"Well, it's not the best timing," she says attempting to smile.

I consider telling Molly that we are both widows and that we share the burden of October 14. But I refrain, consciously concluding that the information would only be an attempt to assuage my guilt and deprive her of whatever feelings she might have about again being deserted. Today, my conclusion still seems valid, although I do wonder if the amazing coincidences between me and Molly only added to my need to protect myself from further pain. It is interesting to speculate on what would have occurred if I chose the path of self-disclosure. Would Molly and I have cried together? Would the connection between us have deepened? Would each of us have felt less alone as we went off to grieve separately? Obviously, all unanswerable questions. But throughout Molly's treatment, I continue to feel a press to tell her that I, too, am a widow, a press I resist. Sometimes I even wonder if Molly knows and if we are simply not discussing the elephant in the room. And yet, I say nothing.

I return emotionally bruised and depleted from my two weeks away. Molly's first day back is her wedding anniversary. October is a difficult month for us both.

"I had a hard time, but I got through it. The fourteenth was terrible. Today is too. All I can think of is that it would have been ten years. Our tenth anniversary. We were going to do something special. I looked at all the old cards Mitch had given me.

Sometimes he even wrote little poems. I looked through them all and cried. I suppose I should start getting rid of some of this stuff. But I can't. It's like his clothes. All his work clothes. His shoes. I haven't touched anything in his closet, in his drawers. They're just sitting there. But I can't. I can't bring myself to do it."

Getting rid of George's things. It's like tearing the scab off a deep wound; like throwing George away. Easiest to let go are those things I give to other people. Like George's shoes. Early on I give most of them to Luke, saying that his Grandpa will give him a strong foundation to walk on. We both smile.

Melodee and her youngest son, Mike, the construction person in the family, come down to go through George's garage and ship back the tools they might want. For some unknown reason I do not anticipate how excruciatingly painful this will be for me. I expect that tools and the garage are things devoid of emotional significance. How preposterous! George's tools were a part of him, an expression of his creative self. And they were why and how we met! How could I not have expected myself to grieve? And the emptiness on the shelves in the garage is overwhelming. I can't stand emptiness. I tell Melodee to please spread out whatever is left. It helps a bit.

I give Mike some of George's shirts. That's easier. But the rest of his clothes remain in the closet, a large, walk-in closet that we shared. One day I pack up most everything and call the Vietnam Veterans of America, thinking that George would appreciate such a donation because of his son. But I don't dispose of everything. George's beige wedding suit remains hanging, as do two shirts — one rose-colored, soft and fuzzy, the second, the last shirt he ever wore, black with bright-blue vertical stripes to match his eyes and disguise his added weight. I also keep his warm red robe that I wear on cooler mornings to walk Hadley out back and his long T-shirts that I wear faithfully to bed each night. Still, there's a lot of empty space. I quickly distribute my blouses to the other side of the closet. I don't want any more emptiness than necessary.

After October comes Thanksgiving and Christmas. Firsts for Molly. And not much better seconds for me.

"I'm so sad. All I want to do is get dressed up and go out to dinner with my husband. I think about him all the time. I miss him as much as ever. I feel the pain will never go away. I just want the holidays to be over."

January does not bring relief from her unrelenting grief.

"I hurt so much. It never stops. So it's a New Year. Great!" she says sarcastically. "The year stretches before me like a blank slate. I have nothing to look forward to. Everything feels like blackness. I can't believe he's gone. And I think there's something else. I think sometimes I feel further away from Mitch and that scares me. It's like he's less present. It makes me feel lonelier."

I know exactly what Molly means. She's describing the experience of my second Christmas without George. The house is all lit up and decorated. I'm rushing around finishing the last minute cooking. The house is brimming with friends and family. Although I'm aware of George's absence, I feel less consumed by grief. And suddenly I stop, aware that I'm not at all comfortable in that diminishment of pain. It's as though George is slipping further away from me. At least the unrelenting grief provides a sense of connection, what a widowed friend of mine meant when she said, "Grief is my friend."

"I think what you're saying, Molly, is that when you feel the pain of Mitch's death even a little less intensely, your emptiness feels greater, as if you need your pain to stay connected to Mitch."

"Yes, I think you're right. I think that's exactly what I feel. I don't know why, but that actually makes me feel a little better."

Time moves on and so does the journey around the circular staircase.

"I'll never forget Mitch," she says. "I want to make him proud, but maybe I have to stop treating him as if he's still alive. Maybe I really have to let go of things and move forward." She decides to put his picture on the headboard, rather than continuing to sleep with it.

I've put some of George's pictures away, mostly what I call his "sick" pictures, pictures taken after he looked visibly ill. I remember how he looked then, bloated by medication, absent facial hair, a dull cast to his eyes. But that's not how I want to remember George. So I put them away, keeping instead the dozens of pictures of both him and us that line bookshelves, desks, and bureaus, pictures that recall the happier times, the George with the radiant smile and sparkling eyes. But still, I recall how wrenching it felt to remove even one picture. Was it a betrayal? A loss? Perhaps a bit of both.

Then Valentine's Day approaches, as does the second anniversary of Mitch's death, and Molly's pain returns as acutely as ever.

"Saturday was really hard. I was going through it all hour by hour, wondering about all the 'if onlys.' I know Mitch didn't take care of himself, but I shouldn't have left him. I bought him a Valentine's card and took out all his cards and poems and read them."

For months, for years, passing the card section in supermarkets, in drugstores, wherever, left me in a bucket of tears. "Birthday for Husband." I have no husband. "Birthday for Wife." I am no longer anyone's wife. "Anniversary." There will be no more anniversaries.

"Is it comforting for you to read the cards or are you torturing yourself?" I ask, a question born of knowing how intolerable it would feel to me.

"I'm not torturing myself. It's more comforting," Molly responds, reminding me that despite the similarities in our grieving process, there are differences between us.

Getting past the second anniversary is helpful to Molly. She cuts and styles her hair, highlights it red. She carries herself with greater assurance, smiles more readily. She eyes the mountain of Mitch's work clothes. A week before his birthday she says, "I cleaned out Mitch's closet. It was very hard. It made me feel depressed and angry all over again. One of Mitch and my good friends said that he had a tear in his eye thinking about my cleaning out that closet, but that it was time."

Several weeks later, Molly makes a big decision.

"I finally decided what to do about my wedding ring. I've known it's been time to take it off. But I couldn't just take it off! I couldn't take it off and leave it in a drawer. For one birthday, Mitch gave me a necklace, a cross. I'm definitely not wearing a cross again! It has small diamonds in it. I'm going to bring it to a jeweler. I want him to take both pieces and put them together so that I'll have one ring I can wear on a different finger, whatever finger will work. I know that means I'm going to have to take it off, to give it to the jeweler, but I think I can handle that as long as I know I'll be getting it back."

Wedding rings. I wonder if there is any widow who doesn't agonize about what to do or not do about her wedding ring. For me it has been a long saga that even now is not completely resolved. Anne Roiphe, in her beautiful memoir, Epilogue (2008), describes a similar journey: "On my fifth or sixth or eighth attempt I take the ring off and keep it off. I look at it in its box. I hold it in my hand but I do not replace it on my finger. I am not married anymore" (p. 54). I still marvel at her resolve. My ring went from the ring finger of my left hand to the ring finger of my right hand. Except sometimes, like on the first anniversary of George's death, when I put it back on my left hand. Then back onto my right hand. It was a see-saw I kept up for quite some time. Meanwhile, George's wedding ring – which I bought for him for our tenth anniversary – I wore for over two years on a gold chain around my neck whenever I wasn't wearing the wedding necklace I gave him the day we married. And when I finally put my wedding ring in the jewelry box, I placed another ring on my right finger. To this day, now four years after George's death, I still have difficulty being without some ring on my finger, even if I'm at home or at the gym. I can do it, but I'd rather not. I don't like going "bare."

Despite difficulties in her day-to-day life – her son is not doing well in school, her business goes through hard times, her house needs repairs – Molly perseveres.

"I was playing pool in a bar. Just a group of us fooling around having a few drinks. There was this guy. He was kind of cute. He asked me if I was married. It stopped me. I didn't know what to say. I said 'no,' but it was almost as though there was a question mark in my answer. I didn't know what to say. I'm not married. But still…"

Several weeks ago a patient in her twenties asked me several questions: Where was I from? Was I married? Did I have children? While we explored what it would mean for me to answer or not answer these questions and why she was asking those particular questions at this specific time, I had ample time to mull over the question, "Am I married?" I realized there was no way I could say "no," regardless of who asked it. To do so would feel like disowning George and our relationship. I just couldn't. My only answer could be, "I'm a widow." I would be telling the truth while still maintaining my connection to George.

170

"How did you feel saying 'no' to that guy?" I ask.

"It was kind of weird," she replies with a half smile.

"Weird in what way?" I persist.

"I mean, it was true. But even though I have been able to move forward, it's not like Mitch is gone from my life. I think about him every day. I don't think I felt disloyal to him. I don't know. It was just weird."

"What about saying, 'I'm a widow?'" I inquire, again wondering about the difference between Molly and me.

"I wouldn't have wanted to do that in that kind of setting. That's for a more intimate conversation. I wouldn't have wanted to say something that would have made him or anyone else uncomfortable."

Two thoughts occur to me. The first is that it remains difficult for Molly to reveal herself, especially if she's unsure of her audience, a holdover from her childhood when there was no one available to truly hear her. The second is that Molly is more able than me to let go and declare herself a single person who is ready for another relationship. I feel glad for her. And somewhat envious.

Indeed, several months later Molly meets a man in a bar. Shortly thereafter they become lovers.

"I really like this guy. But it's weird. I still talk to Mitch every day. I still say good morning and good night. It's still hard for me to go certain places without feeling very sad. And yet, here I am, gaga over this new guy."

"I think it's great! I applaud you," I say, more in the role of Molly's cheerleader. A more thoughtful response might have drawn attention to how Molly is standing in both the past and the present, looking in both directions simultaneously. My unabashed encouragement of Molly is no doubt meant to encourage me along similar lines.

"He's a really nice guy. And he obviously cares for me. We text all the time. We talk every chance we get. He wants to introduce me to his children and to his parents. Sometimes I'm afraid it's just too good to be true."

Molly continues in treatment, continues to remain connected to Mitch in her mind, and continues to engage with the new man in her life. I still wonder how Molly's treatment would have been different if she had known that I too was a widow. I do know that I have continued to want Molly to know and that I have now made sure that she will. Although I have disguised many of the facts about Molly, I did not want to change her husband's birth date or his occupation. I therefore asked Molly for permission to include her in this book, a permission she was more than pleased to give. So she will read these pages and then she will know and then we will see what transpires.

I began treating Paula, a depressed, sixty-two-year-old woman who had been widowed for four years, in the winter of 2009. We are presently in our third winter of working together. The rest of the year she sees a psychiatrist in New York and lives in her home in Park Slope, Brooklyn. As mentioned earlier, Paula's journey around the circular staircase rarely involves her stopping for long on the step of Acceptance before rushing away. Paula's mother was also a depressive, explained as being the result of miscarriages both before and after Paula's birth. Her father was a businessman who had little time for either wife or child, leaving Paula to grow up alone and isolated. When Paula met Robert, the man who was to become her husband, she felt she had met her Prince Charming. Regardless, she continued to become depressed, including having severe post-partum episodes after the birth of two daughters.

Like most depressives, Paula cannot accept the reality of change and loss and cannot, therefore, build the necessary internal structure made up of the memories of herself and her deceased husband, Robert. Paula can, of course, *say* that her husband is dead, but cannot take it in emotionally. "…while the depressed person is virtually completely immersed in a preoccupation with 'loss,' he simply does not experience it as true loss" (Rubens, 1998, p. 227). The depressed person is immobilized, unable to take action or make a decision. From this place of inertia, it is as "if nothing *can* be changed, then nothing *will* change. If I simply cannot tolerate what is happening to me, it will not happen. And …if I refuse to live this new experience as new… I can continue to live the old experience of my inner object world" (Rubens, 1998, p. 226, italics in original).

For Paula, this inner world is filled with negative images of both herself and others. Like all children who are insufficiently cherished, Paula needed to keep her early caretakers "good" since she depended upon them for survival. Also needing to see herself as "bad," so she could strive to become "good" and thereby win her parent's love, she took the "badness" inside herself (Fairbairn, 1943). Unfortunately, this "solution" never works, for the external caretakers remain ungiving and the internal world becomes harsh and abusive. But that inner world is staunchly defended so as to avoid mourning the reality of what never was and never will be (Fairbairn, 1958). This, then, is Paula's dilemma, an inability both to accept the reality of Robert's death and to take in positive memories of him and them so as to find a modicum of peace and comfort.

From the beginning, Paula, short and stocky with straight black hair and eyes that look completely dead, feels immoveable.

"I don't want to be here," she says flatly.

"You mean here in my office or here in Florida?" I ask.

"I don't want to be in Florida. My daughter, Karen, the one who lives in Brooklyn, she just wanted to get rid of me. She figured it was her sister's time to take care of me. Not that I blame her. I'd like to get rid of me too. I don't mean I want to kill myself, although sometimes I do want to, but I'm too afraid of dying." She shakes her head with a quizzical look on her face. "I can't remember what I was saying. I can't think straight. I hate when I get like this. I hate myself."

"You hate yourself?" I say, feigning surprise, trying to convey my sense that hating herself is not the logical next step to losing her husband and being depressed.

"I do. I hate myself for being depressed. It's a long time now, a long time since Robert died. Everyone tells me I should be better by now and I agree, I should be. Everyone tells me about all the widows they know who have lost their husbands a year ago or two years ago and are already seeing someone, or working or involved in all these volunteer activities. That's just great for them. But I'm just weak, weak and worthless that's all I am."

"Wow! You're not exactly your own best friend," I say, while thinking to myself that I could never tell Paula that I, too, am a widow, for fear of giving her yet another reason to despise herself. Here again, as with Molly, my conclusion is not unfounded for Paula could indeed see me as another of those widows who a little over a year after her husband's death is functioning quite well, working, going on with her life, completely able to cope. Of course, this would be a very incomplete picture and, if I had been willing to reveal more of my struggles, it is possible that Paula could have benefited from such a disclosure. Again, it's impossible to know, but is a question worth asking. Additionally, I am not caught up in the intensity of Paula's despair, nor personally discouraged by her depression that lingers with her now four years after her husband's death. Perhaps this is a defensive response on my part, an example of my need for protection, as I distance myself from Paula to protect myself from the black cloud of her grief.

"No, I'm definitely not my best friend," Paula says, tearing up. "That's why I miss Robert so much. He was my best friend. My daughters certainly aren't. I mean, I know I can't expect them to take care of me. I know I should be better. I don't know what's wrong with me. Robert would be so disappointed in me. I can't stop crying. All I do is cry. And I hate being here. I hate being in Florida. Oh yes, that's what I was talking about. I hate it. I hated leaving my house. It's where Robert and I lived for so much of our married life. It wasn't so bad when I was staying with Janice – that's my daughter who lives here – for two weeks, but now that I'm in my condo, I hate it. Those long, empty corridors. I never see people. When I close the door to the apartment it's like locking myself in a coffin. People say I should be happy. I'm living right on the ocean. Right! Who cares about the ocean?!"

"Sounds like you feel pretty angry."

"Just at myself. I'm angry at myself for being depressed."

"You're not angry at Karen for sending you to Florida or at Janice for not having you stay in her home or, for that matter, at Robert for dying?"

"I couldn't possibly be angry at Robert! He's the one who's dead! He didn't want to die. It wasn't his choice."

Despite her denial, Paula seems filled with anger, her inner world a cacophony of voices that rail against her as bad and unworthy, displaying her attempt to keep those in her external world good by seeing herself as the bad one. Paula berates herself for anything and everything: for not having spent more time with Robert, for not having been more attentive, for not having been more aware of the preciousness of their time together.

It is a crystal clear, bitterly cold winter night in Michigan. I am walking our dog, Brenna, shivering. Suddenly I think, "Linda, as cold as you are, savor this time, for these are the best years of your life. One day George will be gone. Every day must be cherished."

"I've always been afraid of death," Paula says one day. "It was as if it was always with me, this thing. I don't know why. No one close to me died. My grandfather, but we hardly saw him. And my father didn't seem all that sad when he passed."

"What about the miscarriages your mother had? It sounds as though she was always in mourning for her lost children."

"Oh yes. Other therapists have brought that up. I don't know why I always forget. It's not like I forgot as a kid. I always felt I had to be perfect, perfect so that I could make up for everything my mother lost. I could never be perfect enough. I could never stop her from being depressed. I guess that's where I get it from."

"How did you feel about not being able to 'cure' her depression?"

"Bad. Like there was something wrong with me. Like I wasn't good enough."

How interesting, I think. Is Paula unconsciously inducing in me a feeling similar to the one she felt as a child? Does the tenacity of her depression lead me to feel as helpless and worthless in my attempt to "cure" her depression as she felt trying to "cure" her mother's?

"Sounds like quite a burden to put on a child," I say.

"I guess. I think I was just grateful that it wasn't me. That I was the one who lived. Although I could never figure out why, why it was me."

"Did you feel bad that you lived and they didn't?"

"Oh yes, definitely."

"Kind of like how you feel about Robert?"

"Yes. Except that's worse. If I find myself laughing at something funny on TV or notice how pretty the clouds are here, I immediately feel guilty. Like how could I be laughing when Robert is dead? Why is it that I get to see the clouds and he doesn't? It's not right."

Here again we see Paula's determination to maintain her own "badness" and the condemning status quo of her internal life. Taking in a positive voice that would alter her internal world must be resisted at all cost so that she is not left with the pain of mourning not only Robert, but the disappointing parents of her childhood (Fairbairn, 1958).

Still, I try. "You say that you feel better when you're in the office with me, that you feel understood by me. Can you take me with you when you leave? Can you think about talking with me and feeling somewhat better?"

"But you're not with me. What I feel is that you're not there. So why should I feel better?" she asks, clearly dumbfounded.

"But if you heard my voice inside your head or had a picture of me or of being in this office with me you might find that comforting," I say, trying to coach her along.

"That just sounds crazy," she replies, unable to understand.

"And is the same true for Robert as well? Do you not hear his voice or have images of him, or have images of the two of you together?" I persist.

"Not really. And when I do, they just make me sad," she says, starting to cry. "I don't want to think about them, about him, because they just remind me of what I don't have. He's not here anymore. He's not here to enjoy his life. He's not here to help me out of my depression. I don't know what I'm going to do," she says plaintively.

Paula cannot internalize Robert and their relationship in a way that would build a comforting, internal connection between them. Instead she is left with a never-ending void that is impossible to fill. I feel sadness for Paula while being immensely grateful that I do not share this difficulty. I can't imagine what it would be like to not carry George within me, not to have all the wonderful memories, memories both ordinary and exotic. And, yes, they sometimes bring me sadness in my awareness of their absence, but more often they bring a smile to my face and a feeling of warmth to my body. Could I have shared with Paula this difference between us, demonstrating that it is possible to build such a comforting structure? Perhaps, although I do think the tenacity of Paula's closed system, her need to see herself as bad while others remain good, would not have given way so easily to modeling from her therapist and, in fact, might well have made her feel even more weak and damaged.

Despite Paula's difficulty in taking Robert in, she is attached to some concrete objects that were associated to him, although they too sometimes bring her more sadness than comfort.

Shortly after the start of our second winter together, Paula comes in looking particularly distressed. She starts sobbing as soon as she sits in the chair, unable to speak and soon gasping for breath. She grasps her right wrist, shaking it back and forth. I think of the possibility of a suicide attempt, but see no blood. Still, I'm becoming alarmed.

"Paula, can you try and tell me what's going on? You're obviously so distraught. Did something happen?" I ask gently.

Continuing to clutch her wrist she manages to eke out a sentence punctuated with sobs. "I … lost … it! I lost the bracelet. How could I? How could I be so stupid? He gave it to me. He gave it to me on our first anniversary. I've had it for all these years. I hate myself. I want to die!"

I remember. It was less than a month after George's death. In those early days I never took off George's wedding necklace except to shower. It's an oblong jasper stone in tones of brown and gold set in a silver frame. Although a stone, it looks like a scene – the setting sun highlighting the mountains and valleys in the foreground. At least that's how George and I always saw it. It went around George's neck, and now mine, with a braided leather strap that clipped in back with a hook and eye. I'm putting away groceries I just brought into the house from the garage. And it's gone!! The necklace is gone! I was concerned about losing it. The hook and eye didn't seem secure. I was going to change the clasp. I thought I remembered taking it off, just to be on the safe side. But did I? Or did it fall off? I begin crying, near hysteria, as I ransack my car, walk the short distance between the car and the house a dozen times. The phone rings. Despite my distress I answer it. It's Ann, my friend from Ann Arbor. When I hear her voice I cry even harder. "What's wrong?" she asks, alarmed. Not even when we scattered George's ashes did Ann hear me crying so desperately. "I lost George's necklace," I wail. Calmly, carefully, she encourages me to retrace my steps, to think where I was. I can't stay on the phone with her. I have to keep looking. I promise I'll call her back. Now I'm looking in the pantry, in drawers, in cabinets. I'm desperate. Then a thought occurs to me. I did take it off. I remember. Right when I pulled the car into the garage. But I looked in the car. I looked in my purse. The bag from the drugstore. Where did I put the bag from the drugstore? I walk into the living room. There's the bag. But no necklace. But wait. Behind the cushion of the couch. There it is!! There it is! Now I'm crying even harder. I'm crying with relief. I must call Ann. I must let her know.

I bring myself back to the present, to my role here as Paula's therapist. "Oh Paula," I say, with more empathy than she will ever know, "I'm so sorry. How horrible for you. Are you absolutely sure? Can you remember the last time you saw it?"

Paula stops crying immediately and stares at me. Mucous dripping from her nose, she reaches for a tissue. "I thought you'd think I was being silly, being so upset over a bracelet."

I give her a half smile and reply, "No, not at all. It's a precious possession. Of course you'd be distressed about its loss."

"My daughters would never think so. They'd just think I was over-reacting, being foolishly sentimental. It's like Karen made me stop wearing my wedding ring after Robert's unveiling."

I always wondered about Paula not wearing her ring. It seemed so unlikely a choice for her. I want to challenge her premise that Karen could make her do something she didn't want to do, but decide that is better left for another day. What I say instead is, "It sounds like my understanding your feelings was helpful for you. It can't take away the loss, but perhaps it helped you feel less alone."

"Yes, I think it did."

But again, this is not a connection she is able to take with her once she leaves my office and her despair continues.

"This never stops. Nobody helps me. I just sink further and further down."

"Are you saying you feel angry with me because I'm not helping you?"

"I'm angry with myself. For being so weak. For not being able to get myself out of this."

"But what do you feel first? When you say, 'Nobody helps me,' aren't you saying that you're disappointed in me, angry with me that I can't make you better?"

"Yes, yes I feel angry. You came so highly recommended. I placed my trust in you. But I'm the same. But I know it's not you. You try. It's my fault. I'm just too weak."

"So let's look at what just happened here. You were able to say you were angry at me. Then what happened?"

"I felt bad. Like I was blaming you and then maybe you'd be angry with me and give up on me."

"So you felt angry at me and then immediately felt scared and guilty and turned the anger on yourself, the same thing you've done your entire life."

"That's true. I could never be angry with my parents. It felt way too scary."

"Can you say more?" I prompt.

"I don't know. Like I might hurt them. Or they'd leave me. I don't know. It just wasn't possible. They were good. They loved me. They took care of me. I couldn't be mad at them."

Here again Paula is giving voice to the notion that the dependent child has no choice but to take the badness inside herself, so that the parents she needs for survival can remain "good" (Fairbairn, 1943). It is a difficult dilemma, for changing that closed internal system, taking in the good and recognizing that one's early caretakers were not a model of perfection, involves a painfully slow process of mourning that which never was and never will be.

Now into her seventh year of widowhood and our third winter of working together, there are glimmers of Paula making some progress.

"I know it sounds stupid after all these years, but I think most of the time I do believe that Robert is dead. I don't want to believe it, but I usually do."

"It doesn't sound stupid to me at all. It's been very difficult for you to accept the reality of his death."

"I don't like it when you say it! Then I'm not sure. I can think it. I guess I can even say it, but when you say it out loud it sounds too cruel to be true."

"Hearing me say it makes it feel too real."

"I guess. But I do know it's true – usually. I brought some of Robert's pictures down with me this year. Every so often I can even look at one without crying. There's one of us someone took on our cruise through the Panama Canal. It was a wonderful trip," she says, her lip beginning to quiver.

"So starting to accept Robert's death has made it possible for you to look at his photographs. Do you remember that trip?" I ask.

"Oh yes, definitely."

"What are some of your specific memories?" I prod.

"Well, I remember not being too thrilled about all that fuss about going through the locks. That seemed kind of boring to me. But then that night, it was a beautiful night, Robert and I actually danced outside on the deck with him humming in my ear," she says with a half smile.

"It sounds like that's a very positive memory, a memory of you and Robert together, enjoying each other. And it sounds like you have that memory with you, that it brings you comfort."

"A little. But I can't think about it for long, 'cause then I'll only get sad."

This is the paradox Paula must face. In order to take in Robert and hold positive memories of him which would, in themselves, provide her with comfort, she must risk altering the negativity of her internal world, opening up still more mourning, this time for the childhood she never had. Paula has a long road ahead of her, but she does seem to be able to place more than a toe on the step of Acceptance as she continues her journey around the circular staircase.

Flora, a tall, thin, seventy-year-old, retired teacher who was recently widowed for the second time, began treatment with me in March of 2009. Since her husband died in early September, she found herself extremely anxious and unable to comfortably be in her townhouse by herself. Her internist had prescribed Xanax which she occasionally took, but said that she didn't like how it made her feel and that she didn't want to be "dependent" on medication. She kept two radios and two televisions on at all times and tried to "run" with her friends as much as possible. When forced to be at home she played Solitaire on the computer or continually worked puzzles. Although she had four children and seven grandchildren they were scattered throughout the country, leaving her feeling alone. Flora had been in therapy once before when her first husband died suddenly in an accident. Then, too, she had found herself to be very anxious, but attributed it to being left to raise four young children on her own.

Flora's background was extremely traumatic. Her parents were believed to be Polish Jews who placed their infant daughter in a Catholic nunnery to protect her from the Nazis. Flora remembers nothing of her parents and little of her early years. Her first memory is of being in a Catholic school in Belgium, surrounded by imposing figures in black garments, some kind, most stern. She doesn't remember longing for her parents or even thinking about them. She does remember being cold and hungry and huddling with some of the other girls to keep warm. She also remembers the times the girls were instructed to stand to attention and strangers would arrive to look them over. These strangers were always in couples and always spoke a language Flora could not understand. She knew the girls were supposed to pass some kind of test and the one who won got to go home with the strangers. And so it was, when Flora was five years old, she went "home" with her "new parents."

Thus began the next chapter in Flora's life, learning to adjust to a family that already existed: a meek, depressed, but caring mother, who had lost much of her extended family in the Holocaust and looked to Flora as a connection to those who were dead; a harsh, rejecting father who had only grudgingly agreed to his wife's request to adopt a European child; and two much older sisters who resented Flora's intrusion into their well-established family. Then there was the language. Flora spoke only French and had to quickly make the transition to English or be taunted for her "stupidity" by her father and sisters.

As I listened to the recitation of these facts from Flora's background, I found myself overwhelmed with sadness for this poor, orphaned, neglected, traumatized child. But I was the only one in the room who felt those feelings. Flora reported them as though she were an impartial observer, and any attempt on my part to encourage her to reach for the feelings behind her words were met with statements such as, "It was a long time ago." Or, "I've worked through that already." Or, "I need to focus on the present, not the past." My suggestion that the past might be impacting her present or that her anxiety might be a safer feeling than those she was sheltering underneath was met with staunch resistance.

So we moved on to somewhat more current history. As she was expected to do, Flora graduated from college with a degree in education. She taught for two years. Her first husband was the brother of one of her fellow teachers. He was "tall, dark, and handsome and I fell hard," Flora says. "He was also a child who was totally self-centered. He had all kinds of other women. It was impossible. But before I knew it I had four children and I wasn't going anywhere. Not that he ever made lots of money. In fact, my father helped us out. I have to give my father that, he came through for me even though he despised my husband. When he got killed – my first husband, that is – in a motorcycle accident of all stupid things. So typical. What father of four gets on a motorcycle? Anyway, my father helped me out then too. I wanted to go back to teaching, but I was a nervous wreck. That's when I went into therapy. And then when I was forty I met Harvey. It wasn't like it was any passionate romance or anything, but look where passionate romance got me the first time. I knew he'd be a good father and he was. And I was a good wife. We had almost thirty years together and then he got pancreatic cancer and died in six months. It wasn't pretty. It was a hard way to die. But I took care of him 'til the end. I didn't expect to be so anxious when he died, but here I am again."

I certainly know about anxiety. I have lived the past three years in a state of almost constant anxiety, first with George, then my mother, and now my cat, the repeated ups and downs of hope followed by the threat of loss, followed again by hope and the threat of loss. And finally the horror of the loss itself. Without question it is George's loss that fills me with the greatest terror, the biggest void, the most encompassing aloneness. Then the roller coaster with my mother, not knowing when the next seizure would strike or how much more debilitated she would become. But her death, now only two months past, actually brought some relief, some feeling of necessary closure. And now Pippin's illness. For the sweet being who has shared my life for fifteen years and for all she may represent – George, my mother, or the helpless, vulnerable part of myself – my anxiety is soaring once again.

"What do you see as the reason for your anxiety, both now and when your first husband died?" I ask.

"I was scared of raising four children on my own. And I guess I'm still afraid of being on my own."

"Does that surprise you?" I ask.

"What do you mean?"

"Well, in many ways you've spent most of your life alone. You don't remember your biological parents or any particular nun or child in the orphanage. I don't know how easy it was for you to feel connected to your depressed adoptive mother, and certainly not to your rejecting father or sisters. You did feel an attachment to your first husband, but he was totally unavailable to you. And Harvey, well, he was 'good,' but it doesn't sound like you really loved each other."

"Oh we loved each other. It's just that something was missing. And that's why I decided it's time to take off my wedding ring and go on JDate. This is my last chance, my last chance to find a truly loving relationship."

In my mind I yell, "Whoa! Not so fast. You're flying by all the steps of the circular staircase, trying to land on Acceptance and not even realizing the staircase is circular." JDate. I can't believe she's ready for Internet dating so soon after her husband's death.

It's now well over two years since George's death, and I have just coaxed myself onto Internet dating with much anxiety, even more doubt, and the company of three supportive friends. I'm just not sure. Can I do it? Am I ready? I still can't quite imagine dating. What about kissing another man? I don't think so. Having sex with him? That's totally inconceivable. So far it's not a problem that's presented itself. No man I'm even vaguely interested in is interested in me, and those who might be interested in me seem totally unsuitable. I'm not even sure how a new man would fit into my life. What would I do with all of George's pictures? I can't imagine putting them away. I know the goal isn't to replace George, but to add to him. Except I haven't yet figured out how that's possible.

Attempting to put myself aside, I respond to Flora's announcement. "I understand your feeling that this is your last chance, Flora, but I'm concerned about the man you might choose."

"You mean because I haven't made such great choices in the past?"

"Yes," I say tentatively. "But I'd say that a little differently. Perhaps it's because I'm not sure you understand why you chose the men you did."

"Well, I was head over heels for the first one, and sure Harvey would be a good father."

"But the question still remains why you fell head over heels with the first one and why you didn't keep looking for someone who could be a good father and who was also capable of loving you deeply."

"Well, what do you think? Why do you think I made the choices I did?"

"I think you chose your first husband because you're attracted to unavailable men, men who unconsciously remind you of all the people in your life who were or became unavailable to you – your biological parents, the nuns, your adoptive father. And by the time that relationship was over I think you had had more than enough pain and suffering and closed yourself up and chose a 'safe' relationship, a relationship that would neither give nor demand too much closeness." Even in this long interpretation, I have not told Flora all that I believe. I think that given the horrible traumas of her early life, Flora was closed off long before she met her first husband and that she chose him because unconsciously she preferred his unavailability, both because it was familiar to her and because it did not demand that she open herself up, something she was incapable of doing. Starved for love as a child, Flora has totally closed herself off, afraid of her own infantile neediness and the destructive power of her overwhelming need for love (Fairbairn, 1941). Unlike Paula who fears the destructiveness of her anger, Flora fears the destructiveness of her love.

I say none of this to Flora, just as I do not say that I very much sense her difficulty in connecting to me, in allowing me to matter. Today, even with my re-found insight about needing protection from my widowed patients as well as connection, I believe that Flora maintains too much distance for my comfort level, that she is so afraid of her own neediness that she cannot allow a deeper connection and that I am, with her, the one who yearns for a closer relationship.

Flora is soon involved in a whirlwind of dating. Four months later, seventy-nine-year-old Morty, also a retired teacher, moves into her house. She is sure she has finally found the man who will love her unconditionally and without reservation. I am less confident. I question my pessimism. Am I jealous? Jealous of Flora's attachment to Morty rather than to me? Or perhaps of Flora's apparent ease at stepping off the circular staircase of grief into another relationship? Perhaps. But despite my personal feelings, Morty, who has been divorced twice, does not sound like a man who is forthcoming with his feelings or unconditionally available. In fact, as Flora describes him, he sounds rather depressed, spending endless hours on the computer playing poker or going for long, solitary walks. Flora does not complain. Morty's presence has allayed her anxiety and, for the moment, that is sufficient. She begins to talk about termination. I encourage her to keep coming and she agrees. I'm heartened. She values our time together. Perhaps she is even moving towards allowing herself to value our relationship.

Not surprisingly, before long, Morty wounds Flora severely and she is thrown back into her anxiety. Underneath all her accomplishments and seeming ability to function in the world, Flora is indeed that scared, dependent, rejected child who seeks connection, albeit with unsatisfying others, to keep her from feeling entirely adrift and alone in the universe. She remains determined to make the relationship with Morty work.

"He's better than nobody," she says. "I don't want to go back to being alone. I don't want to be anxious."

I think, but do not say, "You're not alone, you have me," for I know Flora is far from accepting me as a significant relationship in her life. Instead I reply, "Maybe if we were able to confront the origins of your anxiety, your fears from the past, your overwhelming pain from the past, we could help you to be less anxious."

"Maybe," Flora answers skeptically. "But I don't know if I'm ready for that. Why would I want to revisit all that pain? There's no guarantee that I wouldn't stir all that stuff up and get stuck in it and that my anxiety wouldn't be worse than ever. Besides, I'm seventy years old. I'm too old to change."

"I don't think anyone is too old to change, Flora. But you're right. There are no guarantees. And it's true, you've suffered a tremendous amount and I'm sure looking at all that would be very painful. Still, you might find yourself able to lead a much fuller life, a life with a greater intensity of connection, not only to the man in your life, but also to your children, your grandchildren, and perhaps even to me."

I seem unable to not assert my desire to be a significant person in Flora's life. I want connection. Perhaps this is partially true because I sense both the pain and the potential in Flora and wish to give her the opportunity to live out her life to the fullest. And perhaps it is also true because I am a widow. Because I am without George I desire an intensity of connection which can sometimes be realized with patients. Am I then using my patient for my own gratification? Yes, I suppose that is true. And I suspect that is true for all analysts, at all points in their lives, although in different forms and to different degrees. Am I now at a place of particular need? Yes,

I think that too is true, but I do hope that my awareness of my desire for an intensity of connection helps me to keep, as much as possible, my patients' needs and defenses foremost in my mind.

And so, Flora and I continue, now almost three years into her treatment. She has made considerable gains, although she still skitters between examining her past and running from it; between opening up and closing off. Morty is long gone, but William isn't much of an improvement. She will talk about our relationship, but still keeps me at a distance, unsure what it really means to feel close to me. I'm not in a rush. I've learned to push less, to accept more. I'm here, however she may need to use me.

While in the process of writing this chapter, I attend Luke's graduation from the Fire Academy. He is now an EMT, paramedic, firefighter, an extraordinary accomplishment. I am extremely proud and inexplicably anxious. On the way, I cause the first accident in my life and will be forever beholden to the man whose car I hit who lets me go on my way so that I will not miss the graduation. Then I can't find its location, despite huge signs that are blatantly obvious. But I make it. I get to kiss Luke as he walks off the stage with his certificate, making all the previous problems inconsequential. On my way home it hits me. George should have been there. George should be here. I can't stop my tears. I don't want to stop my tears. I'm no longer anxious. Grief is my friend.

EPILOGUE

Legacies

It is the Sunday after Thanksgiving, a little over four years since George's death. I spent the holiday with Melodee, her husband Dan, and her children and their families on the outskirts of Cleveland. I gave much thought to this trip before buying my ticket. How would I feel returning to a place I had not been since celebrating George's eightieth birthday seven years ago? How would I feel returning to a place I had never been without him?

Except for a new pond, not much had changed at Melodee's home, a 175-year-old farmhouse on three acres of land. The flat, treeless landscape never felt particularly inviting to me, but the interior of the home, filled with overstuffed furniture, antiques, and family heirlooms, counteracts the starkness of the outside landscape and welcomes me. I am relieved to learn that I will be sleeping in the downstairs den, a small Victorian room filled with doilies, portrait silhouettes, and a keepsake box depicting a mailbox complete with fence and mailman that George had made as a young man. I was concerned that Melodee and Dan would give me their upstairs bedroom, the room George and I had slept in when we came to visit. I didn't want to sleep there anymore.

Thanksgiving had not been as difficult as I had feared. George's absence did not loom constantly in my mind. On the contrary, I felt embraced by family, George's family, now my family as well.

On Friday I borrowed Melodee's car and drove to Ann Arbor to celebrate my friend Ann's seventieth birthday. I had never made this drive without George. Although under three hours, it seemed endless, George's absence weighing heavily. Being with Ann is a relief, a warm hug, a loving embrace, connected again rather than floating in space. Ann's home, which I've always loved, couldn't be more different than Melodee's – a modern, open, split-level house that sits in the middle of a forest. It is filled with her artwork – abstract paintings and whimsical, metallic figures of women, horses, and unicorns. This time I have an added treat: colorful paintings of our trip to Costa Rica, capturing her favorite bird – the shiny black grackle – as well as the dense variegated forest that had surrounded us. Once again I am pleasantly surprised. Being here feels comfortable, even when it is filled with celebrating people, just as it was for George's birthday.

On the other hand, being with two of Ann's adult children is more painful than I anticipated. Her youngest daughter says, "It's great to have you here, Linda, just like old times." Her son talks about all the Thanksgivings and Christmases we spent together, the seven of us – the three children, both parents, and George and me. There is a wistful quality to their words, a longing for the time when they were little, before their parent's painful divorce. Their yearning for the past, for the men who are no longer present, envelops me and encourages my own drift towards feelings of loss and longing. Driving through Ann Arbor is similarly painful. Every street evokes a memory – the first office George remodeled for us, the restaurant where George and I went for lunch, the second office George remodeled for us, the homes of friends we visited.

And all the trees look dead. It is after all November in Michigan. There is no green. I've become accustomed to green. Is it possible that Ann Arbor is no longer home? Is Florida home? I don't know. I am adrift, untethered. I quickly return to Ann's home. That's better. Our connection grounds me.

On Sunday I drive back to Melodee's. The skies are gray and rainy, the traffic congested. I'm forced to attend to my driving. It's actually a welcome distraction from the inner workings of my mind. Soon enough I'm again anchored at Melodee's home where the delicious aromas of cumin and coriander greet me, a Mexican soup that Melodee has created from the leftover turkey. Perfect for warmth on a dreary fall night; perfect for warmth to welcome me back from what has felt like a long journey.

After dinner, the plan is to go first to Mike's house – George's youngest grandson – and then to Angie's – his eldest granddaughter – to see the renovations they've made to their homes since my last visit. When I cross the threshold of Mike's home onto the cream-colored tile and stand in the middle of the dining room looking up, I am in a contemporary cathedral. Stretching high above me is a barrel-shaped ceiling, its variegated peaks and valleys cascading down into the living room with its recessed lighting, see-through fireplace and glass shelves. In its openness it is simultaneously freeing and embracing.

Eight years ago George and I gave Mike the down-payment on this then small, 1950s ramshackle house with rotting walls and crooked floors. When we first saw the house, Mike was busily at work, tearing down one room at a time and jacking up the unattached garage one block at a time so that all six feet, four inches of him could stand upright. That one story, diminutive house is now three thousand square feet with a six hundred pound oak staircase that connects the two stories, the old crooked floors now a rich cherry wood that shades from blonde to copper. And that dilapidated garage has evolved into a five-bay, attached garage, one bay equipped with a car lift.

George would be so proud. But George is not here. In the moment, however, my admiration for Mike's skills and their obvious legacy from his grandfather, bring me pleasure, the pain of absence less present.

Then we're off to the home of Angie and Bruce, her husband, where George's second granddaughter, Michelle, with her husband, Kenny, will also be waiting.

Four of George's great-granddaughters are also present, ranging in age from nine to seventeen. We sit in the small dining area adjacent to the kitchen. I'm on a bench, my back to the staircase, George's family all around. I feel cocooned.

I look above Michelle's head. On the wall is a large, multi-colored framed needlepoint of trees with a Mom and Dad and four children on the bottom. The saying reads: "Count your age by friends, not years/ Count your life by smiles, not tears." I know George did the needlepoint. It was one of his hobbies before we met. Sadness begins to creep over me. I struggle to shrug it off. Pointing to the needlepoint, Angie says, "People are always surprised when I say my Grandpa, with an emphasis on the 'pa,' did that. But then I tell them that he also did those," she says, gesturing to the balusters, the spindle-shaped wood pieces that support the upper railing of the staircase behind me. Balusters with a story. George made them, piece by piece, almost one hundred of them, after also hand-making the lathe that would create their shape – square on both ends, followed by circular ridges, flaring out towards the middle. Designed for the banister around Melodee's porch, only a few of the original ones remained and the cost of reproducing them was prohibitive. So her Dad came to the rescue. He made them, a long and painstaking labor of love. But no one built the railings around the porch to hold the balusters and twenty years later they remained unused. When Angie and Bruce were remodeling, Angie asked if they could have some of them to put in their banister. Melodee agreed. Later Melodee tells me that Angie and her youngest daughter, Kristina, who was only two when she last saw George, sometimes walk up the stairs running their hands over the balusters saying, "Grandpa, Grandpa."

George's needlepoint is in front of me, his balusters behind me and his family around me. What only a short while ago felt comforting, now feels suffocatingly painful as I struggle to keep my feelings at bay. I am relieved when Angie suggests a tour of the house. The gloom settling over me subsides. Then it's time to leave. I will return to Florida early the next morning. Hugs and kisses all around. I don't feel terribly sad, even though I'm not sure when I'll see them again, perhaps because I carry them with me, or perhaps because I need some alone time.

Back at Melodee's, I close the door to the den, pack a few items, move the small tables and magazine rack to enable me to open the green velour hide-a-way bed. Tasks completed. I sit down on the open bed and sob – quietly. I don't want anyone to hear me. I don't want Melodee to come to comfort me. I'm not even sure why I'm crying, why I feel swallowed by my grief.

I'm on the circular staircase going round and round. I want George! I can't have George. I want George!! But George is no more. I want to escape these feelings. I can't escape. I'm trapped. I struggle to add thoughts to what feels like an increasing morass of despair. Mike's house. I think about Mike's house and sob even harder. Why? I felt pleasure when I stood in Mike's house. Why such overwhelming sadness now? "Count your age by friends, not years/ Count your life by smiles, not tears." So George. "Grandpa, Grandpa." The memory of these experiences is more painful than living their reality. Yes. That's it. My memories. It's not the house itself. It's not the needlepoint itself. It's not the baluster itself. It's when these "things" join with the image of George I carry within me, the image of the man who George was: the man who could create anything; the man who believed in smiles, not tears; the giving, generous, loving man, George.

I want George! But George is no more.

No, that's not true. Again and again this trip has shown me that George lives on. He lives on in Mike's talent, in Angie's memories, and in the love of family connection imparted to his great-granddaughter, Kristina. So why doesn't that thought comfort me? Why doesn't my grief tonight bring me closer to George? Why doesn't it lead to my feeling held by George as it so often does? Maybe there's been too much of almost-George this weekend. Like a tease. George is here in the memory of Ann's children, but not in reality. George is here in Mike's house, but unable to take pride in it. George is everywhere and nowhere. Not here. Not anywhere.

But ... tomorrow will be a new day. Tomorrow I will return to the warmth of Florida and to the joy of Hadley, the fluffy bundle of love I call my happy dog. Tomorrow I will return to the pleasure of my work, to the creativity of my writing, and to my friends and family in Florida. And, as always, George will be with me.

ACKNOWLEDGEMENTS

There is another family that has had a profound effect upon this book, one that I mentioned earlier, but now takes center stage in my acknowledgements: the New Directions writing program. The program, which meets for three weekends a year, was begun by two analysts, Robert Winer, M.D. and Sharon Alperovitz, MSW, with the intent of providing a community of clinicians, academics, and writers who were all interested in developing and honing their writing skills. I entered the program in 1999, my father's voice firmly embedded in my mind, convinced that I had nothing to say and no ability to say it. From the first weekend, I found a warm, welcoming, supportive community that immediately began to chip away at my long held belief in my incompetence as a writer. Those whose writing I held in high esteem actually thought I wrote well and that what I had to say was worthwhile. Soon my first paper was accepted for publication. Then my second. And then my third! I must be a writer after all!

Although I graduated from the program in 2002, I continued to return until George's illness and death, during which time I neither attended nor wrote. A year after his death, I made my first tentative return to New Directions. In my mind I was playing with the idea of writing a book about George and his death, but I wasn't yet sure I wanted to subject myself to all the pain I knew that would entail. However, I was back in New Directions. I had to write about something. Soon, five of us formed an alumni writing group, three hopeful writers, and an analyst and writer as co-leaders. I had indeed made another three-year commitment to New Directions and a commitment to myself to write a book. It is this group of people who helped birth *Love and Loss in Life and in Treatment* and to whom I can never give sufficient thanks for their love, support, and careful reading of every word of my manuscript.

My fellow alumni and frequent roommate, Sheila Felberbaum, LCSW, who shared my interest in end-life caretaking, while daring to challenge herself with different forms and styles of writing, was a constant source of encouragement and inspiration. Sylvia Flescher, MD, whose struggle and determination to overcome her own writing inhibition, provided me with a similar determination when I became bogged down in either the tedium or pain of writing. Nan Heneson, the writing co-leader for the first two years of our group, had penetratingly incisive insights and suggestions for which I will always be grateful. Kathie Hepler, MA, the writer in the third year of our group, was an extremely nuanced reader, whose careful suggestions often had a profound effect on the manuscript.

Which brings me to the last co-leader in our group, Sharon Alperovitz, MSW. I fear that my talent as a writer is not sufficient for me to say all that I would wish to say both to and about Sharon. I see Sharon as my writing mentor, the person from New Directions who, almost from the start, has been my most helpful reader, not only for this book, but for most of my papers as well. Sharon has a clear and incisive mind that enables her to read a paper or a chapter and know what is missing or wrong or somehow off. She also has the capacity to put those insights into words so that I as the writer can understand the difficulty and make the necessary changes. This book truly would not have been the same were it not for Sharon. In fact, I'm not sure it would have existed at all, had Sharon not been both such an enthusiastic supporter and astute critic of my writing from the beginning. I am forever in her debt.

There are other people from New Directions who have helped me along the way, both with this book in specific, and with my writing in general. Although I apologize to those I am sure I am omitting, in no particular order, I would like to thank: Harvey Rich, MD, Bo Winer, Robert Winer, MD, Jeanne Lemkau, Ph.D., MFA, and Sara Taber, MSW, Ed.D. I would also like to offer my heartfelt appreciation to Richard Fritsch, Ph.D., for his unwavering support and wise counsel.

In addition to New Directions, the person who has provided me with the greatest support for my writing through the years is Donnel Stern, Ph.D. When he was editor of *Contemporary Psychoanalysis* he accepted four of my articles for publication, providing helpful suggestions regarding the content and positive feedback about the writing itself. When I went to hear Don Stern speak in Miami – one of the few conferences I attended while George was ill – he told me he was the editor of a new book series, Psychoanalysis in a New Key, and encouraged me to think about writing for it some day. Although this book was not born at that moment, the possibility that I might someday write a book was and for that I am greatly appreciative.

My thanks go out to Kate Hawes and Kirsten Buchanan at Routledge, for their appreciation of my book and for their help in ushering it and me through the process of publication.

My appreciation is extended to the following publishers who have given permission to use previously published work in this book: Sherby, L.B. (1989). Love and hate in the treatment of borderline patients. *Contemporary Psychoanalysis*, 25: 574–591; Sherby, L.B. (2004). Forced termination: When pain is shared. *Contemporary Psychoanalysis*, 40:69–90; and Sherby, L.B. (2005). Self-disclosure: Seeking connection and protection. *Contemporary Psychoanalysis*, 41:499–517. Journey by Linda B. Sherby, *Psychoanalytic Perspectives*, Volume 6 Issue 2 (November 2009), pp. 113–119. Reprinted by permission of Taylor & Francis (http://www.tandfonline.com).

The Five Stages of Grief, from *The Five Stages of Grief* by Linda Paston. Copyright © 1978 by Linda Pastan. Used by permission of W.W. Norton & Company, Inc.

The Five Stages of Grief: used by permission of Linda Pastan in care of the Jean V. Naggar Literary Agency, Inc. (permissions@jvnla.com).

NOTES

INTRODUCTION

1 Psychoanalysis (analysis) and psychotherapy (therapy) are often used interchangeably throughout this book. Although psychoanalysis can be seen as a more intensive form of therapy, since my work is always informed by psychoanalytic concepts, I have chosen not to maintain a clear distinction.

JOURNEYS

1 First published under the title, Journey, by *Psychoanalytic Perspectives* (2009), 6(2): 113–119. Minor changes have been made to the text.

1   FALLING IN LOVE IN TREATMENT AND IN LIFE

1 This chapter and the following one are a revised and lengthened version of Love and hate in the treatment of borderline patients (1989), *Contemporary Psychoanalysis*, 25:574–591.

4   FORCED TERMINATION

1 This chapter is a revised and lengthened version of an article by the same name that appeared in *Contemporary Psychoanalysis* (2004), 40:69–90.

5   SELF-DISCLOSURE

1 This chapter is a revised and lengthened version of an article by the same name that appeared in *Contemporary Psychoanalysis* (2005), 41:499–517.

6   FROM DISCONNECTION TO RECONNECTION

1 For a detailed explanation of these concepts see W.R.D. Fairbairn (1952). *Psychoanalytic Studies of the Personality*. London: Routledge and Kegan Paul; and H. Guntrip (1968). *Schizoid Phenomena, Object Relations and the Self*. London: Hogarth Press.

REFERENCES

Abend, S. (1990). Serious illness in the analyst: Countertransference considerations. In: *Illness in the Analyst*, eds. H.J. Schwartz and A.-L.S. Silver. Madison, CT: International Universities Press, pp. 99–113.

Adler, G. (1985). *Borderline Psychopathology and its Treatment*. Northvale, NJ: Jason Aronson.

Akhtar, S. (2000). Mental pain and the cultural ointment of poetry. *International Journal of Psychoanalysis*, 81:229–243.

Aragno, A. (2003). Transforming mourning: A new psychoanalytic perspective on the bereavement process. *Psychoanalysis and Contemporary Thought*, 26:427–462.

Aron, L. (1996). *A Meeting of Minds*. Hillsdale, NJ: The Analytic Press.

Baker, J. (2001). Mourning and the transformation of object relationships: Evidence for the persistence of internal attachments. *Psychoanalytic Psychology*, 18:55–73.

Balint, M. (1950). On the termination of analysis. *International Journal of Psychoanalysis*, 30:196–199.

Balint, M. (1968). *The Basic Fault*. New York: Brenner/Mazel.

Beatrice, J. (1982–1983). Premature termination: A therapist leaving. *International Journal of Psychoanalytic Psychotherapy*, 9:313–336.

Bromberg, P.M. (1998). *Standing in the Spaces: Essays on clinical process, trauma, and dissociation*. Hillsdale, NJ: The Analytic Press.

Bromberg, P.M. (2006). *Awakening the Dreamer: Clinical journeys*. Hillsdale NJ: The Analytic Press.

Bromberg, P.M. (2011). *The Shadow of the Tsunami: And the growth of the relational mind*. London: Routledge.

Chasen, B. (1996). Death of a psychoanalyst's child. In: *The Therapist as a Person*, ed. B. Gerson. Hillsdale, NJ: The Analytic Press, pp. 3–20.

Clewell, T. (2004). Mourning beyond melancholia: Freud's psychoanalysis of loss. *Journal of the American Psychoanalytic Association*, 52:43–67.

Cooper, S.H. (2000). *Objects of Hope: Exploring possibility and limit in psychoanalysis*. Hillsdale, NJ: The Analytic Press.

Cooper, S.H. (2010). *A Disturbance in the Field: Essays in transference-countertransference engagement*. London: Routledge.

Davies, J.M. (1994). Love in the afternoon: A relational reconsideration of desire and dread in the countertransference. *Psychoanalytic Dialogues*, 4:153–170.

Davies, J.M. (1998). Between the disclosure and foreclosure of erotic transference-countertransference: Can psychoanalysis find a place for adult sexuality? *Psychoanalytic Dialogues*, 8:747–766.

Davies, J.M. (2001). Erotic overstimulation and the co-construction of sexual meanings in transference-countertransference experience. *Psychoanalytic Quarterly*, 70:757–788.

Davies, J.M. (2006). The times we sizzle, and the times we sigh: The multiple erotics of arousal, anticipation and release. *Psychoanalytic Dialogues*, 16:611–616.

Dewald, P.A. (1965). Reactions to the forced termination of therapy. *Psychoanalytic Quarterly*, 39:102–126.

Dewald, P.A. (1966). Forced termination in psychoanalysis: Transference, countertransference, and reality responses in five patients. *Bulletin of the Menninger Clinic*, 30:98–110.

Dewald, P.A. (1982). The clinical importance of the termination phase. *Psychoanalytic Inquiry*, 2:441–461.

Dewald, P.A. (1990). Serious illness in the analyst: Transference, countertransference, and reality responses – And further reflections. In: *Illness in the Analyst*, eds. H.J. Schwartz and A.-L.S. Silver. Madison, CT: International Universities Press, pp. 75–113.

Dobija, J. (2007). Sky light. Personal communication.

Edwards, N. (2004). The ailing analyst and the dying patient: A relational perspective. *Psychoanalytic Dialogues*, 14:313–335.

Ehrenberg, D.B. (1992). *The Intimate Edge: Extending the reach of psychoanalytic interaction.* New York: Norton.

Ehrenberg, D.B. (1995). Self-disclosure: Therapeutic tool or indulgence? *Contemporary Psychoanalysis*, 31:213–228.

Epstein, L. (1995). Self-disclosure and analytic space. *Contemporary Psychoanalysis*, 31:229–236.

Fairbairn, W.R.D. (1940). Schizoid factors in the personality. In: *Psychoanalytic Studies of the Personality.* London: Routledge and Kegan Paul, 1952, pp. 1–27.

Fairbairn, W.R.D. (1941). A revised psychopathology of the psychoses and psychneuroses. *International Journal of Psychoanalysis*, 22: 250–279. Also in *Psychoanalytic Studies of the Personality.* London: Routledge and Kegan Paul, 1952, pp. 28–58.

Fairbairn, W.R.D. (1943). The repression and return of bad objects (with special reference to the "war neuroses"). In: *Psychoanalytic Studies of the Personality.* London: Routledge and Kegan Paul, 1952, pp. 59–81.

Fairbairn, W.R.D. (1952). *Psychoanalytic Studies of the Personality.* London: Routledge and Kegan Paul.

Fairbairn, W.R.D. (1958). On the nature and aims of psychoanalytic treatment. *International Journal of Psychoanalysis*, 39:374–385.

Firestein, S. (1978). *Termination in Psychoanalysis.* New York: International Universities Press.

Freud, S. (1912). Recommendations to physicians practicing psychoanalysis. *Standard Edition*, 12:109–120, London: Hogarth Press, 1958.

Freud, S. (1917). Mourning and melancholia. *Standard Edition*, 14: 243–258.

Freud, S. (1923). The ego and the id. *Standard Edition*, 19: 12–66.

Gabbard, G. (1996). *Love and Hate in the Analytic Setting.* Northvale, NJ: Jason Aronson.

Gaines, R. (1997). Detachment and continuity: The two tasks of mourning. *Contemporary Psychoanalysis*, 33: 549–571.

Gerson, B. (1996). An analyst's pregnancy loss and its effects on treatment: Disruption and growth. In: *The Therapist as a Person,* ed. B. Gerson, Hillsdale, NJ: The Analytic Press, pp. 55–69.

Ginot, E. (1997). The analyst's use of self, self-disclosure, and enhanced integration. *Psychoanalytic Psychology*, 14:365–381.

Giovacchini, P. (1986). *Developmental Disorders.* Northvale, NJ: Jason Aronson.

Gorkin, M. (1987). *The Uses of Countertransference.* Northvale, NJ: Jason Aronson.

Greenberg, J. (1995). Self-disclosure: Is it psychoanalytic? *Contemporary Psychoanalysis,* 31:193–211.

Guntrip, H. (1968). *Schizoid Phenomena, Object Relations and the Self.* London: Hogarth Press.

Hagman, G. (1995). Mourning: A review and reconsideration. *International Journal of Psychoanalysis,* 76: 909–925.

Hoffman, I.Z. (1998). *Ritual and Spontaneity in Psychoanalytic Process: A dialectical-constructivist view.* Hillsdale, NJ: The Analytic Press.

Hinton, A., Sherby, L. and Tenbusch, L. (1982). *Getting Free: Women and psychotherapy.* New York: Grove Press.

Horowitz, M. (1990). A model of mourning: Change in schemas of self and other. *Journal of the American Psychoanalytic Association,* 38: 297–324.

Kahn, N.E. (2003). Self-disclosure of serious illness: The impact of boundary disruptions for patient and analyst. *Contemporary Psychoanalysis,* 39:51–74.

Kaplan, L. (1995). *No Voice is ever Wholly Lost.* New York: Simon and Schuster.

Kernberg, O. (1975). *Borderline Conditions and Pathological Narcissism.* Northvale, NJ: Jason Aronson.

Kernberg, O. (2010). Some observations on the process of mourning. *International Journal of Psychoanalysis,* 91:601–619.

Klass, D. (1988). *Parental Grief: Solace and resolution.* New York: Springer.

Lasky, R. (1990). Keeping the analysis intact when the analyst has suffered a catastrophic illness: Clinical considerations. In: *Illness in the Analyst,* eds. H.J. Schwartz and A.-L.S. Silver. Madison, CT: International Universities Press, pp. 177–197.

Limentani, A. (1982). On the "unexpected" termination of psychoanalytic therapy. *Psychoanalytic Inquiry,* 2: 419–440.

Maroda, K.J. (1991). *The Power of Countertransference.* New York: Wiley.

Maroda, K.J. (1999). *Seduction, Surrender, and Transformation.* Hillsdale, NJ: The Analytic Press.

Maroda, K.J. (2009). *Psychodynamic Techniques: Working with emotion in the therapeutic relationship.* New York: Guilford Press.

Martinez, D. (1989). Pains and gains: A study of forced terminations. *Journal of the American Psychoanalytic Association,* 37:89–115.

Mendelsohn, E. (1996). More human than otherwise: Working through a time of preoccupation and mourning. In: *The Therapist as a Person,* ed. B. Gerson, Hillsdale, NJ: The Analytic Press.

Mitchell, S.A. (1988). *Relational Concepts in Psychoanalysis: An integration.* Cambridge, MA: Harvard University Press.

Mitchell, S.A. (1993). *Hope and Dread in Psychoanalysis.* New York: Basic Books.

Mitchell, S.A. (1997). *Influence and Autonomy in Psychoanalysis.* Hillsdale, NJ: The Analytic Press.

Mitchell, S.A. (2003). *Relationality: From attachment to intersubjectivity.* Hillsdale, NJ: The Analytic Press.

Morrison, A.L. (1990). Doing psychotherapy while living with a life-threatening illness. In: *Illness in the Analyst,* ed. H.J. Schwartz and A.-L.S. Silver, Madison, CT: International Universities Press, pp. 227–250.

Morrison, A.L. (1997). Ten years of doing psychotherapy while living with a life threatening illness: Self-disclosure and other ramifications. *Psychoanalytic Dialogues,* 7:225–241.

Novick, J. (1997). Termination conceivable and inconceivable. *Psychoanalytic Psychology*, 14:145–162.

Ogden, T. (1982). *Projective Identification and Psychotherapeutic Technique*. New York: Jason Aronson.

Pastan, L. (1998). The five stages of grief. In: *Carnival Evening*. New York: W.W. Norton.

Pizer, B. (1998). *Building Bridges: The negotiation of paradox in psychoanalysis*. London: Routledge.

Pollock, G. (1961). Mourning and adaptation. *International Journal of Psychoanalysis*, 42: 341–361.

Renik, O. (1995). The ideal of the anonymous analyst and the problem of self-disclosure. *Psychoanalytic Quarterly*, 64:466–495.

Renik, O. (1999). Playing one's cards face up in analysis: An approach to the problem of self-disclosure. *Psychoanalytic Quarterly*, 68:521–539.

Roiphe, A. (2008). *Epilogue: A memoir*. New York: HarperCollins.

Rubens, R. (1998). Fairbairn's theory of depression. In: *Fairbairn, Then and Now*, eds, N. Skolnick and D. Scharff. Hillsdale, NJ: The Analytic Press, pp. 215–234.

Scher, M. (1970). The process of changing therapists. *American Journal of Psychotherapy*, 24:278–287.

Schlachet, P.J. (1996). When the therapist divorces. In: *The Therapist as a Person,* ed. B. Gerson. Hillsdale. NJ: The Analytic Press, pp. 141–157.

Schuchter, S.R. (1986). *Dimensions of Grief.* San Francisco, CA: Jossey-Bass.

Schwaber, E.A. (1998)."Traveling affectively alone": A personal derailment in analytic listening. *Journal of the American Psychoanalytic Association*, 46:1045–1065.

Schwartz, G. (1974). Forced termination of psychoanalysis revisited. *International Review of Psychoanalysis*, 1:283–290.

Searles, H. (1979). *Countertransference*. Madison, CT: International Universities Press.

Searles, H. (1986). *My Work with Borderline Patients*. Northvale, NJ: Jason Aronson.

Shapiro, E. (1994). *Grief as a Family Process: A developmental approach to clinical practice*. New York: Guilford Press.

Sherby, L.B. (1989). Love and hate in the treatment of borderline patients. *Contemporary Psychoanalysis*, 25: 574–591.

Sherby, L.B. (2004). Forced termination: When pain is shared. *Contemporary Psychoanalysis*, 40:69–90.

Sherby, L.B. (2005). Self-disclosure: Seeking connection and protection. Contemporary Psychoanalysis, 41:499–517.

Sherby, L.B. (2007). Rediscovering Fairbairn. *Contemporary Psychoanalysis*, 43:185–203.

Sherby, L.B. (2009). Journey. *Psychoanalytic Perspectives*, 6:113–119.

Silver, A.-L.S. (1990). Resuming the work with a life-threatening illness – And further reflections. In: Illness in the Analyst, eds. H.J. Schwartz and A.-L.S. Silver. Madison, CT: International Universities Press, pp. 151–176.

Singer, I. (1977). The fiction of analytic anonymity. In: *Human Dimensions in Psychoanalytic Practice*, ed. K. Frank. New York: Grune & Stratton, pp. 181192.

Slochower, J.A. (1996). *Holding and Psychoanalysis: A relational perspective*. Hillsdale, NJ: The Analytic Press.

Slochower, J.A. (2006). *Psychoanalytic Collisions*. Hillsdale, NJ: The Analytic Press.

Stern, D.B. (2003). *Unformulated Experience: From dissociation to imagination in psychoanalysis*. London: Routledge.

Stern, D.B. (2009). *Partners in Thought: Working with unformulated experience, dissociation, and enactment.* London: Routledge.

Viorst, J. (1982). Experiences of loss at the end of analysis: The analyst's response to termination. *Psychoanalytic Inquiry,* 2:399–418.

Weigert, E. (1952). Contribution to the problem of terminating psychoanalyses. *Psychoanalytic Quarterly,* 21:465–480.

Weiss, S. (1972). Some thoughts and clinical vignettes on translocation of an analytic practice. *International Journal of Psychoanalysis,* 50:711–716.

Winer, R. (1994). *Close Encounters.* Northvale, NJ: Jason Aronson.

Winnicott, D.W. (1949). Hate in the countertransference. *International Journal of Psychoanalysis,* 30:69–75.

INDEX

195